Bill Tuck
A Political Life in Harry Byrd's Virginia

Bill Tuck

A Political Life in
Harry Byrd's Virginia

William Bryan Crawley, Jr.

University Press of Virginia
Charlottesville

THE UNIVERSITY PRESS OF VIRGINIA
Copyright © 1978 by the Rector and Visitors
of the University of Virginia

First published 1978

Frontispiece: Tuck in front of Washington statue on the Capitol grounds.
(Courtesy of the Richmond *Times-Dispatch*)

Library of Congress Cataloging in Publication Data

Crawley, William Bryan, 1944–
  Bill Tuck, a political life in Harry Byrd's Virginia.
  Based on the author's dissertation, University of Virginia.
  Bibliography: p. 271
  Includes index.
   1. Tuck, William M., 1896–   2. Virginia—Gover-
nors— Biography.   3. Virginia—Politics and govern-
ment 1865–1950   4. Legislators—United States—Biog-
raphy.   5. United States. Congress. House—Biography.
I. Title
F231.T82C72.   975.5′04′0924   [B] 78–16751
ISBN 0–8139–0766–7

Printed in the United States of America

To my parents,
who personify the best in
Bill Tuck's Virginia

Preface

The political history of Virginia in the middle half of the twentieth century was dominated by the unostentatious but powerful Democratic organization of Harry Flood Byrd. During that period no Virginian approached Byrd's status as a political leader; so predominant was his influence that one of his adherents once claimed, with no great exaggeration, "Byrd *is* Virginia!"

There was during the Byrd era, however, one state politician—William Munford Tuck by name—whose career rivaled in length, if not in eminence, that of Harry Byrd himself. In a political life which spanned almost fifty years and included more than twenty undefeated appearances before the electorate, Tuck fashioned a career which coincided remarkably with the life of the Byrd organization itself. Having entered politics in the early 1920s, just when Byrd was establishing himself, Tuck worked his way up the political ladder while the organization grew to maturity and was elected governor as the organization reached its "golden age"; by the time Tuck retired from active political life, the organization was moribund.

In many ways Tuck was the archetypical organization politician; no one was more dedicated to the conservative philosophy which Byrd espoused, or more devoted to Byrd personally, than he. Yet he was also distinctive. Most organization leaders, reflecting the unobtrusive manner of Byrd himself, tended to be models of genteel deportment—i.e., dull. Not Bill Tuck. A country boy and not ashamed of it, he possessed an extravagantly outgoing, fun-loving personality which sometimes produced conduct shocking to the bluenose crowd, but which fascinated the generality of Virginians. Accordingly he became one of the state's most colorful—and to his admirers, most beloved—political figures of his, or any other, generation.

In his prizewinning biography of Huey Long, T. Harry Williams relates that on one occasion newspaper reporters surrounded the Louisiana "Kingfish," questioning him about his political style. Unable to articulate a satisfactory self-description, Long finally growled, "Oh, hell, just say I'm *sui generis* and let it go at that." So it was with Bill

Tuck. Though not to be confused by any means with Huey Long in terms of his philosophy of government, Tuck was, like the Louisiana potentate, truly *sui generis*—one of a kind—in the politics of his own state. The purpose of this study is to examine Tuck's public life and in the process to illumine, at least inferentially, the life of the Byrd organization of which he was an integral part.

The work is based largely on primary sources, including newspaper accounts, personal interviews, and collections of the papers of various participants in the period. Two disclaimers should be entered concerning my use of such sources. First, regarding interviews with Tuck himself (of which there were many), I have felt it unnecessary to cite the date of each interview since ofttimes the same subject was discussed in several interviews; specific documentation is in the author's files. Second, with regard to the use of personal papers, citation of the source is complete in almost every case; however, there are a very few instances in which the source is not specified, because anonymity either was requested by one of the persons involved or was deemed appropriate by the author in order to prevent the possibility of needless embarrassment to some private individuals. Such are the hazards of writing about the relatively recent past; however, I believe that this procedure, used as infrequently as it is, does not detract materially from the validity of the work.

In the course of this project I have amassed debts of gratitude too extensive to enumerate, let alone repay. I shall therefore be constrained to mention only the most prominent of them. To more than any single person, I am indebted to Professor Edward Younger of the University of Virginia. It was he who initially interested me in the study of Virginia history and who patiently directed the present study as it metamorphosed, haltingly, from term paper, to master's thesis, to doctoral dissertation, to book. He provided me throughout with insights and encouragement, often when there was little to warrant much encouragement. I deeply appreciate his scholarly guidance and, even more, his personal friendship.

Special note must be made of my appreciation for the role played by the principal of the study, William M. Tuck. It is rare for the historical investigator to have the benefit of such direct contact with his subject as was possible in my case. Tuck's cooperation over a period of years was complete: he allowed unrestricted access to his personal papers, promptly answered every one of numerous letters, and generously granted time for interviews. Moreover, he exhibited throughout a much appreciated, and one suspects unusual, restraint in not attempting to influence the author's judgments. In the course of many hours spent with Tuck in interviews, and in what might more properly be called informal conversations, I concluded that his reputation as a raconteur was well deserved; there were times when, under conditions hardly conducive to strict scholarship, I was regaled with stories which, though they do not necessarily appear in this volume, served to enrich my understanding of Virginia politics in the Byrd era.

The study has benefited from the advice of several persons who have read the manuscript in whole or in part: Professor David A. Shannon of the University of Virginia, who brought to the subject a comprehensive knowledge of modern American history; Professor Weldon Cooper, also of the University, who offered suggestions based upon a long and intimate acquaintance with Virginia government; and Professor Joseph C. Vance of Mary Washington College, who contributed the criticism of a practiced researcher and skilled writer. There are a number of additional persons whom I would like to acknowledge for a diversity of contributions: Virginius Dabney and Francis Pickens Miller, for granting me access to their personal papers, and Senator Harry F. Byrd, Jr., for permitting me to use the personal papers of his late father; the staffs of all the libraries in which I worked, for their cooperation, and especially Margaret Cook, Curator of Manuscripts at the Earl Gregg Swem Library of the College of William and Mary, for her unfailing assistance; Virgil Carrington (Pat) Jones, former administrative assistant to Tuck, for allowing me to use his manuscript, "Behind the Scenes with a Governor"; James Latimer of the Richmond *Times-Dispatch*, for allowing me to use his manuscript, "Virginia Politics, 1950–1960"; Marvin Garrette, also of the *Times-Dispatch*, for his aid in obtaining photographs; Richard S. Gillis, Jr., Executive Vice President of the Virginia State Chamber of Commerce, for his interest in the publication of the work; Janet Rader and Cynthia Ingham, two of my students at Mary Washington College, for helping with the research on Tuck's congressional career; Una Crist, for a masterful typing performance; Frances Hallam Hurt, a gracious lady and gifted writer, for volunteering for the tedious task of proofreading; and Theresa R. Young, also for proofreading—but mainly for just being Terrie.

Finally, as connoisseurs of such esoterica will realize, prefaces are not quite complete without the obligatory acknowledgment of the inestimable assistance rendered by the author's wife (or husband, as the case may be). This poses a serious hardship for those who, like myself, happen to be single. In the hope of surmounting this lamentable literary deficiency, I would like to end—not too enigmatically, I trust—by thanking those special friends who in sundry ways helped (or hindered) me in the course of this project. Without them, I would have finished much sooner—and much less enjoyably.

WILLIAM BRYAN CRAWLEY, JR.

Fredericksburg, Virginia
July 1977

Contents

Illustrations

Introduction

I was like the little boy who was fishing on the river bank when he felt the hot breath of a bear on the back of his neck. It was a huge bear. The boy looked around and there was just one tree in sight. He ran for it with the bear right on his tail, but the lowest limb was twenty feet up.

"Did you make it, boy?" the game warden asked later.

"Well, sir," the lad replied, "I missed it going up, but I cotched it coming down."

—*William M. Tuck, describing his political career*

The Political Setting

I. Harry F. Byrd and His Organization

> Understanding the "Byrd Machine" is a little like understanding metaphysics. Known simply as the Organization, it has no organization. It is identified with Senator Byrd, but Mr. Byrd, *in propria persona*, often is remote from it. As a political force, it operates as gently as a zephyr; it cannot be defined, bounded, described in a single crisp sentence any more than a cloud can be trapped in a bottle.
>
> —*James J. Kilpatrick (1959)*

> They that govern the most make the least noise.
>
> —*John Selden (1689)*

From the time that William Byrd I was appointed to the colonial Governor's Council in the seventeenth century, the Byrd family had been intimately associated with public affairs in Virginia, but never was that association more evident than during the middle decades of the twentieth century when the Democratic organization of Harry Flood Byrd exercised almost complete control over the politics of the state. So powerful was the organization and so pervasive was its influence that from the 1920s until the 1960s, it seemed almost redundant to speak of "Harry Byrd and Virginia politics." To contemporaries it sometimes appeared that Harry Byrd was Virginia politics.

One of the most articulate observers of state affairs during the Byrd years, Virginius Dabney, editor of the Richmond *Times-Dispatch*, commented privately that Byrd "carries the state around in his vest pocket, and has a machine which is probably the hardest to beat in the United States." [1] The longevity of the organization seemed, as the years passed, to impart to it a patina of legitimacy and to inculcate the idea that the organization was somehow preeminently "Virginian." In the

---

[1] Dabney to Marquis Childs, April 30, 1946, Virginius Dabney Papers, University of Virginia Library, Charlottesville.

homely phrase of one observer, the organization by the late 1940s had become "as much a fixture in the comfortable, cloistered life of the people of the state as, say, their faith in the Confederacy or their addiction to buttermilk biscuits and Smithfield ham." It was this widely accepted notion of Byrd's predominance which prompted veteran Virginia journalist Guy Friddell to state the matter succinctly: "In Virginia politics, in the beginning, there was Byrd. And the word was Byrd's."[2]

The thoroughness with which Byrd and his adherents came to control Virginia politics did indeed tend to make the organization seem almost coeval with the Commonwealth itself. In reality, although the state had been dominated by a powerful Democratic machine since shortly after Reconstruction, it was not until the 1920s that Harry Byrd emerged as the central figure. The original machine dated from the political turmoil of the 1880s, growing out of the successful attempt of conservative Democrats to oust William Mahone and the "Readjusters." The victorious conservative cabal was directed by Senator John S. Barbour, a wealthy railroad magnate who became the first real "boss" in Virginia politics. After Barbour's death in 1893, the machine was directed for the next quarter-century by Thomas Staples Martin, who gained preeminence by defeating the popular Confederate hero and former governor Fitzhugh Lee in a controversial election to fill Barbour's vacant Senate seat.[3]

During the period of Martin's domination, there were but few lapses in the control exercised by his machine. The first break occurred in 1901 when a progressive independent Democrat, Andrew Jackson Montague, defeated the machine's candidate, Congressman Claude A. Swanson, for the gubernatorial nomination. A second and more serious

[2] Cabell Phillips, "New Rumblings in the Old Dominion," *New York Times Magazine*, June 19, 1949, p. 10; Guy Friddell, *What Is It about Virginia?* (Richmond: Dietz Press, 1966), p. 72.

[3] James Tice Moore, *Two Paths to the New South* (Lexington: University of Kentucky Press, 1974); Allen W. Moger, *Virginia: From Bourbonism to Byrd, 1870–1925* (Charlottesville: University Press of Virginia, 1968); Virginius Dabney, *Virginia: The New Dominion* (Garden City, N.Y.: Doubleday, 1971), pp. 411–58; James A. Bear, "Thomas Staples Martin: A Study in Virginia Politics, 1883–1896" (M.A. thesis, U.Va., 1952).

disruption came in 1917 with the election of another "outsider," Westmoreland Davis, to the governorship. In a contest much influenced by the Prohibition issue, Davis—a political neophyte who was personally a teetotaler but politically a "wet"—was elected largely because the machine divided its support in the primary between two "dry" candidates, Lieutenant Governor J. Taylor Ellyson and Attorney General John Garland Pollard. Within two years the machine was further staggered by the death of Senator Martin, and the prospect of its demise was increased by Governor Davis's appointment of Carter Glass (theretofore an ascerbic opponent of the machine) to fill the vacant seat.[4] In short, by 1920 the once potent Democratic faction seemed on the brink of total collapse. It was at that point, however, that the organization underwent a metamorphosis resulting in new leadership and renewed strength—a development in which Harry Flood Byrd was the protagonist and the catalyst.

By birth, by vocation, and by personal philosophy, Byrd was perfectly equipped for political success in the Virginia of his age. Born into a state where ancestry was of prime importance, at a time when worldly success was the hallmark of acceptability, he possessed to a unique degree both the lineage and the business reputation which twentieth-century Virginians so admired. To be a member of the Byrd family was to be, in one writer's opinion, "as close to noble birth as is possible for an American."[5] Yet the economic status of the aristocratic clan had declined perilously by the time of Harry's birth, and it was he who undertook the task of recouping the family's fortunes. Leaving school at the age of fifteen, he was able by dint of hard work and extraordinary frugality to restore the solvency of the family newspaper, the Winchester *Star*, as well as to develop what eventually became the

---

[4] Jack Temple Kirby, "The Democratic Organization and Its Challenges, 1899–1922," *Virginia Social Science Journal* 1 (1966): 35–45; William Larsen, *Montague of Virginia* (Baton Rouge: Louisiana State University Press, 1956); Henry C. Ferrell, Jr., "Claude Swanson of Virginia" (Ph.D. diss., U.Va., 1968).

[5] Gerald Johnson, "Senator Byrd of Virginia," *Life* 27 (Aug. 7, 1944): 83. The early history of the Byrd family is traced in Clifford Dowdey, *The Virginia Dynasties* (Boston: Little, Brown, 1969), and in Alden Hatch, *The Byrds of Virginia* (New York: Holt, Rinehart and Winston, 1969).

largest one-family apple-producing operation in the world. Thus it was that Byrd emerged as a "self-made aristocrat."[6]

Since the Byrds had remained prominent politically even while in decline economically, it was not surprising that young Harry was attracted to public life. His father, Richard E. Byrd, Sr., served as Commonwealth's attorney of Frederick County for twenty years and in the House of Delegates for eight more, from 1906 until 1914. His uncle, Henry DeLaWarr (Hal) Flood, for whom he was named, served in the state Senate for nine years and in the United States House of Representatives from 1900 until 1921, rising during that time to a lofty position within the Martin organization. As one observer wrote, "If [Harry] Byrd's formal education was somewhat sketchy, his political education was conducted by experts and he graduated *magna cum laude.*"[7]

Having barely reached the age of twenty-one, Byrd was first elected to public office in 1908 when he was chosen to the Winchester city council; seven years later he was easily elected to the state Senate. Displaying in that position the same quiet efficiency which characterized his business career, he won the favor of the Martin machine to such an extent that when Hal Flood died in 1921, he was named to replace his deceased uncle as chairman of the state Democratic party. By successfully directing a campaign to defeat a proposed highway bond issue in 1923, he positioned himself for a victorious gubernatorial bid two years later against G. Walter Mapp, who was strongly supported by the outspoken Prohibitionist leader, Methodist Bishop James Cannon, Jr., and by former governor Westmoreland Davis.[8]

Byrd's governorship proved to be remarkably progressive and innovative (especially in light of his subsequent, and well-deserved,

---

[6] The story of Byrd's business success, reflecting the very essence of the Horatio Alger legend, has been recounted so often that it has itself become almost a part of Virginia folklore. For a typical account, see William S. White, "Meet the Honorable Harry (the Rare) Byrd," *Reader's Digest* 82 (April 1963): 207–9.

[7] Hatch, *Byrds of Virginia*, p. 414. See also John A. Treon, "The Political Career of Henry DeLaWarr Flood: A Biographical Sketch, 1865–1921," *Essays in History* (University of Virginia Department of History), 10 (1964–65): 44–65.

[8] Moger, *Bourbonism to Byrd*, pp. 334–42. See also Ronald E. Shibley, "G. Walter Mapp: Politics and Prohibition in Virginia, 1873–1941" (M.A. thesis, U.Va., 1966).

reputation as a conservative). He promoted efficiency by reorganizing the executive branch so as to consolidate some one hundred agencies, accountable to various authorities, into fourteen departments responsible directly to the governor; further streamlining was achieved by instituting the "short ballot" by which the governor, lieutenant governor, and attorney general became the only officials chosen by statewide election. Under the rubric of his "Program for Progress," he secured passage of a strong antilynching law, implemented tax reforms, sponsored conservation and tourism efforts, and increased funds for education, highways, and mental hospitals. The sudden enactment of such a sweeping program prompted one observer to comment that Byrd had "rushed Virginia, as breathless as a girl going to her first ball, into the twentieth century. He gave the Old Dominion a new deal before the New Deal." [9] Significantly, it was all achieved within the framework of a balanced budget; Byrd's opposition to public borrowing was adamant, and the "pay-as-you-go" policy was destined to remain an integral, and inflexible, part of Virginia government so long as Byrd directed the affairs of the Commonwealth.

At the end of his gubernatorial term Byrd was clearly the dominant force in Virginia politics—a position which was solidified when he engineered the victory of his chosen successor, John Garland Pollard, despite the machinations of his persistent adversary, Bishop Cannon. [10] By 1930, then, Byrd was firmly established as the leader of the Democratic organization: Carter Glass, an earlier antagonist, had formed a rapprochement with the Byrd faction following his elevation to the Senate; Westmoreland Davis, decisively defeated for the other Senate seat in 1922 by Claude Swanson, was fading into political

[9] Friddell, *What Is It about Virginia?*, p. 74. The Byrd administration is astutely examined in Robert T. Hawkes, Jr., "The Emergence of a Leader: Harry Flood Byrd, Governor of Virginia, 1926–1930," *Virginia Magazine of History and Biography* 82 (July 1974): 259–81. For a contemporary assessment, see Virginius Dabney, "Governor Byrd of Virginia," *Nation* 126 (June 6, 1928): 632–33. Byrd's own account may be found in his article, "Virginia through the Eyes of Her Governor," *Scribner's Magazine* 83 (June 1928): 684–88.

[10] John S. Hopewell, "Politics in Virginia, 1928–1929" (M.A. thesis, U.Va., 1968); Alvin L. Hall, "Virginia Back in the Fold: The Gubernatorial Campaign and Election of 1929," *Virginia Magazine of History and Biography* 83 (July 1965): 280–302.

obscurity; and Bishop Cannon had twice demonstrated that he could not use Prohibition politics to topple Byrd.

In 1933, upon Swanson's departure to become secretary of the navy in the Roosevelt administration, Governor Pollard appointed Byrd to the Senate, where he remained until illness forced his retirement thirty-two years later. From Washington he continued to direct his organization, perfecting it to such an extent that it was never broken so long as he remained active in politics. Though there were many assaults upon it, the organization was seriously rebuffed only once during that time—in 1937, when James H. Price was elected governor without Byrd's blessing. That setback proved only temporary, however, and from 1941 until his demise in 1966, Byrd dominated Virginia politics as had no man before him in the history of the Commonwealth.

As the Byrd organization waxed in strength it elicited increasingly hostile criticism from its opponents, both Republican and Democratic. Henry W. Anderson, one of the state's most influential Republicans, once expressed his belief that Virginia had "the most tyrannical government of any state since the Stuarts were driven from England and the most inefficient of any state in the western hemisphere, not excepting Mexico, Nicaragua or Venezuela."[11] An antiorganization Democrat later lamented, with somewhat less hyperbole, that "we have here in Virginia a machine that is as ruthless as any machine headed by Pendergast, Crump, or Hague or anywhere in America for that matter."[12]

However appropriate such assessments may have been with respect to the organization's power, they were not indicative of its character. Not only did the Virginia organization under Byrd differ from the urban machines to which it was occasionally compared, it also differed qualitatively from the old Martin machine which spawned it. As Virginia historian Hamilton Eckenrode explained: "The Democratic organization under Barbour and Martin had been a machine; but under Byrd it ceased to be a machine and became a union of leaders. Byrd was

[11] Quoted in Harry F. Byrd, *The Real Issue in This Campaign*, reprint of speech delivered at Richmond, Oct. 1, 1928 (Richmond: Democratic Central Committee, n.d.), p. 8, copy in Harry F. Byrd Papers, University of Virginia Library.

[12] Curry P. Hutchinson to Martin A. Hutchinson, Oct. 16, 1949, Martin A. Hutchinson Papers, University of Virginia Library.

no autocrat. He did not . . . dictate policies. When consulted, he gave his advice, and his advice was usually followed; but he never thrust it unasked on the leaders." [13]

The Byrd organization thus bore little resemblance to the machine stereotype. Newspaper columnist Marquis Childs claimed that the Byrd-dominated party constituted "just as tight an organization as was ever put together in the crowded river wards on the other side of the railroad tracks in any American city you care to name not excluding Kansas City," but he was quick to point out that in Virginia "the controls are not exercised in the same way, of course. It is quieter and much more polite." A contemporary Virginia historian was more direct in his characterization: "This," he said "is a gentleman's machine." [14]

The organization was outwardly unobtrusive in its operation, reflecting the reserved style of its guiding genius. So few were the visible indications of "bossism" that those who sought to fathom the organization's mechanism were often moved to speak of its "elusive, almost phantom-like, quality." The absence of concrete signs of direct control baffled observers. "To relate Senator Byrd to this . . . monolith," mused one journalist, "is a little like debating the divine origin of the Scriptures. You know the answer, but try to prove it." A Washington *Post* investigator was similarly confounded: "There is," he confessed, "almost no palpable evidence of its existence—no hall or clubhouse such as Tammany maintains, no letterheads, and . . . no one even willing to acknowledge leadership in it." [15]

Publicly, Byrd himself was always coy about his alleged organization. His own innocuous description, usually delivered with a benign smile, was that the ruling group was only "a loose organization of friends, who believe in the same principles of government"—or, as he put it on one occasion, "Some people say I run a political machine in

[13] Hamilton J. Eckenrode, "History of Virginia since 1865," unpublished MS, Hamilton J. Eckenrode Papers, University of Virginia Library, p. 407. For a different interpretation of the nature and extent of Byrd's control, see Alvin L. Hall, "James H. Price and Virginia Politics, 1878 to 1943" (Ph.D. diss., U.Va., 1970), p. 44.

[14] Washington *Post*, Mar. 13, 1948; Marshall Fishwick, *A New Look at the Old Dominion* (New York: Harper and Brothers, 1959), p. 252.

[15] Phillips, "New Rumblings in the Old Dominion," p. 34; Washington *Post*, June 9, 1957, pp. A–1, A–17.

Virginia. All I do is offer a little advice now and then."[16] Privately, however, he often referred to "the organization," making frequent mention of it in his personal correspondence. Writing to a prominent Democrat, Byrd specifically defended such a device: "I have always looked upon a political organization as a means to an end," he explained, "namely that through the effectiveness of a political organization, the advancement and progress of the people can be made."[17]

Moreover, Byrd was at times not nearly so shy about the use of naked political power as his disclaimers would have indicated. There is evidence that, particularly in the early years when Byrd was just establishing his control, his insistence upon loyalty within the organization resulted in the use of tactics which could sometimes be heavy-handed.[18] In short, if the accoutrements of power were lacking to Byrd and his followers, the substance was not. It was with justification that Richard E. Byrd once said of his son: "Don't ever cross my boy Harry. He has the face of an angel and the heart of a tiger."[19]

In actual practice the organization did not usually find it necessary to resort to blatant machine tactics. Owing partly to the organic framework of the state's government, partly to the composition of the party itself, and partly to the peculiar ambience of the state of Virginia, the Byrd faction was generally able to retain its control by more subtle methods.

Several features of the state's governmental structure facilitated organization control.[20] One such feature was the extensive power held by the governor, especially after the reorganization carried out at Byrd's direction in 1928. Far more than just the titular head of the state

[16] Clifford Dowdey, "Harry Flood Byrd: Defender of the Faith," *Virginia Record* 78 (Jan. 1956): 64; *Wall Street Journal*, April 11, 1952.

[17] Byrd to Leonard G. Muse, Nov. 22, 1939, Byrd Papers. Letters exchanged among Byrd and his lieutenants contain numerous references to "the organization," none to "the machine." For examples, see Byrd Papers and the William Munford Tuck Papers, Earl Gregg Swem Library, The College of William and Mary in Virginia, Williamsburg.

[18] Confidential source.

[19] Friddell, *What Is It about Virginia?*, p. 74.

[20] The most perceptive and lucid explanation of the mechanics of the organization is J. Harvie Wilkinson III, *Harry Byrd and the Changing Face of Virginia Politics, 1945–1966* (Charlottesville: University Press of Virginia, 1968); see especially pp. 30–38.

government, the governor was responsible for the appointment of almost all boards, committees, and department heads. Second, there was the extensive appointive power vested in the circuit court judges. These men, elected to eight-year terms by the General Assembly, were charged with highly important duties within their circuits, including the appointment of the electoral boards which supervised all county elections. A further aid to organization control lay in the formidable leverage of the State Compensation Board, a three-man panel appointed by the governor. The basic purpose of the board was to determine, within certain previously defined limits, the salaries and expense allowances for local officials who conducted various state functions (e.g., treasurers, commissioners of revenue, Commonwealth's attorneys). Termed the "heart and soul of the Byrd machine" by organization opponents, the board was condemned by critics as a "powerful political persuader." Although investigations of the board never discovered evidence of corruption or political influence in its decisions, the potential for intimidation remained.[21]

At the core of the organization's power were the so-called "courthouse rings," composed chiefly of the five constitutional officers of each county: the clerk of court, county treasurer, commissioner of revenue, Commonwealth's attorney, and sheriff; these might be joined by the members of the county board of supervisors. By virtue of their incumbency, which was frequently long, and their honored standing within their community, such men provided effective sustenance for the organization at the local level. Their support for Byrd organization candidates was so general that adversaries of the organization sought signs of "arm-twisting" from the hierarchy. The search was largely in vain. As J. Harvie Wilkinson III has noted, the adherence of the courthouse crowds to Byrd was achieved mostly by a "remarkable similarity of viewpoint among organization members, which, in the long run, unified them far more effectively and fundamentally than any pressure or patronage ever could have."[22]

Organization dominance was facilitated by the existence of a consis-

[21] Richmond *News Leader*, Aug. 8, 10, 1955; Francis Pickens Miller, *Man from the Valley: Memoirs of a 20th Century Virginian* (Chapel Hill: University of North Carolina Press, 1971), p. 176.

[22] Wilkinson, *Harry Byrd*, p. 6. See also Clifford Dowdey, "The Winds Change," *Virginia Record* 92 (Jan. 1970): 5.

tently small active electorate. The diminution of voter participation was largely attributable to the stringent suffrage requirements—including, most notably, a poll tax provision—established by the 1902 constitution. In the avowed purpose of "purifying" state politics, the framers of that document deliberately undertook to restrict Negro suffrage—in the words of Carter Glass, to "eliminate the darkey as a political factor in this state." At the same time, and not unwittingly, many poor whites were also disfranchised.[23] So restrictive was the new constitution that in the first statewide election following its adoption, the total vote was less than half of what it had been in the preceding election; as late as 1940 less than ten persons in every 1,000 were voting. It was with but little exaggeration that political scientist V. O. Key, Jr., claimed that "by contrast Mississippi is a hotbed of democracy."[24]

Although the poll tax was partly responsible for the low vote totals, that tax alone did not explain the continued lack of voter participation through the years. At work in Virginia was a subtler, more complex phenomenon—a reciprocal, self-perpetuating process through which the organization, by its very successes, tended to breed voter apathy which, in turn, made future successes even more likely. This process induced a sort of fatalism on the part of organization opponents and helped to produce an increasingly torpid electorate.

The overall effect of the process was the creation of a "voting elite," a segment of the population which was attached either economically or spiritually to the organization. Such people admired the fiscal conservatism, administrative efficiency, and ostensible integrity of the organization. If, as critics claimed, the Byrd leadership was too often

[23] Raymond Pulley, *Old Virginia Restored: An Interpretation of the Progressive Impulse, 1870–1930* (Charlottesville: University Press of Virginia, 1968), p. 84. The framing of the 1902 constitution is examined in Wythe W. Holt, Jr., "The Virginia Constitutional Convention of 1901–1902," *Virginia Magazine of History and Biography* 76 (Jan. 1968): 67–102, and in an older work, Ralph C. McDanel, *The Virginia Constitutional Convention of 1901–1902* (Baltimore: Johns Hopkins Press, 1928).

[24] V. O. Key, Jr., *Southern Politics in State and Nation* (New York: Knopf, 1949), Vintage edition, p. 20; Pulley, *Old Virginia Restored*, pp. 84, 182. See also Herman L. Horn, "The Growth and Development of the Democratic Party in Virginia since 1890" (Ph.D. diss., Duke Univ., 1949), pp. 293–341. The poll tax, including attempts to modify or repeal it, is further discussed in Chapter 8.

delinquent in providing needed public services, it was also true that it was seldom guilty of serious misconduct. "No one can truthfully say that it is bad government," noted one observer, "nor can anyone truthfully say that it is an inspired one. It is honest and it is dull."[25]

The allegiance of the voting public to the organization was not based only upon tangible factors; it was attributable in some degree to a peculiarly "Virginian" milieu in which much (some would say too much) emphasis was placed upon honor, decorum, and, especially, family. There existed such a "deliberate cult of the past," suggested Richmond author and editor Douglas Southall Freeman, that many Virginians seemed to be "Shintoists under the skin."[26] In such an environment Harry Byrd—whose very name, according to one writer, "bespoke an almost mystical communion with the state's folklore"— appeared to have virtually a hereditary right to govern. "No Virginian, probably including Robert E. Lee," asserted the New York *Times*, "was so widely and even reverently regarded in the Old Dominion as a symbol of a courtly, comfortable, honorable and unharried past."[27]

Since the Byrd organization thus met the metaphysical as well as material expectations of the upper class, it is easy enough to understand its appeal to that group; it is less easy to ascertain why such a "government of the gentry" was not opposed more vigorously by the lower classes. Indeed, the organization usually drew its greatest majorities in the rural Southside, the very section of the state where the average income was lowest. Even if the black population (which was then largely nonvoting) is discounted, it remains to be explained why there was such general acceptance of the Byrd hegemony by those whites whose interests appeared to have been poorly served by organization policies.

Part of the answer seems to be that the rural folk, being on the whole poorer, less mobile, and less educated than their urban contemporaries, were tied more than any other group to the past, to the "old Virginia" which Byrd represented. Moreover, the remarkably homogeneous ethnic composition of the state meant that many of these

[25] Richard Cope, "The Frustration of Harry Byrd," *The Reporter* 3 (Nov. 21, 1950): 23.

[26] Virginia Writers Project (WPA), *Virginia: A Guide to the Old Dominion* (New York: Oxford University Press, 1940), p. 4.

[27] Wilkinson, *Harry Byrd*, p. 343; New York *Times*, Oct. 21, 1966, p. A–29.

people were also influenced by the "Virginia mystique" which affected their "betters."[28] To be a Virginian, one journalist wryly commented, was to "impute a certain modest elegance to one's genes and chromosomes, to suggest a superior quality of character, breeding and gentility." Somewhat more soberly, H. L. Mencken, who seldom found anything worthy of praise south of the Potomac, grudgingly observed that Virginia was "by long odds, the most civilized of the Southern states," and that its inhabitants, "even the worst of them, show the effects of a great tradition."[29] Whatever the cause, there was little evidence of class antagonism within the state, despite manifest social inequities. Historian Marshall Fishwick put it perceptively. "In rural Virginia," he wrote,

class is not so much a matter of economic position as personal description. Among the poorest Virginians . . . there is a self-respect and sense of worth as men, regardless of what they have done or accumulated, which sets them apart from many Americans who recognize no price but that of achievement. . . . Yet here the old-time aristocracy has not given up, or sunk into decadence. . . . The Snopses may come to town, sit on their haunches and tell ribald stories about jackasses; but they will quiet down when the Colonel walks up. Unless he approves a change or a crusade, they will not endorse it either.[30]

Translated into its political effect, all of this meant that the Byrd organization, once established, was difficult to dislodge. To the despair of organization opponents, the mass of Virginians evinced little animosity toward the ruling clique and, indeed, little concern even for the franchise. One survey of the state's electorate in 1946 revealed that there were many adults, some past middle age, who had never voted; when pressed for reasons, they typically replied that they "just never

[28] The population of Virginia in 1940 was 63.2 percent rural, and almost totally native born; the foreign-born population constituted a minuscule 0.9 percent of the total (U.S. Bureau of the Census, *Census of Population: 1950*, vol. 2, *Characteristics of the Population*, Pt. 46, *Virginia* [Washington, D.C.: U.S. Government Printing Office, 1952], pp. 23–31).

[29] Phillips, "New Rumblings in the Old Dominion," p. 18; H. L. Mencken, *Prejudices: Second Series* (New York: Knopf, 1920), p. 144.

[30] Marshall Fishwick, "F.F.V.'s," *American Quarterly* 11 (Summer 1959): 154–55.

thought much about elections." [31] "A good many white Virginians," the survey concluded, "think that voting is something only for the elite, the 'quality folk.'" [32] Alluding to the apparent ossification of the body politic, North Carolina editor Jonathan Daniels chided his Virginia neighbors by writing in 1947: "Come with me to old Virginia and see at one time and for one price the birthplace and the grave of democracy." Other contemporaries, farther removed than Daniels, were similarly struck by the stagnant—not to say static—condition of the Commonwealth's politics. A French observer, for example, concluded that the most salient characteristic of Virginia was its "resistance to change," while the English historian Arnold Toynbee described the state as presenting "the painful impression of a country living under a spell, in which time has stood still." [33]

In sum, Virginia during the middle decades of the twentieth century was thoroughly dominated by Harry Byrd and his organization. With tradition reinforcing economic and ideological predilections among the elite, with the lower classes deferring to the political judgment of their superiors, and with blacks effectively dissuaded from voting, Byrdism gained virtually the force of a secular religion. It became "downright un-Virginian to oppose the organization," wrote one observer, "and those who had the gall to do so had to be somewhat irrational and unstable"—or, as another appropriately put it, any criticism of Byrd came to be viewed as "a sort of breach of etiquette." [34]

[31] The study, conducted by historian Robert D. Meade, appeared in the Richmond *Times-Dispatch* in a four-part series, Mar. 31, May 12, July 7, and Aug. 4, 1946.

[32] Indicative of such feeling was an incident related by Col. Francis Pickens Miller, one of the foremost opponents of the Byrd organization during the 1940s and 1950s. According to Miller, he once asked a painter (white) who was then working for him if he had qualified to vote in an upcoming election. The painter, incredulous, replied, "Colonel, you know I don't belong to the folks who vote" (Miller, *Man from the Valley*, p. 169).

[33] Richmond *Times-Dispatch*, Feb. 26, 1947; Friddell, *What Is It about Virginia?*, p. 79; Arnold Toynbee, *A Study of History*, abridgement by D. C. Somervell (New York: Oxford University Press, 1947), p. 315.

[34] Virginius Randolph Shackleford III, "The 'Liberal' Movement in Virginia Politics, 1945–1954" (B.A. thesis, Princeton Univ., 1968), p. 11; Richmond *Times-Dispatch*, Oct. 19, 1975.

In the years of Byrd's domination there was one politician whose career remarkably paralleled that of Byrd himself. That politician, who, because of his reputation for brash behavior was at first viewed skeptically by Byrd, eventually won the confidence of the senator to the extent that he became perhaps Byrd's closest ally. In short, from the beginning of the Byrd hegemony until the end, it is likely that no political figure in the Commonwealth better personified the essence of organization politics than did William Munford Tuck.

I   *The Early Years*

Political Apprenticeship
2. *The Development of an Organization Man*

I am a Democrat one hundred per cent.

—*William M. Tuck (1936)*

You can politicate all day and find fifty straight people for you.
But one man against you just ruins the whole day.

—*Tuck (1967)*

Woodrow Wilson once remarked that "Southerners seem born with an interest in public affairs."[1] Such an observation may have been especially valid for Virginians, and it was peculiarly applicable to Virginians of the state's rural Southside. There, in an area redolent of black-eyed peas, turnip greens, and cornbread, the aroma of politics was traditionally in the air. From this region a disproportionately large number of the state's leaders in the early twentieth century had emerged, among them such stalwarts as Andrew Jackson Montague, John W. Daniel, Claude A. Swanson, Henry D. Flood, and Carter Glass; the same area produced such later figures as governors Thomas B. Stanley, Albertis S. Harrison, and Mills E. Godwin, Jr. Throughout the entire life of the Byrd organization this portion of the state provided the organization with much of the leadership and many of the votes that sustained it in power.

In the Southside, the Bible and black belt of the state, old-time politics as well as old-time religion remained vigorous long after both had languished in the more sophisticated urban areas. There, well after the middle of the twentieth century, a political rally could still take on the fervor of a camp meeting; election night in the county seat, with anxious candidates and their eager partisans milling around the Confederate monument in the courthouse square, was a social event of

---

[1] Quoted in Richard Hofstadter, *The American Political Tradition* (New York: Alfred A. Knopf, 1948), Vintage edition, p. 245.

considerable importance. To the inhabitants of a region which offered little diversion from a generally humdrum existence, politics in the Southside was as much an entertainment as a necessary adjunct of government.

It was in the heart of the politically sensitive Southside, in Halifax County, that William Munford (Bill) Tuck was born and reared. Family tradition, perhaps apocryphal, maintained that Tuck's birth on September 28, 1896, came in the midst of a violent storm; but whatever the possible portents of the weather at the time may have been, the genealogy of the family into which he was born augured well for Tuck's future success in public life. Although the Tuck lineage was not as fabled as that of the Byrds, it was, even by Virginia standards, highly respectable. Bill Tuck could trace his ancestry with surety for five generations and, less precisely, to the English Tucks who emigrated from County Kent in the seventeenth century. Since the middle of the eighteenth century the Tuck family had been substantial landowners in Halifax County. The farm on which Bill Tuck was born and which he later owned, Buckshoal Farm, had been in the family since the time of his great-grandfather.[2]

Over the years the Tucks had become recognized not only as respected, modestly prosperous landowners but also as influential political leaders in the Halifax area. William Munford Tuck, the paternal grandfather for whom Bill Tuck was named, served as a captain in the Civil War, commanding Company K, Third Virginia Regiment of Kemper's Brigade at Pickett's Charge, where he was taken captive and imprisoned until the end of the war; in his home county, he served on the Board of Supervisors. Tuck's father, Robert James Tuck, was a tobacco warehouse owner by occupation who served in the House of Delegates for three sessions, 1899–1901, and on the local school board for twenty-five years, during which time he became an acknowledged political savant in Halifax County. By the time of Bill Tuck's birth, one writer aptly observed, "politics was as much a staple with the Tucks as tobacco."[3]

---

[2] Alethea Jane Macon, *John and Edward Tuck of Halifax County, Virginia, and Some of Their Descendants* (Macon, Ga.: Southern Press, 1964), p. 182 and passim; interview with Tuck.

[3] Richmond *Times-Dispatch*, Nov. 20, 1960. The account of Tuck's early life which follows is taken, unless otherwise noted, from interviews with Tuck and from four

The Tuck family was large, consisting of nine children—five boys and four girls—of whom Bill was the youngest except for one girl. Since his mother died when he was only twelve years old, the major influence on Bill's adolescent years was exerted by his father. In later years Tuck recalled his father as a "ruggedly honest" man who often admonished him to "tell the truth, whether it hurts or helps." When he didn't, it often hurt, literally, because the elder Tuck did not spare the rod.

Despite the respected position which the family enjoyed within the community, Tuck's early life on the farm was by no means one of ease. For much of the year, from January until late fall, the tobacco crop demanded almost constant attention: preparing the plant beds, transplanting to the field, cultivating, suckering, harvesting, and stripping in readiness for the market—all had to be done by hand. In the absence of chemical pesticides even the large green hornworms which infested the plants had to be removed one by one and killed by pulling off their heads. It was not a life-style which appealed to young Tuck. "Ours was an austere existence," he recalled. "We worked from early Monday morning to late Saturday night. Growing tobacco was the most laborious of tasks, requiring a strong back, a strong will and a great amount of skill. Not only that," he added, "it was hard as hell."

In Halifax County, as in most of the rural South at that time, there were few opportunities for diversion. Such social life as there was usually revolved around the church, in the form of picnics, covered-dish suppers, and occasional square dances. Nor was there much opportunity to escape, even temporarily, since automobiles were rare. Tuck was almost ten years old before he witnessed any form of conveyance that was not horse-drawn. "I was coming out of the front door of the church when I first heard the sound of an automobile," he remembered. "People were running everywhere trying to catch and quiet the horses before they ran off. And then it rolled into view, a shiny mechanical contraption with wheels like a bicycle. What a stir it created!"

For the young Tuck, politics was the nexus with the larger and more

---

newspaper feature articles: Richmond *Times-Dispatch*, Dec. 21, 1941, and Nov. 20, 1960; Norfolk *Virginian-Pilot*, June 8, 1969; and Halifax *Record-Advertiser*, May 23, 1974.

exciting world beyond the farm. Because of his father's role in county affairs, prominent state politicians, traveling by horse and buggy, frequently stopped to spend a night at the Tucks' house. The impressionable boy was fascinated by the visitors, most of whom were lawyers. They wore better clothes and comported themselves with more grace than the neighboring farmers, he noticed, and their conversation was always stimulating. He decided early that he too wanted to be a lawyer and to have a part in the excitement of public life.

The course toward fulfilling his ambitions began in a one-room school which had been built by his father on a corner of the family farm. Though barely adequate by most standards, the little school was a source of satisfaction to Bob Tuck. As his son later recalled, "He was about as proud of that school as Jefferson was when he founded the University." Conditions in the one-room school were hardly conducive to scholarship, but the discipline was sure. "Everybody was in the same room, from the primer to the big geography," Tuck remembered, "so you heard the same thing all day long. If anybody misbehaved, the teacher took a switch and wore him out."[4]

By his own admission young Tuck often merited a "wearing out." His early years in school, as well as most of his later ones, were not distinguished by academic excellence. Though intelligent and ambitious, Tuck came to be better known, euphemistically, as "a real boy" than as a scholar. In an attempt to direct his energy into more productive channels, the spirited youth was sent to Chatham Training School (later renamed Hargrave Military Academy), a military preparatory school located in neighboring Pittsylvania County. Despite the tighter discipline, Tuck's rambunctious nature was not totally curbed. "I didn't behave too well there either," he confessed. "Chatham was a 'dry' school. Another county boy and I got thirsty one day so we picked up a gallon jug and hiked to a nearby distillery. We hid our prize in the woods off the school grounds, but somehow we got

[4] The one-room school at "High Hill" also produced, in addition to Tuck, another figure who attained national prominence: Oscar Chapman, a distinguished lawyer whose twenty years in government affairs was culminated by his service as secretary of the interior in the Truman administration (Morell Clarke, "A Salute to Bill Tuck," *Virginia and the Virginia County* 7 [June 1953]: 5).

The Tuck family, circa 1898. William Munford is on his father's knee.
(Courtesy of William M. Tuck)

Tuck (fourth from left, in foreground) in 1908 with his four brothers and
three cousins. (Courtesy of William M. Tuck)

caught and received enough demerits to keep us digging up stumps on the school grounds for a month." All the while, however, he maintained an avid interest in politics, sometimes walking several miles into the country merely to gaze awestruck at the mansion of one of his heroes, Governor (subsequently Senator and Secretary of the Navy) Claude Swanson.

After a one-year sojourn in military school, Tuck attended William and Mary Academy for two years before enrolling in the College of William and Mary. As a collegian he was intensely interested in sports as well as in politics, and played for two years on the football team. Having not yet acquired the expansive girth which later characterized his physique, he weighed a svelte 150 pounds when he entered college and had to eat excessively in order to gain weight for football. The highlight of his athletic career came, not in football, but in track, when, in 1917, he won the two-mile race at the state intercollegiate meet.

At William and Mary, Tuck evinced more athletic ability than intellectual prowess. After two years in residence he left the college to become a teacher-principal in Northumberland County during the 1917–18 session. He was doubtful of his pedagogical talents from the outset, admitting that he "wasn't much of a teacher" and preferring to say that he "kept," rather than taught, school. "Fortunately, I didn't stay there but one year," he later recalled, "because if I'd stayed much longer, I would have impressed that whole section with a lot of ignorance."

Believing that he would attain no more success as a teacher than he had as a student, Tuck soon began to look for a more promising, or at least more exciting, livelihood. American involvement in World War I provided just such an opportunity, and the energetic Tuck, for reasons partly patriotic and partly adventurous, enlisted in the United States Marines. Much to his disappointment, his wartime service was limited mainly to the Dominican Republic, where he was assigned until his discharge in July 1919.

Out of military service Tuck resumed pursuit of a legal career with greater seriousness of purpose by entering the school of law at Washington and Lee University. It was while there, in 1920, that he made his first political speech. The occasion was a debate between the partisans of presidential candidates James M. Cox and Warren G.

The twenty-year-old college student at William and Mary. (Courtesy of William M. Tuck)

Harding; Tuck, reared in an area where Republicanism still reeked of the horrors of Reconstruction, lustily supported the Democrat, Cox. His predilection for politics over books nearly cost Tuck his law degree as he failed a course necessary for graduation. He was redeemed only through the personal intervention of the dean of the law school who, after perusing the offending exam paper and taking into account qualities other than pure scholarship, announced his verdict to an anxious Tuck: "You didn't miss it by much," he said, "and, hell, I think you're going to be a good lawyer. I'll pass you." The law degree, the only degree of any kind which Tuck ever earned, was thus duly conferred in June 1921. The only possible remaining impediment to a legal career was the state bar examination and, perhaps conditioned by lack of academic success in the past, Tuck was certain that he would fail it. He later recalled that when he spied his name in the Lynchburg *News*, indicating that he was among those who had passed, he was as thrilled as at any time in his life. Shortly thereafter the new attorney opened his office in the Halifax town of South Boston.

It was not long before Tuck gravitated toward active politics. It was somewhat surprising, considering his family's attachment to the old Martin machine, that he was not totally in alignment with the organization at the outset. In the crucial gubernatorial contest of 1921, for example, Tuck gave his support in the primary to the independent-minded Henry St. George Tucker, a man whom he much admired and who was, in Tuck's words, "too much of a gentleman to be a politician." When, however, Tucker was defeated by organization candidate E. Lee Trinkle in the primary, Tuck dutifully supported the latter in the general election.

An even more blatant apostasy—and one which was potentially more injurious to any future political ambitions—came two years later in 1923 when, at the age of twenty-seven, Tuck made his political debut by running for one of the two Halifax County seats in the House of Delegates. The hottest campaign controversy across the state that year involved the proposed highway bond issue, and Tuck, recognizing the need for improving the frequently muddy and impassable roads in his area, took his stand in favor of the bonds. To his chagrin, he came to realize in the course of the campaign that he had erred politically. "As I got around," he explained, "I could feel more and more that the people in the county were overwhelmingly opposed to the bonds. And there I was, *for* the bonds, running for the House of Delegates!"[5] The young candidate's solution to the problem was to announce that even though he personally favored the bonds, he would, if elected, be bound in his

[5] Richmond *Times-Dispatch*, Sept. 28, 1975.

voting by the outcome of the referendum in Halifax. The overwhelming defeat of the bonds left little doubt in Tuck's mind that the people
of his area wanted no part of state indebtedness.

Although he had been on the losing side of the bond referendum,
Tuck's own candidacy did not suffer as a consequence; in a three-way
race for the House seat, he led the ticket. The victory marked the
beginning of a long and often tempestuous public career—one which
would last almost a half-century without ever being tarnished by
electoral defeat. It also meant the learning of a valuable political lesson:
from that point onward, Tuck would seldom be found in opposition to
the policies of the Democratic organization.

In January 1924 Bill Tuck climbed the long white steps of the
Capitol in Richmond, surveyed the premises, and searched for his seat
in the House of Delegates. It was the first time he had ever seen the
inside of the legislative hall. "My father," he explained, "didn't believe
in going anywhere unless you had *business*." For the next four years the
Halifax delegate had ample opportunity to learn his way around the
Capitol as his constituents twice returned him to office.

Just as he seemed to be establishing himself as a permanent fixture in
the legislature, he decided to retire from active politics. The reason was
quite simple, he explained, and could be stated in three words: Eva
Lovelace Dillard. "She was the prettiest thing I ever saw, and I fell so
desperately in love with her that I'd have done anything for her." It
appeared for a while that his feelings for the South Boston widow
would go unrequited. "She was reluctant to marry me," he said, "as I
asked her many times. I think she thought I was kind of rough."
Ultimately his entreaties were successful, and on February 26, 1928,
the two were married.

New family responsibilities soon caused Tuck to realize that his
penchant for politics was working to his financial disadvantage. He
therefore decided not to seek reelection to the legislature in order to
devote full time to his law practice. However, when his successor in the
House died shortly after the General Assembly convened in 1930,
Tuck found himself eminently available. "I inaugurated the first draft I
ever heard of," he explained. "I persuaded the people to draft me."

With, then, the exception of one brief hiatus, Tuck remained for
seven years in the House of Delegates, where he served on several
important standing committees, including the General Laws and

Privileges and Elections Committees. In 1931, following the death of his father the previous year, he decided to offer for the state Senate. A close friend and political mentor, Marshall B. Booker, advised him: "Bill, your father was a helluva sight more popular than you are. Make a list of everybody you ever heard him mention and look up every one of them." Tuck followed the advice and was successful. "I reckon," he said, "my daddy got me 1200 votes, from the grave."[6]

Although the identification with his father may well have helped, Bill Tuck was by that time acquiring a substantial reputation of his own. Ruggedly, robustly handsome, he possessed a somewhat roguish, yet gentle, wit and a simple rustic charm that deeply appealed to his predominantly rural constituency. He was an indefatigable campaigner with an uncanny faculty for remembering names. The air of genuine friendliness which he exuded led those whom he met to regard him not so much as a politician soliciting a vote but as an old friend renewing an acquaintance. And, if subtler methods failed, Tuck was not adverse to employing more tangible, potable inducements; in the days of Prohibition he found that it was sometimes helpful "to ride the back roads with a few jars of white lightning in a black satchel."[7] Parlaying his considerable natural abilities with the acquired wiles of his chosen profession, Tuck remained in the state Senate throughout the 1930s, during which time he developed into a formidable politician of potential statewide appeal.

The caliber of Tuck's service in the General Assembly was disparaged by some critics who claimed that throughout his long tenure he was responsible for little significant legislation. While it was true that he did not flood the hopper with bills, his legislative career was not undistinguished, nor was it, as his detractors argued, devoid of enlightened proposals. The esteem in which he was held by his colleagues was evidenced by his appointment to the important seven-member Senate Steering Committee at the very beginning of his freshman term in the upper chamber. In succeeding sessions he served on the Committees of Finance, Privileges and Elections, and Nominations and was chosen to be chairman of the General Laws Committee. Most advan-

[6] Virginia, *Manual of the Senate and the House of Delegates, 1930* (Richmond: Division of Purchase and Printing, 1930), pp. 26–29; Norfolk *Virginian-Pilot*, June 8, 1969.
[7] Richmond *Times-Dispatch*, May 7, 1967.

tageous in the wielding of political power was his rise to the chairmanship of the Democratic caucus, a position which made him the effective
leader of the Senate.[8]

Most of Tuck's service in the state Senate took place during the
presidency of Franklin D. Roosevelt and, consequently, necessitated
Tuck's taking a stand on various New Deal proposals. Initially better
disposed toward the Roosevelt program than were many of his peers,
Tuck often voted in favor of measures designed to extend the New Deal
into Virginia. Among such measures was an important bill sponsored
by Tuck at the 1933 extra session which authorized the expenditure of
state funds "for the purpose of co-operating with the government of the
United States in reducing and relieving unemployment and in conserv-
ing natural resources." Although in later years a more conservative
Tuck expressed reservations about the wisdom of spending public
money for such purposes, it was his bill which gave the major impetus
to the development of the state's park system.[9]

At the regular session of the legislature in 1936 Tuck supported
several measures designed to provide relief and reform in Virginia,
including a new child labor law. He was unavailing in his support of a
bill to provide for unemployment compensation in the state, a measure
which proved to be one of the most controversial of the entire session. If
enacted, the bill would have allowed workers to partake of the benefits
of the fund, provided by federal legislation, to which employers
already had to contribute irrespective of individual state action; defeat
of the bill would mean that even though employers were obligated to
participate in the program, the workers of Virginia would not reap the
benefits. Tuck was among the slim majority of Senate members who
voted, 18–17, in favor of the unemployment compensation bill. The
House, however, defeated the measure. When it became clear that the
state would lose all benefits from the federal program unless it acted

[8] *Manual of the Senate and House of Delegates, 1938*, p. 22; interview with Tuck. The
chairmanship of the caucus was of great strategic importance because the holder of
that position appointed the Steering Committee which, in turn, appointed all other
committees of the upper house.

[9] Ronald L. Heinemann, "Depression and New Deal in Virginia" (Ph.D. diss.,
U.Va., 1968), pp. 51–52; Virginia, *Journal of the Senate of Virginia, Extra Session,
1933* (Richmond: Division of Purchase and Printing, 1933), pp. 152–53, 175;
interview with Tuck.

favorably on the state bill, an extra session was called (at the cost of some $70,000) which hastily approved virtually the same piece of legislation which it had rejected earlier in the year.[10]

Tuck's voting record in the 1938 General Assembly included support of several measures deemed to be progressive, among them the Old Age Assistance Act and a jail reform bill. In response to a legislative study commission report which revealed the state's prison system to be antiquated and overcrowded, Tuck cosponsored a measure designed to reduce the number of inmates and establish a more orderly penal structure. Although the proposal was generally hailed in the press and won easy approval in the Senate, the House of Delegates failed to act on the bill, thus indefinitely postponing Tuck's prison reform plan.[11]

Except for his initial gaffe in supporting the proposed highway bond issue in 1923, Tuck remained throughout his tenure in the state legislature well within the ambit of the organization then being consolidated by Harry Byrd. From the outset Tuck had found the Byrd philosophy of "sound government" congenial to his own conservative way of thinking. On the eve of Byrd's gubernatorial term he assured the governor-elect that he was "thoroughly in accord" with his program and urged Byrd to "call upon me freely to support the policies of your administration."[12]

Such a call was not long in coming. Although most of Byrd's program was enacted forthwith by a complaisant legislature, one of his recommendations—a measure which would have required that uniforms be worn by all officers making arrests or searches on the highways of the state—was defeated in the House. Since Tuck had been absent on the day the vote was taken, he was eligible to move reconsideration of the vote by which the bill had been defeated. Tuck's motion

[10] *Journal of the Senate,* 1936, pp. 320–411; *Journal of the Senate, Extra Session, December 14, 1936 – January 11, 1937,* p. 52.

[11] The bill provided for extending bail procedures, improving the probation system, instituting recognizance, and allowing installment payment of fines (*Journal of the Senate,* 1938, pp. 127–28, 610–11; Virginia, *Journal of the House of Delegates of the Commonwealth of Virginia,* 1938 [Richmond: Division of Purchase and Printing, 1938], pp. 877, 1056–57; Richmond *Times-Dispatch,* Feb. 3, 1938).

[12] Tuck to Byrd, Dec. 8, 1925, Tuck Papers.

prevailed and the legislation passed. "Governor Byrd," noted Tuck, "seemed to be quite grateful for it." [13]

In other ways, too, Tuck ingratiated himself with the new governor. In 1926, at the first session of the General Assembly under Byrd, Tuck threw his support behind Thomas W. Ozlin of Lunenburg in his contest against James H. Price of Richmond for the speakership of the House of Delegates. The narrow victory by Ozlin, who had been a leader in the fight against highway bonds, was interpreted by contemporaries as a victory for the organization, an opinion shared by Price's biographer, who termed the incident "another step in Byrd's consolidation of power." [14] Throughout Byrd's governorship Tuck avidly supported the "Program of Progress" which the governor espoused. He was particularly interested in the proposed reorganization of the state government and encouraged Byrd to call the special legislative session in 1927 which expedited that reform. [15] By the end of Byrd's term as governor there had evolved between the two men a political relationship which was cordial, though not intimate.

Following Byrd's departure for the United States Senate in 1933, Tuck continued to devote himself to the interests of the state organization. Much of his work was carried out sub rosa. ("A real leader," he once explained, "works behind the scenes.")[16] His activities in behalf of Prohibition repeal typified such covert maneuvers.

By both personal inclination and governmental philosophy, Tuck was opposed to Prohibition. "It was just unworkable," he declared years later. "Prohibition agents trampled the people's rights. They violated the principle that a man is presumed to be innocent until guilt is established beyond reasonable doubt." In addition there were practical problems. "Prohibition generated gangsters like Al Capone. There were shootouts on the highways. People got killed. Resentment grew and grew." [17]

Such resentment culminated in February 1933 with congressional

---

[13] *Journal of the House of Delegates*, 1926, p. 1003; Richmond *Times-Dispatch*, Oct. 19, 1975.

[14] Hall, "Price," p. 43.

[15] Tuck to Byrd, Dec. 2, 1926, Tuck Papers.

[16] Interview with Tuck.

[17] Richmond *Times-Dispatch*, Oct. 12, 1975.

passage of the Twenty-first Amendment, which provided for the repeal of Prohibition. With the decision on ratification then in the hands of the states, it became necessary for the Byrd organization to take a position on the issue of repeal in Virginia. There were a number of antiorganization politicians in the state, led by Vivian Page of Norfolk and C. O'Conor Goolrick of Fredericksburg, who demanded that a special session of the General Assembly be called in order to expedite the ending of the "noble experiment." The governor, organization man John Garland Pollard, a noted "dry" who could scarcely have been expected to embrace repeal with enthusiasm, refused their pleas, however, and most organization spokesmen initially followed Pollard's lead. Tuck, in a response typical of the organization leadership, announced by telegram on March 27 that he was "opposed to a special session of the General Assembly at this time for any purpose." [18]

Tuck and other organization men appear to have acted as they did from two main considerations. First, they did not believe that the advantages to be gained from an early repeal would be sufficient to offset the costs of an extra Assembly session; second, many organization leaders came from rural sections of the state where Prohibition had been most popular and were therefore solicitous of the "dry" tendencies of their constituents. Tuck later explained that even though he personally was "known to have been wet in sentiments," he responded negatively at first because "I was generally at that time opposed to special sessions and also my constituents had always voted dry. . . . [I] naturally had to follow the known sentiments of my own people." [19]

Gradually, though, the organization detected increasing public favor toward repeal. "There is right much dissatisfaction now," Tuck informed Byrd, "more than I have ever seen, and right many are criticizing me for my telegram opposing an extra session." With the gubernatorial election scheduled for later that same year, the organization was especially sensitive to the changing public temper, and anxious to arrange itself on the appropriate side of the repeal issue. The organization candidate for the governorship, former Ninth District congressman and member of the State Corporation Commission

[18] Ibid., Mar. 28, 1933.
[19] Letter from Tuck to author, Jan. 28, 1972.

George Campbell Peery, was an advocate of temperance, but the exigencies of Prohibition politics led to an amelioration of his antiliquor posture. Sensing the shift in public feelings, Tuck advocated Peery's accommodation to the new repeal sentiment. "I believe there will be a revolt,"he warned Byrd, "unless there is some modification, and I advised Judge Peery last week to come out as wet as his conscience would permit him." [20]

Peery's opponents in the August primary were both "wets," state Senator W. Worth Smith of Louisa and former Second District congressman Joseph T. Deal of Norfolk. As the election approached, with Prohibition bulking large as an issue, Peery came out in favor of repeal. The organization leadership, in order to give support to the repeal movement, had by early summer reversed itself and had begun to express interest in an extra legislative session. As Tuck recalled, "There was such a howl over the state that it became almost necessary to take some action." [21]

The great impediment to a special Assembly meeting was the long-avowed Prohibition stance of Governor Pollard. Unwilling to renounce his "dry" position openly, Pollard let it be known that he would summon a special session to effect repeal only upon the petition of at least two-thirds of the members of the legislature. It was at that juncture that Bill Tuck received a call from Senator Byrd asking if he would do what he could to rally the support of the requisite number of members to force the extra session. Tuck gladly obliged. He left Halifax immediately for the capital, took a room in the Hotel Richmond, and from there communicated with every member of the General Assembly either by telephone or wire, exhorting each one to request the governor to convene the legislature. His diligence was rewarded when the required number of appeals reached Governor Pollard, who proceeded to call a special session to meet in August. With the "wet" candidates, Smith and Deal, thus effectively robbed of

[20] Tuck to Byrd, Mar. 29, 1933, Tuck Papers. "The loud mouth wets around here have quieted down considerably," Tuck continued, "but the feeling is still there and they are demanding some change."

[21] Letter from Tuck to author, Jan. 28, 1972. The most complete account of the 1933 gubernatorial primary is Joseph Andrew Fry, "George Campbell Peery: Conservative Son of Old Virginia" (M.A. thesis, U.Va., 1970), pp. 37–52.

one of their most potent issues, George Peery easily triumphed in the gubernatorial primary.[22]

The August meeting of the General Assembly quickly set up the machinery for deciding the question of repeal by ordering a dual referendum on the proposed Twenty-first Amendment and on the continuance of state Prohibition under the Layman Act. The Assembly also approved a measure which permitted the immediate sale of state-taxed beer, a measure which Tuck actively supported. The propriety of the organization's decision to support repeal was made clear when the October referendum resulted in the resounding defeat of Prohibition: of the 157,976 votes cast, roughly 100,000 were cast in favor of repeal.[23]

Tuck's efforts toward repeal showed him to be a shrewd and energetic worker and did much to elevate him in the esteem of the Byrd hierarchy. During his subsequent years in the state Senate he worked for the strengthening of the organization, using his vantage point to keep a perceptive eye on state affairs. Periodically he passed his observations along to Senator Byrd. Of some concern to Tuck was the possibility that Byrd might acquire the reputation of a heavy-handed political boss. He advised caution, therefore, in making political appointments since blatant dispensing of patronage, he warned the senator, "makes it appear that you are the absolute political dictator." The admonition did not mean, however, that Tuck disapproved of strict control by Byrd—indeed, he thought it desirable. "I believe," he wrote Byrd, "that you should name every person, but the public should not know this, and that no one should be given a position of any sort unless they are tried and true Byrd men, and they should know from what source their appointment comes." Once men were appointed, Tuck suggested, Byrd should "instruct them to take the

---

[22] Richmond *Times-Dispatch*, Mar. 27, Aug. 17, 1933, Oct. 12, 1975; letter from Tuck to author, Jan. 28, 1972; Fry, "Peery," pp. 50–52.

[23] Eckenrode, "Virginia since 1865," pp. 422–23. At the regular session of the General Assembly in 1934, the Alcoholic Beverage Control Board was established to oversee the sale of liquor by issuing licenses for the sale of beer and wine and by dispensing liquor through state-operated stores (Virginia, *Acts of the General Assembly of the Commonwealth of Virginia, 1934* [Richmond: Division of Purchase and Printing, 1934], p. 100).

blame for everything that is unpleasant and give you the credit for everything that is good." [24]

When Byrd was first challenged for his Senate seat in November 1933, Tuck proved his worth as a political ally in the Southside by helping to deliver Halifax to the incumbent by the largest majority of any county in the state. [25] Tuck was heartened by the result, especially because he had heard rumors during the campaign that Byrd was "losing out with the people," owing perhaps to growing skepticism regarding Byrd's support of Roosevelt's New Deal. "I think it is a strong tribute to the way in which you have administered the affairs of Virginia," Tuck told the senator, "that we have passed through the depression, the worst that has ever been known, without the state organization losing any prestige." The magnitude of the election victory seemed to Tuck to be a good omen for the future of the Byrd hegemony. "If the affairs of Virginia are continued to be managed as they have been, in a cautious and intelligent way," he predicted, "it will be a long time before our friends are overthrown, if ever." [26]

Tuck's airy optimism, induced by Byrd's overwhelming victory, was tempered somewhat during succeeding years as Byrd, along with his Senate colleague, Carter Glass, became increasingly strident in opposition to the New Deal. In no portion of Virginia was Roosevelt more popular than in the Southside. The inhabitants of that region, having suffered more perhaps than most Virginians during the early years of the depression, regarded Roosevelt with deep admiration, and regularly gave him larger majorities than did the state as a whole. [27] As a representative of that rural area, Tuck was sensitive to Byrd's attitude

[24] Tuck to Byrd, Sept. 14, 1933, Tuck Papers.
[25] In Halifax, Byrd received 1,668 votes while his Republican opponent, Henry A. Wise, received a mere 82 (Alexander Heard and Donald S. Strong, *Southern Primaries and Elections, 1920–1949* [University, Ala.: University of Alabama Press, 1950], p. 199).
[26] Tuck to Byrd, Nov. 10, 1933, Tuck Papers.
[27] Edgar Eugene Robinson, *They Voted for Roosevelt* (Stanford, Calif.: Stanford University Press, 1947), pp. 44, 170–74. For an analysis of the relationship between Virginia's senators and the Roosevelt administration, see Robert F. Hunter, "Carter Glass, Harry Byrd, and the New Deal, 1932–1936," *Virginia Social Science Journal* 4 (Nov. 1969): 91–103; and Robert T. Cochran, Jr., "Virginia's Opposition to the New Deal" (M.A. thesis, Georgetown Univ., 1950).

toward farm legislation, especially that which affected tobacco, the main agricultural commodity of the region. Initially Byrd had supported the Roosevelt farm program, but by 1934 he had come to oppose the administration's plan for broadening the Agricultural Adjustment Act. Fearing that the proposed changes would result in making the secretary of agriculture a veritable "Hitler of American agriculture," Byrd fought the plan vigorously and, in one analyst's opinion, "was largely to blame for the defeat of the amendments of AAA in 1934." [28] When Byrd voiced opposition to the Kerr-Smith Tobacco Control Act, Tuck was perplexed, as well he might have been since a referendum on the act in his home county of Halifax revealed that fully 99 percent of the farmers approved of the measure. [29]

Although he never revealed any personal disagreement with Byrd, Tuck did evince some anxiety as a result of the senator's apparent failure to adhere more closely to the will of his Southside constituents—a particularly dangerous practice in light of the importance of that region in maintaining organization control. Writing to Fifth District Congressman Thomas G. Burch, Tuck expressed his alarm. "There is strong sentiment for Roosevelt in this section of the state," he warned, "and from what I hear, in nearly all other sections of the state. Unless the situation is treated in the proper way, the future success of the state organization will be placed in jeopardy." [30]

For his own part Tuck continued to support the Roosevelt administration for some time after Byrd had soured on the New Deal, and his activities in the Virginia legislature reflected his acceptance of much of the national relief and reform program. In November 1936 Tuck assured a labor leader that as a member of the state Senate he had "voted for every measure that would enable the state to enjoy the full benefits of the Roosevelt program." During the presidential campaign of that same year Tuck's enthusiasm for the Democratic incumbent exceeded

[28] Heinemann, "Depression and New Deal in Virginia," p. 157. Evidence of Tuck's wariness toward Byrd's stand on New Deal agricultural programs can be found in Tuck to Byrd, June 7, 1934, June 22, 1938, and Tuck to Thomas G. Burch, Mar. 13, 1935, Tuck Papers.

[29] Tuck to Byrd, June 7, 1934, Tuck Papers. Heinemann, "Depression and New Deal in Virginia," p. 160, notes that the flue-cured tobacco growers of Halifax voted in favor of the Kerr-Smith Act by a margin of 3,000 to 9.

[30] Tuck to Burch, Aug. 17, 1935, Tuck Papers.

that of Byrd, although the senator did campaign perfunctorily for the ticket himself. In private, responding to a Norfolk attorney's condemnation of New Deal banking policies, Tuck appeared incredulous, pointing out that

the Democratic policies enunciated by Roosevelt and made a reality by the Democratic Congress saved what banks were left. Strange to say, however, most of the large bankers of the country are opposing the re-election of Roosevelt, and one of the main reasons for this is that he has made it possible for the ordinary distressed landowner and homeowner to secure an adequate amount of credit at a low rate of interest. . . . The Republicans, on the other hand, during the administration of Hoover operated and controlled the affairs of government so that certain persons enjoyed privileges that were not extended to the rest of the country.[31]

Publicly the Halifax legislator extended his defense of the first Roosevelt administration. Speaking at a rally of Young Democrats in his home county, Tuck heatedly denounced the self-styled "Jeffersonian Democrats" who opposed Roosevelt's reelection. Such persons, he said, were the "descendants of the already discredited American Liberty League, . . . who clothe themselves in the habiliments of democracy, and slander the memory of Jefferson by devoting it to base and unworthy purposes." He pleaded that the leadership of "these Democratic apostates" be rejected and that the Roosevelt program be supported because it represented fundamental American goals: "It is certainly in accordance with the spirit, if not the letter, of the Constitution that our governmental affairs should be so regulated and controlled that every honest citizen could have an opportunity to find useful employment and earn an honest living."[32]

Election returns in Halifax demonstrated the extent of Tuck's influence. The 91.1 percent of the votes which Roosevelt received in that county was the highest percentage which he achieved in any political subdivision of the state in which over 2,000 ballots were cast. The overwhelming margin left Tuck exultant. "I am a Democrat one

[31] Tuck to W. D. Anderson, chairman of the State Legislative Committee of the Virginia Federation of Labor, Nov. 20, 1936, Tuck to Garrett Baxter, Oct. 1, 1936, Tuck Papers. For Byrd's attitude toward Roosevelt and his program, see Heinemann, "Depression and New Deal in Virginia," pp. 189–227.

[32] Richmond *Times-Dispatch*, Sept. 23, 1936.

hundred per cent," he said shortly after the election, "and one who believes that Roosevelt has revamped and revitalized the Democratic party and made it stand for something great. I have supported him throughout every hour of his administration."[33]

Tuck evinced some concern that his more favorable predisposition toward the New Deal, at least in its early form, might cause a misunderstanding with Senator Byrd. His anxiety was revealed in a letter to his political confidant, Congressman Burch, when he emphasized that he wanted Byrd "to know that I have never broken away, and do not intend ever to break away from the political moorings to which I was born and have adhered to all these years." Despite any differences in their attitudes toward the national administration, there was no hint of friction between the two men; indeed, their association grew closer as time passed. Tuck took every opportunity to praise the senator and to defend him whenever he came under attack. Byrd, in turn, was effusive in his admiration for Tuck. "There is no friend I have," he assured him, "whose friendship I value more than yours. I feel to you like I feel toward my brother."[34]

It was not long after Roosevelt's reelection in 1936 that Tuck's view of the New Deal began to coalesce with Byrd's. As the president seemed bent on arrogating more personal power, and as heavy deficit spending continued, Tuck became increasingly wary. By 1938 he was in direct opposition to much of the Roosevelt program. "I congratulate you," he wrote Byrd in April of that year, "on your fight against the Administration Reorganization Bill. . . . I am glad also that you are against any further 'pump-priming.' I hope you will be equally successful in your opposition to this wild orgy of spending."[35]

On the state level, meanwhile, the possibility of organization trouble, of which Tuck had forewarned, had come to fruition in 1937 in the person of James H. Price. For seven consecutive terms Price had represented Richmond in the House of Delegates until, in 1929, he was elected lieutenant governor, a position which he held for two

[33] Tuck to W. D. Anderson, Nov. 20, 1936, Tuck Papers. For a convenient summary of vote distribution, see Robinson, *They Voted for Roosevelt*, pp. 170–74.

[34] Tuck to Burch, Aug. 17, 1935, Byrd to Tuck, Aug. 23, 1935, Tuck Papers. Byrd sometimes appealed directly to Tuck for help in countering criticism. See, for example, Byrd to Tuck, July 25, 1934, Tuck to Byrd, July 26, 1934, ibid.

[35] Tuck to Byrd, April 13, 1938, ibid.

terms. Throughout his lengthy service he never became a member of
the inner circle of the organization, as evidenced by his loss to Ozlin in
the House speakership contest in 1926. Byrd's own disenchantment
with Price was increased in the 1930s by the lieutenant governor's
tendency toward independence and by his open advocacy of many of
the New Deal programs. Price's manifest desire for political advancement presented the organization with its greatest challenge since Byrd
had established himself as leader. When Price announced himself as a
candidate for the governorship in 1937, the organization hierarchy was
faced with the choice of accepting him as its own or opposing him and
taking a considerable risk of defeat.[36]

Tuck by this time was becoming an influential organization
member, and he, like many of the other insiders, was opposed initially
to Price's candidacy. According to Tuck the gubernatorial aspirant
"looked the part of a governor—he was a very handsome man—but he
didn't give the impression of much strength." Even Tuck, though,
conceded the lieutenant governor's immense popularity. Unable to
devise a stratagem for staying Price's candidacy and fearing that he
might prove impossible to defeat openly, most of the leaders of the
organization eventually accommodated themselves to him. "I did
support Price," Tuck later recalled, "but I was right late coming out for
him."[37] With the grudging acquiescence of the Byrd coterie and aided
by his association with the popular New Deal, Price was easily
elected.[38]

Although the support of the organization, timid as it was, served to
smooth the way for Price's election, his most important financial

[36] The best account of Price's rise to prominence is Hall, "Price," pp. 27–159; his
gubernatorial race is analyzed in Carl J. Vipperman, "The Coattail Campaign: James
H. Price and the Election of 1937 in Virginia," *Essays in History* (U. Va. Department
of History), 8 (1964): 47–61.

[37] Interview with Tuck. It is clear that the organization endeavored to circumvent
Price and that Tuck was in complete accord with that attempt. For evidence, see
Harry F. Byrd, Jr., to Tuck, June 4, 1948, Tuck Papers.

[38] It has been suggested that one of the reasons for the continued success of the
organization was its willingness to adapt itself to political realities, even if it meant
embracing a candidate not totally to its liking. V. O. Key, Jr., for example, in
Southern Politics (p. 23), points out that "the high command usually accepts those that
it probably could not defeat." The thesis of Vipperman, "The Coattail Campaign," is
that Price was greatly aided by his known support of the Roosevelt administration.

backing came from sources outside the Byrd faction, from such organization adversaries as Ninth District Congressman John Flannagan, former governor Westmoreland Davis, and former secretary of the Democratic State Central Committee Martin Hutchinson. Once in office Price embarked upon a course which revealed his antiorganization bias. As Tuck explained it: "He commenced kicking off everybody who had been friendly to the organization—men like T. McCall Frazier [chairman of the ABC Board] and E. R. Combs [chairman of the State Compensation Board]. I didn't like that a bit and Senator Byrd didn't either."[39]

Particularly galling was Price's dismissal of "Ebbie" Combs. Known in the organization affectionately and appropriately as "The Chief," Combs was regarded by consensus as the most powerful figure in the Byrd hierarchy save the senator himself. A native of southwest Virginia, Combs became a close personal and political friend of Byrd's in the 1920s, owing partly to the help which he rendered to Byrd in defeating the highway bond issue. When Byrd was elected governor, he appointed Combs comptroller of Virginia. The main source of Combs's power derived from his position as chairman of the State Compensation Board, a position to which he was appointed in 1934 immediately after the board was created. In the view of its critics that agency was the organization's "Hindenburg line as far as defense of political patronage in Virginia is concerned."[40] With Byrd in the Senate after 1933, Combs became the "field general" of the organization's operations, presiding over political matters both large and small. According to James Latimer, the knowledgeable political writer for the Richmond *Times-Dispatch*, "Combs was 'the man to see' for clearance of things political with Byrd or entree to Byrd. It became almost a ritual for any aspiring young Democrat who wanted to run for office to make a pilgrimage to Richmond to meet Combs and talk things over." When Combs informed party members as to what was "satisfactory to the

---

[39] Interview with Tuck. Principal contributors to the Price campaign are listed in an undated memorandum in the Charles J. Harkrader Papers, University of Virginia Library.

[40] Horn, "Democratic Party in Virginia," p. 430; Richmond *Times-Dispatch*, Feb. 24, 1938.

state organization and the state administration," his words bore the imprimatur of Senator Byrd himself.[41]

It was the removal of Combs which marked a conclusive break between Jim Price and the organization. Thereafter, for the duration of Price's administration, the Byrd faction was mainly concerned with thwarting the governor's program. In the words of one member of the General Assembly, the Byrd-controlled legislature devoted itself to "naming bridges and bedeviling Jim Price." In that obstructionist course of action few persons were more energetic than Tuck, who as chairman of the Democratic caucus in the Senate played a large, if usually unseen, part.[42]

Early in his governorship Price had revealed a fatal flaw as a politician: lacking the temperament of an effective political manipulator, he was independent enough to remove some of his enemies, but not vindictive enough to remove them all. The result was that he antagonized his opponents but did not weaken them sufficiently to prevent their retaliation. Thus by the end of his first two years in office the Byrd forces were sensing a renascence at the conclusion of his term, including the recapture of the governorship in 1941. Bill Tuck was fully aware that the political signs were propitious for an organization candidate, telling Byrd that although he had been "very much worried two or three years ago," he now found the situation "most encouraging."[43] With almost two decades of legislative service behind him and believing that the time was ripe for him to move up the *cursus honorum*, Tuck embarked upon a determined campaign to ensure that he himself would be that candidate.

The process by which the Byrd organization bestowed its endorsement—or, in the usual political parlance, "gave the nod"—was a rather mysterious one. According to one student of state politics, "One day nobody would have any definite opinion on an important issue or

[41] James Latimer, "Virginia Politics, 1950–1960" (unpublished MS, Latimer's personal files), p. 26. For examples of Combs's influence, see Combs to Charles J. Harkrader, Mar. 22, 1935, Harkrader Papers; Combs to Tuck, Dec. 6, 1941, and Tuck to Robert P. Bagwell, Jan. 16, 1943, Tuck Papers.

[42] Roanoke *World-News*, Oct. 5, 1945; Hall, "Price," p. 182; interview with Tuck.

[43] Tuck to Byrd, Jan. 9, 1939, Tuck Papers.

election; then Harry Byrd would make a speech or a few telephone calls, and soon opinions of near uniformity would abound." As a result, claimed another observer, gubernatorial contests in Virginia were "little more than ceremonial acknowledgements of *faits accomplis*. It could scarcely be said that gentlemen 'run' for the governorship in the Old Dominion. By an obscure and rarely challenged process they have emerged, one by one, each in his season, and succeed to that high office unopposed and by what has amounted to acclamation." [44]

Despite the persistent insinuations that the organization dictated the choice of a governor, the decision was never made imperiously by Byrd alone. The process included, among other factors, a sounding of the local courthouse cliques to ascertain their inclinations. According to J. Harvie Wilkinson, the ultimate decision resulted from an amalgam of "the informal give and take of courthouse preferences, the Senator's own wishes, and the choice of the Senator's closest advisers." [45] Still the sine qua non was Byrd's own benediction, and gaining of his favor constituted the crucial part of the gubernatorial quest.

Owing to his lengthy service to the organization in the General Assembly and, more recently, to his endeavors in opposition to the Price program, Tuck was invariably named as a possible choice for the Byrd mantle. He was particularly encouraged in April 1940 when informed by David K. E. Bruce, an important conduit to Byrd, "From everything I have heard, your prospects are very bright." During the spring and summer, however, he became dismayed by continuing press reports that several other Byrd partisans intended to enter the race— among them House Speaker Ashton Dovell, former Speaker Thomas Ozlin, and Second District Congressman Colgate W. Darden, Jr.— and that Byrd was leaning toward Darden. Nevertheless, writing to Bruce, he expressed his belief that "if my friends will at the proper time press him [Byrd] hard enough, it will work out all right." Bruce agreed, counseling Tuck to bide his time; the best policy, said Bruce, was simply to "sit steady." [46]

---

[44] Shackleford, "The 'Liberal' Movement in Virginia Politics," p. ix; Phillips, "New Rumblings in the Old Dominion," p. 10.

[45] Wilkinson, *Harry Byrd*, p. 14.

[46] Bruce to Tuck, April 1, Oct. 22, 1940, Tuck to Bruce, Oct. 26, 1940, Tuck Papers. Bruce cautioned Tuck specifically not to "make any favorable references to those items of New Deal legislation which have been opposed by . . . Byrd."

Such advice proved increasingly difficult for Tuck to take. With Darden's candidacy snowballing and state newspapers suggesting that the Halifax senator would be shunted aside, Tuck admittedly grew discouraged, lamenting to Congressman Burch that "this talk is pretty general over the state . . . and I am unable to track it down to its source."[47] Finally, determined to have the matter resolved, Tuck appealed directly to Byrd. "I am most anxious to see you at the earliest practicable date," he wrote, adding that "a word from you will be appreciated." When the meeting took place in Washington shortly thereafter, the hoped-for word, to Tuck's dismay, was not forthcoming. Although the senator remained as cordial as ever personally, from a political standpoint, Tuck recalled, he seemed "cold as an iceberg. I could see that he preferred Darden. . . . It was the first thing Byrd ever did to hurt me."[48]

There were several factors which may have influenced the senator's thinking. One student of Virginia politics during that period has suggested that Tuck was bypassed because Byrd feared that Tuck's vigorous opposition to Governor Price's program would cause the defection of the more moderate elements of the party should he be the organization's gubernatorial candidate.[49] Although Byrd surely applauded Tuck's opposition to Price, it may have been that the senator's political pragmatism led him to opt for a candidate less likely to antagonize the Price faction. Then, too, Colgate Darden had peculiarly commendable qualifications to Byrd's way of thinking. Known as a man who often sustained vindictive political grudges, Byrd was a genuine admirer of Darden from the time of Darden's 1938 defeat of anti-Byrd Congressman Norman Hamilton.[50] It was also

[47] Tuck to Burch, Nov. 4, 1940, ibid. Tuck placed heavy reliance on Burch, a venerable organization man whom some believed to have been Byrd's personal choice for governor in 1937 (see Richmond *Times-Dispatch*, Sept. 28, 1975).

[48] Tuck to Byrd, Nov. 8, 1940, Tuck Papers; interview with Tuck.

[49] Jonathan J. Wolfe, "Virginia in World War II" (Ph.D. diss., U.Va., 1971), p. 26.

[50] Interview with Tuck. Richard Cope, "The Frustration of Harry Byrd," p. 21, claims that Byrd's abiding dislike for his enemies was "the deep-seated, genteel passion of a man with ruffles at his wrists. His patient treasuring of feuds and enmities, some of which go back so far that nobody (except Harry Byrd) remembers quite how they began, would have been understood by Thomas Jefferson and John Randolph."

believed by some observers that Byrd had an inordinate preference for candidates who were wealthy—a requirement which Darden clearly fulfilled. Finally, among Darden's numerous political assets was a gleaming military record in World War I; although Tuck had also served in that war, Darden had emerged as a full-fledged hero who might prove especially attractive to voters as the nation veered toward belligerency in 1940–41.[51]

For whatever reasons Byrd reached his conclusion, the decision left Tuck with his ambition frustrated, at least temporarily. Understandably distraught, Tuck returned to Richmond and informed Combs, still the organization wheelhorse, that he was withdrawing from the race. At Combs's insistence, however, he was persuaded not to announce his withdrawal immediately—the strategy being to discourage further challengers to Darden. Several weeks later Combs summoned Tuck to Richmond to meet with Darden, at which time Darden requested that Tuck run for lieutenant governor on what would be in effect, if not explicitly, an organization ticket. At first Tuck demurred; he liked his present role in the Senate and thought that his service might be more valuable in that capacity. Upon reflection, however, and having secured what he regarded as a suitable successor to his Senate seat, he agreed to run. Would-be organization challengers got the message— as Tuck put it, "It was like sending them to Belshazzar's feast to see the handwriting on the wall."[52]

The campaign which followed was bereft of excitement. Thomas Ozlin's candidacy never materialized and Ashton Dovell, realizing that his candidacy was hopeless, withdrew some months before the primary. With the demise of Jim Price's influence, the antiorganization Democrats were left in disarray. Ultimately they divided their support for governor between two rather ineffectual candidates, Vivian Page and Hunsdon Cary; for lieutenant governor, against Tuck, they supported Moss Plunkett, a little-known attorney from Roanoke.

During the campaign Darden and Tuck worked harmoniously, with

[51] Robert H. Pride to Tuck, July 6, 1944, Tuck Papers. For Darden's war record, including the winning of the Croix de Guerre, see Jonathan J. Wolfe, "The Virginia Gubernatorial Election of 1941" (M.A. thesis, U.Va., 1968), pp. 16–17, 26, 38.

[52] Thomas R. Morris, *Virginia's Lieutenant Governors: The Office and the Person* (Charlottesville: University of Virginia Institute of Government, 1970), p. 64; interview with Tuck; Richmond *Times-Dispatch*, Sept. 28, 1975.

Darden most effective among the urbanites and Tuck at his best among the rural folk. The two men spoke together at political rallies throughout the state, giving the organization a united front. To the surprise of no one, the pair easily triumphed in the primary, with Darden polling over three times as many votes as Page and Cary combined and Tuck defeating Plunkett by a margin of more than four to one. As expected, the overwhelming victories were repeated in the November general election as Darden and Tuck defeated their relatively unknown Republican challengers, Benjamin Muse and Dr. I. C. Wagner respectively, by margins of approximately five to one.[53]

The amicable relationship established between Darden and Tuck during the campaign grew into a fast political and personal friendship over the ensuing four years. The closeness of the bond was the more remarkable in light of their contrasting backgrounds and personalities. Although they were almost exactly the same age (Tuck was five months older) and both had been Marines, there the similarity ended. Darden was erudite and urbane, while Tuck was ever the "country boy," concealing his considerable intelligence behind a facade of rustic simplicity.

It was Tuck's political savvy which made him an invaluable asset to Darden, particularly as a liaison between the governor and the General Assembly. An able practitioner of backroom politics, Tuck was at his persuasive best in those informal gatherings of legislators where the real decisions frequently were made. According to one account, he "spent many nights during Assembly sessions partaking of tobacco, bourbon, and political bargaining in hotel rooms packed with delegates and senators," exhibiting in so doing "endurance and capacity which were almost legendary." Combining his skill at behind-the-scenes maneuvering with his constitutional powers as president of the Senate, Tuck indeed proved a great boon to Darden. "I turned to him time after time for advice and help," Darden related, "and he was no end of assistance to me."[54]

The Virginia over whose public affairs Darden and Tuck presided

---

[53] Wolfe, "Virginia Gubernatorial Election of 1941," pp. 36–37; Hall, "Price," p. 342.
[54] Wolfe, "Virginia in World War II," pp. 51–52; letter from Darden to author, Jan. 27, 1972.

was a state generally absorbed in the war effort. The nation had entered World War II little more than a month before Darden's inauguration and left that war only a few months before his term ended. In the interim the state experienced significant social, economic, and demographic changes. The heavy infusion of federal money into the state as a result of war-related needs led to unaccustomed prosperity for many Virginians and served to hasten the movement of the population from the farms to the cities. In the midst of the bustle of wartime activity, interest in politics was minimal. The successful prosecution of the war assumed paramount importance. Virginians, like most Americans, considered the war "a dirty business," according to Darden, "and wanted to get the damned thing over with."[55]

Public attention to the war did not mean, however, that politics was "adjourned" on the state level. In a few instances there arose acrimony as fierce as might have arisen had there been no war in progress. Perhaps the most nettlesome of such issues confronting Darden and the organization was the problem of providing for the soldier vote; in solving the problem satisfactorily, Bill Tuck played a significant part. That the issue ever cropped up was largely attributable to Virginia's rather complex voting laws which made it difficult for the state's servicemen to vote. The American Legion, which had considerable power in World War II Virginia, took up the soldiers' cause and demanded that the 1944 General Assembly pass legislation enabling servicemen to vote without impediment. The Byrd organization initially resisted the idea, but ultimately relented, and the so-called American Legion War Voters Act was passed—only to be found unconstitutional by the state Supreme Court of Appeals shortly after the November election.

Although so few soldiers had taken advantage of the act to vote that it hardly seemed worthwhile to devise another plan, the matter had by that time become a political football. The problem was that no solution short of a constitutional amendment seemed feasible, and the calling of a constitutional convention presented perils of its own— namely, the possibility that such a body might insist upon other revisions, perhaps including the larger matter of the poll tax. Caught in this dilemma, the organization eventually decided to risk the calling

[55] Wolfe, "Virginia in World War II," p. 62.

of a constitutional convention. At a special session summoned by Governor Darden in December 1944, the General Assembly passed an act providing for a referendum on the question of calling a constitutional convention; but in order to guard against unwanted tampering with such matters as the poll tax, the act specified that the proposed convention be limited to dealing only with the matter of the soldier vote. That restriction led to widespread criticism of the plan and of the Byrd organization which had devised it. The Richmond *Times-Dispatch* asserted that the organization had "seldom been so high-handed in its disregard of the popular will," and the Richmond *News Leader* agreed: "Everywhere in Virginia there is new hostility toward the machine. Resentment is higher now than we have known it to be in many years."[56]

Despite vociferous opposition, Governor Darden was determined to see his plan through. In this he relied extensively upon Lieutenant Governor Tuck, who was entrusted especially with securing support among the country people. It was Tuck who was called upon to deliver the opening speech in the administration's referendum campaign. Having noted that the whole issue had become confused in the minds of some, Tuck declared: "There should be no confusion. There is only one issue at stake: 'Should we permit our servicemen and women to vote?' On this issue there can be no compromise. . . . They have bought that right with their courage and their blood." In answer to the charge of critics that the convention would involve too much "red tape," the lieutenant governor responded, in typically graphic fashion, that any trouble incurred would be trifling "compared to a single hour on patrol duty by a single doughboy moving into enemy territory with his life literally hanging in the balance minute by minute as he advances."[57]

With both Tuck and Darden expending much energy in its behalf, the administration plan for a limited convention succeeded, though the results of the referendum were not overwhelming. The margin by which the referendum passed (54,515 to 30,341) would have been much closer had the rural counties not favored the proposal by a heavy

[56] Richmond *Times-Dispatch*, Dec. 15, 1944; Richmond *News Leader*, Dec. 16, 1944.
[57] Richmond *Times-Dispatch*, Feb. 6, 1945.

vote—an outcome which revealed Bill Tuck to be an important force in Virginia politics. As one writer observed, "This election indicated how deeply the organization stood in Tuck's debt. He was instrumental in amassing those county totals."[58]

Another factor which enhanced Tuck's growing political stature was the ability which he exhibited in presiding over the Senate. Conscientious in his desire to succeed in his job, he reviewed each day's proceedings at night and checked to see if his parliamentary rulings had been correct; if they were not, he began the next day's session by pointing out that he had been in error on certain points and endeavored to correct his mistakes. Though he worked hard at his task, Tuck later recalled that his tenure as lieutenant governor had been perhaps the most enjoyable of his public career.[59]

That those years in a generally dull and uninspiring office were pleasant, as well as politically rewarding, was owing to the peculiar conditions which existed at the time. With the war in progress Governor Darden felt compelled to stay in Richmond almost continuously; furthermore, Darden was personally rather reticent and preferred to stay out of the public eye as much as his office permitted. Consequently, Tuck was called upon with inordinate frequency to act in the governor's stead throughout the state, and beyond, as the official representative of the Commonwealth. By Tuck's own admission, and by consensus among students of the period, this experience did much to burnish his image both among party leaders and the ordinary citizenry of the state. Darden "didn't want anybody to forget I was lieutenant governor," Tuck recalled. "He treated me just like a governor."[60]

As the Darden administration neared its end, several political facts became manifest. First, the liberal element, which had once entertained some pretension to power during the Price years, was enfeebled,

---

[58] Wolfe, "Virginia in World War II," p. 78. The convention proceeded to carry out its limited task by approving an amendment which exempted from the poll tax requirement all military personnel who had served or were then serving in World War II. As with the earlier War Voters Act, the new amendment had minimal results: only 3,677 Virginia servicemen voted under its provision (ibid., pp. 79–80).

[59] Interview with Tuck; Morris, *Virginia's Lieutenant Governors*, p. 48.

[60] Wolfe, "Virginia in World War II," p. 43; Morris, *Virginia's Lieutenant Governors*, p. 49; interview with Tuck.

disunited, and without effective leadership. Second, and conversely, the organization had strengthened itself during the popular and effective governorship of Colgate Darden and was approaching the peak of its power. Third, Lieutenant Governor Tuck had emerged as an organization leader possessing a considerable personal following across the state.

From the moment of Tuck's election to the second highest state office there were knowledgeable observers who believed that his ultimate elevation to the governorship was inevitable. Some fifteen months before the 1945 gubernatorial primary, the Richmond *News Leader* indicated that Tuck was the probable front-runner, as evidenced by the approval given to him in a poll of state legislators. Even those politicians who opposed him conceded early that the veteran legislator from Halifax seemed destined to reach the governorship.[61] Tuck was determined that this time, unlike 1941, the opportunity would not be lost.

[61] Richmond *News Leader*, May 25, 1944. For antiorganization comment, see Martin A. Hutchinson to C. S. McNulty, Nov. 17, 1944, Hutchinson Papers.

Uncertain Journey

3. *The Quest for the Governorship*

Governors of Virginia are appointed by Harry Flood Byrd, subject to confirmation by the electorate.

—Benjamin Muse

It is the disappointment of my life that Senator Byrd is reluctant to come to me. . . . I believe in sticking to friends as long as we are confident that our friendship is appreciated and reciprocated. I never have and never will separate from a true friend.

—William M. Tuck (1945)

Bill Tuck possessed impressive credentials as an aspiring gubernatorial candidate in 1945. He had been a member of the General Assembly for almost a quarter century and had risen to a position of great influence within the legislature; few men understood the subtleties of parliamentary maneuver better than he. His service as lieutenant governor had enhanced his reputation and broadened his public following across the state. The record which he had achieved was one thoroughly in accord with the basic tenets of the organization philosophy, and his voice had become increasingly influential in party councils.

Added to his obvious professional accomplishments, Tuck's unique personality was a great asset in making him a figure of commanding statewide appeal. Writers expended a wealth of adjectives in trying to describe the man. To one observer he was "salty, jovial, paunchy, . . . blimplike in his physical contours," while to another he seemed "garrulous, blustery, earthy, [and] stout as a tobacco hogshead." The Richmond *News Leader* pictured him as having "the comfortable appearance of a man who has just dined on a dozen pork chops" and noted that he was "known to chew tobacco, drink whiskey and play a wicked hand of poker. . . . His vocabulary began where the resources of Mark Twain left off."[1] Of all the descriptions applied to Tuck, the most common one was, justifiably, "colorful."

Reared in Southside Virginia, Tuck retained a lifelong appreciation for the traditional fare of that region: collards, chitlins, and cornbread (frequently preceded by the equally traditional "bourbon and branch water"). He also partook freely of the leafy staple upon which the economy of the area depended: in almost any form—smoked in big aromatic cigars, puffed from corncob pipes, or chewed in ample plugs—Tuck enjoyed tobacco. Shortly after his twelfth birthday he had won a reputation of sorts by being acclaimed Halifax County's most accomplished tobacco chewer. His proficiency in that line apparently continued through his law school days. "I remember when you used to spit tobacco by my left ear in classes," a Washington and Lee friend reminded Tuck. "Can you still do this?" "I am sorry to say," Tuck replied puckishly, "that I still have all of my old sins and have acquired a few new ones."[2]

Among Tuck's more endearing qualities was his ability as a peerless raconteur. In one reporter's estimation he was notable as "a lawyer, a gourmet, and an admirer of good bourbon. But most of all he is a conversationalist, a teller of tales, some of them tall, some of them tarnished by truth." This faculty, together with his innate affability, produced a charm which even his enemies found disarming. "Tuck's political success rested on his remarkable understanding of human relations," one writer observed. "He knew just how to make the other fellow feel good." It was this extensive popularity which once prompted a Richmond editor to surmise that nobody in Virginia was called by his first name by so many of his fellow citizens as Bill Tuck.[3]

The public Tuck exhibited much the same ebullience that the private man possessed. On the stump he was uninhibited, delivering with gusto and in rich southern tones speeches compounded of elo-

[1] Dabney, *Virginia: The New Dominion*, pp. 516, 517; Wolfe, "Virginia in World War II," p. 51; Richmond *News Leader*, Jan. 2, 1969.

[2] Wilkinson, *Harry Byrd*, p. 25; J. L. Shaver to Tuck, Mar. 2, 1946, Tuck to Shaver, Mar. 6, 1946, Tuck Papers.

[3] Richmond *News Leader*, Oct. 3, 1967; Wilkinson, *Harry Byrd*, p. 26; Charles McDowell, "Bill Tuck of South Boston," *Virginia and the Virginia County* 4 (Feb. 1950): 8.

quence and emotion. Opponents might be attacked with humor or, if the occasion demanded, with vitriol. Often sprinkling his speeches with biblical allusions and with borrowings from his vast vocabulary of recondite words, Tuck sometimes left audiences to deduce his message as much from the vehemence of his delivery as from the precise meaning of his words. There was nothing wrong, he believed, with adding a little color to political rhetoric. "I would never denounce the forces of evil," he said, "when I could denounce the flagitious forces of evil and their flugelmen and thimbleriggers." The resulting oratorical displays, if somewhat magniloquent, earned Tuck renown as a public speaker and gained him early in his career the sobriquet, "the Halifax word-painter."[4]

Since politics seemed to be as much an avocation as a means of livelihood to Tuck, he had few hobbies other than a casual interest in fishing and in horses. He spent part of his limited leisure time reading, much preferring biographies to novels. "Who cares about something somebody just made up?" he once asked. "A good biography can make a man live again." He was especially fond of Douglas Southall Freeman's *R. E. Lee* and was also quite interested in studies of men who had been national political leaders during his youth, notably Woodrow Wilson, whom he greatly admired, and Warren G. Harding, whom he believed to have been excessively maligned.[5] The one diversion in which Tuck regularly indulged was listening to country music. "It's not hillbilly music I like," he explained, "it's folk music and sweet old hymns." By whatever term he might classify them, his favorite songs included such backwoods classics as "A-Grieving My Heart Out for You" and "The Wabash Cannonball"; his favorite recording artists included twangy vocalists Jimmie Davis (one-time governor of Louisiana) and Roy Acuff. Among local performers he particularly admired a popular country singer from Richmond by the stage name of "Sunshine Sue," who on occasion was invited by Tuck to perform at dinner parties.[6]

[4] Charles Houston, *Virginians in Congress* (Richmond: Richmond Newspapers, Inc., 1966), p. 13; Wilkinson, *Harry Byrd*, p. 26; Richmond *Times-Dispatch*, May 7, 1967, Aug. 18, 1933.

[5] Interview with Tuck; Richmond *News Leader*, Oct. 3, 1967.

[6] Richmond *Times-Dispatch*, April 7, 1946. Music was the one form of public

In response to condescension or outright criticism from those who, like his own wife, regarded his musical taste with some disdain, Tuck defended country music. "[It] makes you forget all of your troubles," he said. "It carries you out into the hills among the people who appreciate the real values of life—people who know nothing of sham or pretense." For him it provided a welcome means of relaxation: "In times of stress," he revealed, "I often tune in the program of the Old Dominion Barn Dance, . . . and find the soothing and uplifting effects a very important factor in enabling me to return to my work with renewed energy." He believed that it was also "the best dance music in the world," and, one observer reported, he could prove that statement "by swinging his wife around and around to mountain rhythm. Both Tucks are fond of dancing and [Mr. Tuck], despite his size, is amazingly light on his feet."[7]

Bill Tuck's obvious delight in simple country pleasures, his rustic joie de vivre, led some critics to feel that he lacked the dignity necessary to hold the state's highest elective office. His unabashed behavior, noteworthy under any circumstances, was thrown into even sharper contrast by the refined manner of his close associate, Colgate Darden. As an aspiring successor to the cosmopolitan Darden, Tuck was regarded by some as "not quite couth—a rough and tumble Southside politician, barrel-bellied and black-hatted, who shaved to hillbilly music in the morning and stomped his feet at the Barn Dance on Saturday nights."[8]

Although he undeniably enjoyed the company and the customs of the common folk, those who dismissed Tuck as a mere "hayseed" misjudged the man. In truth Tuck possessed both civility and charm: his unadorned, simple gentility made him a sought-after guest in the finest homes in Richmond, a city whose "best people" do not suffer rubes gladly. He admitted in later years that if he were forced to choose the company of one or the other social set exclusively, he would

---

entertainment which Tuck thoroughly enjoyed. Once, having gone to a play in the capital, he was observed to have squirmed through the first act and then left. "It doesn't have any music," he commented.

[7] Ibid.; Tuck to Radio Station WRVA, Nov. 5, 1948, William M. Tuck Executive Papers, Virginia State Library, Richmond.

[8] Richmond *News Leader*, May 4, 1967.

probably choose to associate with the plain people. ("They have more fun," he said with a chuckle.)[9] In actual practice he never had to make such a choice because he was welcome among both groups. Indeed, perhaps the most salient characteristic of Bill Tuck as a politician, and as a man, was his ability to feel equally at ease, and make his companions feel the same way, whether he was sitting on a luxurious sofa in a posh West End Richmond drawing room munching hors d'oeuvres from a silver tray or resting on a Pepsi crate in a cluttered country store eating pickled pigs' feet from a gallon jar.

In light of his widespread personal popularity among the masses and his acceptability to the rank-and-file organization members, it was only reasonable that Tuck should emerge as a leading gubernatorial candidate in the 1945 election. Despite his qualifications, however, the road to the executive mansion was not to be without difficulties.

Tuck's main challenger for the organization's nod was Thomas Bahnson Stanley, a wealthy furniture-manufacturing magnate from Henry County. As a member of the House of Delegates in the 1930s, Stanley performed with unvarying conservatism. By taking positions such as his stand against unemployment compensation in 1936, he came to be regarded as one of the most reactionary members of the legislature. Despite his rather insubstantial record (or perhaps because of it), Stanley was mentioned in some circles as a possible gubernatorial candidate in 1941. Although it was pointed out that he was undoubtedly "acceptable to the big money interests" in the state, nothing came of the Stanley boomlet at that time.[10] In 1942, however, he was chosen Speaker of the House, thus indicating his exalted standing within the organization; during the Darden administration he further boosted his status by playing a leading role in the promotion of the governor's program. There were also indications that he made good use of his ample funds by providing lavish entertainment for the legislators.[11] It was becoming clear that Stanley was keenly interested in the 1945

[9] Interview with Tuck.

[10] Roanoke *Leader*, Aug. 15, 1941; copy in Tuck Papers. A brief adulatory account of Stanley's career is Warren W. Riggan, "A Political Biography of Thomas Bahnson Stanley" (M.A. thesis, Univ. of Richmond, 1965).

[11] Wolfe, "Virginia in World War II," p. 52. Although a man of ample means, Tuck could not hope to match Stanley in a contest of wooing politicians through spending money, and he had no intention of trying to do so. "I didn't spend fifty

gubernatorial election, and well over a year beforehand he was receiving some open endorsements of his candidacy.

Tuck recognized early that Stanley had gubernatorial aspirations, and though he was not personally unfriendly to his organization colleague, he was determined that Stanley's challenge be rebuffed. In a letter to Ebbie Combs in May 1944, he made his feelings plain: "I believe that our organization friends should let the word go out as rapidly as possible to the county and city leaders so that they will stymie him in his tracks." As the spring and summer progressed, Tuck was dismayed at reports that Stanley was actively campaigning. He felt that it was too early to begin his own campaign, but he did "not want Stanley to get the jump." The dilemma left Tuck scarcely able to contain his anxiety. Referring to his rival in a letter to Governor Darden's assistant, Colonel Peter Saunders, Tuck fumed: "This man is already a candidate for governor and is frank in telling people so, and in soliciting the support of the public. . . . I think it inadvisable for me to try to offset what he is doing by similar tactics, but I do think our friends in the organization might watch what is going on and not let him get too far." [12]

The primary consideration in Tuck's mind was, understandably, how best to attract the endorsement of Harry Byrd himself. When the senator, as was his wont, played it coy, Tuck was faced with a choice of announcing his candidacy early, in the hope that this would force Byrd to come to him, or waiting, in the hope that Byrd eventually would bestow his endorsement voluntarily. Either alternative offered a danger: the former could be disastrous if the senator chose to endorse someone else; the latter would allow other potential candidates more time to bleed away Tuck's strength.

The situation placed Tuck on tenterhooks. Stanley's continued activity led the lieutenant governor to complain to Saunders that his rival "undoubtedly must be getting some encouragement." Even though he expressed his belief that he would not be betrayed, Tuck was worried by continued reports that the organization, ultimately, would support someone else and complained to Combs: "A strong, concerted

---

cents," he recalled. "I used to tell the legislators, 'I'll be glad for you to take me to lunch, but I can't take you!'" (interview with Tuck).

[12] Tuck to Combs, May 18, 1944, Tuck to Col. Peter Saunders, June 17, June 19, 1944, Tuck Papers.

campaign is being put on to convince the people that I will be pushed out or pulled aside. . . . I hear, wherever I go, people saying that I am not going to run when the time comes; that the 'big boys' are going to push me out and put someone else in." The apprehension which Tuck felt was doubtlessly made more acute by the lingering pain of the snub which he had received in the previous gubernatorial contest. It was that specter of 1941 which was raised directly by his own brother when he told Tuck, "You know the inside track, but they are beginning to say, 'For God's sake, he isn't going to [let] Harry Byrd sidetrack him again, is he?'"[13]

Though obviously somewhat edgy, Tuck bided his time, being careful not to alienate Senator Byrd. The presidential election of 1944 presented a touchy situation, since by that time Byrd's opposition to Roosevelt was adamant. Although Byrd did not deign to speak in behalf of the Democratic nominee—the apple harvest was unusually arduous, he claimed—Tuck did offer Roosevelt some support. Speaking at Wyliesburg, the lieutenant governor declared, "We cannot afford to turn down an administration whose policies are known and approved by the best-thought-of people in America and substitute in its place an administration whose candidates have nothing to commend them to the American people." Lest his announcement be construed by Byrd as advocating New Deal domestic policies, Tuck hastened to explain to Ebbie Combs that his approbation applied only to Roosevelt's foreign policy and that he did not countenance the Democratic domestic program. "I wanted you to have this information," he wrote Combs, "for [I] thought maybe you and Senator Byrd might not understand my having made such a statement."[14]

In the meantime other potential organization challengers were appearing. Most prominently mentioned was John S. Battle, a state senator from Charlottesville, who Tuck believed would be his most formidable opponent should Battle decide to contest for the organization's nod. At one point Congressman A. Willis Robertson of the Seventh District loomed as a possibility, but his return to Congress in

[13] Tuck to Saunders, June 17, 1944, Tuck to Combs, July 27, 1944, Frank P. Tuck to Tuck, Jan. 8, 1945, ibid.
[14] Richmond *Times-Dispatch*, Oct. 29, 1944; Tuck to Combs, Oct. 30, 1944, Tuck Papers.

the 1944 election reduced the chances of his entering the gubernatorial race. Also known to be interested and available was Horace Edwards, a former member of the House of Delegates from Richmond who was then serving as chairman of the Democratic State Central Committee.[15]

With competition growing, Tuck felt the pressure to make his candidacy known publicly. In November 1944 he wrote to his political confidant and adviser, Alton Lacy, "My friends here and all over the state think that it would be unwise for me to delay more than a few days in making an announcement, as some of the press which is hostile to me, as well as others, can use all of that time to build up someone in opposition."[16] While he was still procrastinating the Richmond *Times-Dispatch* asserted that Tuck was "generally regarded as a certain candidate with or without the Byrd support," but that Stanley was "not expected to make the race without the full backing of the junior Senator and his political power."[17] Tuck was quick to point out to "Chief" Combs that such an assertion was erroneous. "I noticed in the *Times-Dispatch* yesterday," he said, "that I was going to run with or without the support of Senator Byrd. I have certainly never made such a statement in my life. The article indicated that Stanley and the Senator were closer; I know that no one in Virginia has for the past twenty years admired Senator Byrd more than I have, and I have been loyal to him in everything which he has stood for and expect to continue to be."[18]

A personal conference with Byrd in mid-November 1944 left Tuck encouraged, despite the senator's unwillingness to bestow a firm endorsement. "I have never talked with a man more frank than he,"

[15] Interview with Tuck; Richmond *Times-Dispatch*, Dec. 10, 1944; Beecher E. Stallard to Tuck, Aug. 17, 1944, Tuck Papers; H. Bayliss Epps to Harry F. Byrd, Jan. 22, 1945, Byrd Papers.

[16] Tuck to Lacy, Nov. 6, 1944, Tuck Papers.

[17] Richmond *Times-Dispatch*, Dec. 10, 1944. As early as May 25, 1944, the Richmond *News Leader* had suggested the possibility that Tuck might run even if he could not secure Byrd's endorsement: "Some of the backers of Mr. Tuck contend that he can beat Mr. Stanley even without the organization 'nod.' The reason for this, they say, is that the Lieutenant Governor has gained great strength during his term in office in second position, and also because he 'stood aside' last time in favor of Governor Darden."

[18] Tuck to Combs, Dec. 11, 1944, Tuck Papers.

wrote Tuck after the meeting. "He did not commit; he indicated he would if I insisted, but that he had promised to get together with others first. In other words, . . . his attitude was all that I could ask." The lieutenant governor's hopes were further buoyed by the report that Byrd's administrative assistant, M. J. (Peachy) Menefee, in a conversation with Alton Lacy, had "said you are the man . . . and that we should make it known definitely that we are for you and present a solid front and head off that . . . crowd who are hoping that we will be divided." [19]

Still, Tuck did not receive Byrd's open endorsement, and in the absence of definite word from the senator concerning whom to support, certain organization members began to fear that a schism within the organization would occur. One of the foremost Byrd lieutenants, "Judge" Howard Smith, congressman from the Eighth District, confronted Tuck directly with that possibility when he warned: "It is getting close to the time when you boys who have your lightning rods up in the governorship matter should endeavor to work out some plan of elimination so that we can present a solid front. Otherwise results may not be so good. I am uncommitted. I am more interested in seeing the organization candidate win than in which one gets the green light. I like them all." Harking back to an earlier debacle, another organization stalwart expressed the same concern to Byrd himself. "We ought to do something about this fight for governor this year before things get out of control," he wrote. "Tom Stanley and Bill Tuck are both our friends and they ought not to run against each other. . . . First thing we know we will have another 'Westmoreland Davis' on our hands." [20]

The reluctance of Byrd to bestow his benefaction deeply worried Tuck, prompting him to admit privately that he was "quite uneasy about the attitude of the Senator." His friends shared that anxiety. "We all have the feeling," one of them confided to Tuck,

that frantic efforts are being made to find a reasonable excuse for calling you in and asking you to stand aside again. If you announce before you are called in, the leaders will be bound to support you. If you delay the matter until the "conference" is had with you, then you are in a bad fix. . . . If you hesitate

[19] Tuck to Lacy, Nov. 18, 1944, Lacy to Tuck, Nov. 14, 1944, ibid.

[20] Smith to Tuck, Nov. 13, 1944, ibid.; Frank Moncure to Byrd, Jan. 6, 1945, Byrd Papers.

and wait for Byrd's nod, you will not be Governor because Byrd has not now, nor has he ever been, inclined to favor you for Governor. You can force him to support you by announcing now.[21]

Although the lieutenant governor was, with good reason, reluctant to take any precipitate action which might provoke Byrd's displeasure, his determination to run in 1945 was such that ultimately he was willing to proceed even without Byrd's formal endorsement. That determination was revealed in a letter to Governor Darden. "I do not want to break with old friends, tried and true," Tuck wrote, "unless and until I have to do it, which situation I hope will not arise." To Darden's assistant, he was even more explicit: "I do not want to embarrass the Governor, but if he is with me in this, I am going to run regardless."[22]

It was a risky decision, but by early February Tuck had come to the conclusion that he had to force the issue. "I got the feeling," he explained later, "that I was just about to be smothered in the closet. I didn't know what to do but announce. So I did. I figured I just had to demonstrate some kind of nerve or will power on my own."[23] However, in order not to antagonize the organization hierarchy unduly, he couched the announcement in tentative terms. What he did, in effect, was to announce informally that he would later announce his candidacy formally!

The preliminary announcement had scarcely been made public before the lieutenant governor began to chastise himself for the timidity of his approach. In a long and tortured letter to Peter Saunders, Tuck poured out his feelings. "I felt somewhat like a weakling," he confessed,

in that after I had made up my mind definitely to press forward, I receded from that position. . . . I certainly had the courage to run, and to take whatever consequences there were, for I don't see how my friends in Washington could have fought me, as I have been so loyal to them throughout many long years. I have loved Senator Byrd and Congressman Burch, and have made many enemies on that account. I have fought many battles that I

[21] Tuck to Alton Lacy, Dec. 26, 1944, Roy B. Shotwell to Tuck, Jan. 29, 1945, Tuck Papers.

[22] Tuck to Darden, Feb. 8, 1945, Tuck to Col. Peter Saunders, Jan. 4, 1945, ibid.

[23] Richmond *Times-Dispatch*, Sept. 28, 1975.

otherwise would have never touched just to protect what I thought was their interests, oftentimes when they had not asked me. It is the disappointment of my life that Senator Byrd is reluctant to come to me. . . . I am not bragging about my courage as above stated, for the more courage a man has, generally the less sense he has, but I do say that I was influenced to recede from [my] position through my desire to preserve if possible harmony within the ranks of the organization, and to avoid breaking with old friends, some of whom I have been associated with for nearly twenty-five years. I hope it may never be necessary for me to break, and I really did not realize that my announcement would cause a break until I talked with Abe [Attorney General Abram P. Staples] and Mr. Combs, and found out from Abe that the Senator was quite mad and fretted over my position. I believe in sticking to friends as long as we are confident that our friendship is appreciated and reciprocated. I never have and never will separate from a true friend.[24]

Tuck was correct in surmising that Byrd was unhappy at the news of his announcement, however hesitant that declaration may have been. To organization intimate J. Frank Wysor, Byrd complained that the announcement had been "premature" and detrimental to the best interests of the organization. He was particularly fearful that Tuck's move portended an organization split. "I have just heard," he informed Wysor, "that Stanley is about to announce himself. . . . It would be a pity to go into a hard battle with many of the leaders of the organization [thinking] that everything is in fine shape and that we have nothing to fear." Byrd was further vexed by the possibility of yet another organization entrant into the race. "John Battle came to Washington yesterday and appears now to be very anxious to be a candidate for Governor. The situation," he noted despairingly, "is certainly most complicated."[25]

The key to the organization's dilemma lay mainly in the actions of Tom Stanley. There were astute political observers who believed that he would be a serious threat to Tuck should he enter the race and that, moreover, he was the first choice of the organization hierarchy. Martin

[24] Tuck to Saunders, Feb. 8, 1945, Tuck Papers. Tuck expressed much the same sentiment to Alton Lacy: "I think the reaction to my statement was fine . . . but the next day after talking with Mr. Combs and Abe I plainly saw that our friends were somewhat offended at my attitude. I did not feel that I wanted to break with them, as I have been with them so long" (Tuck to Lacy, Feb. 10, 1945, ibid.).

[25] Byrd to Wysor, Feb. 21, Mar. 28, 1945, Byrd Papers.

A. Hutchinson, an antiorganization leader in Richmond, reported that he had found "a great many people . . . who do not want to support Tuck and many of these people are within the ranks of the organization. It is my own personal opinion, however, if Stanley would go ahead and announce himself immediately he could easily become the next governor of Virginia." Hutchinson also was informed that Congressman Howard Smith in particular was working diligently behind the scenes for Stanley. "It is my belief," he submitted, "that when Tuck announced his candidacy he thought he did have or would have the support of the organization but it now seems that matters may not be as smoothly worked out as had been hoped by the organization. My own personal opinion is that several congressmen and the Junior Senator [Byrd] have always preferred Stanley to Tuck." [26]

Tuck was dismayed by continuing public reports that he would be spurned by the organization. He complained to Combs that he believed it was mostly "propaganda that is being put out, and I think it should be counteracted in some way by a special effort on the part of our friends high up in the organization to have something to say favorable to me." To his chagrin, not even the formal announcement of his candidacy in March elicited the desired response. Byrd made no public statement and kept his personal feelings to himself. Having tried to fathom the senator's position, Alton Lacy informed Tuck, "I regret to say that I have been unable to pick up anything favorable from that source." [27]

The organization's predicament began to resolve itself somewhat in early April when Tom Stanley bowed out. In the words of an ardent antiorganization state senator, Lloyd M. Robinette, Stanley "took cold feet. He was looking for a nod from Washington, but it never came, and he stepped quickly out of the picture." [28] That turn of events left John Battle as the lone organization threat to Tuck, but a most serious threat he was. One student of the period has flatly stated that "Battle was Senator Harry Byrd's personal preference for the position." However, following a conference with Battle, Tuck was satisfied that he had little to fear from the Charlottesville senator. Robinette was of the same

[26] Hutchinson to W. N. Neff, Feb. 10, 1945, Hutchinson to Rixey Smith, Mar. 27, 1945, Hutchinson Papers.

[27] Tuck to Combs, Feb. 16, 1945, Lacy to Tuck, Mar. 15, 1945, Tuck Papers.

[28] Robinette to Martin A. Hutchinson, April 10, 1945, Hutchinson Papers.

opinion. "Poor old John is not going to do anything," he mused. "He is too scared. He would like to be governor, but he has let the bus leave him."[29] By mid-April, Battle was, in fact, effectively out of contention, leaving Tuck as the consensus organization candidate.

In the weeks which followed, most organization leaders gradually committed themselves to support Tuck but, significantly, one who remained silent was Byrd himself. In light of Tuck's proved ability on the hustings and his long record of service to the organization, Byrd's hesitancy might appear surprising. A man of Falstaffian proportions with a wit to match, Tuck clearly appealed to the voting public. To one city official, he seemed to be "a fellow that once you meet him, you are obliged to like him." Unfortunately for Tuck, however, many of the personal characteristics which endeared him to the masses were the very ones which made him suspect in the eyes of the organization leaders. As J. Harvie Wilkinson has noted, there were some who regarded him as "a playboy and clown who could never be trusted with the responsibility of high office . . . [and] in an organization which . . . generally disdained the vulgar and spectacular, Tuck was regarded in some quarters as downright dangerous."[30] Even though his political philosophy and his legislative record were basically congruent with the principles of the organization, Tuck's temperament set him apart as a man capable of more independence and dash than Byrd was wont to accept.

As a plainspoken, sometimes flamboyant, extrovert, the fun-loving Tuck was obviously not cut from the same cloth as Byrd favorites such as Darden, Battle, or Stanley—all of whom were generally quiet, courtly, and unobtrusive. The problem, according to Tuck, was largely that Byrd was not sure that he had "matured" enough to be governor. "He still thought of me as the same little country bumpkin who came to the House in 1924," he explained, adding, "You know how first impressions are."[31]

Byrd's reluctance to endorse Tuck—while it did indicate a skepti-

[29] Peter R. Henriques, "John S. Battle and Virginia Politics, 1948–1953" (Ph.D. diss., U.Va., 1971), p. 41; Tuck to Alton Lacy, April 10, 1945, Tuck Papers; Robinette to Martin A. Hutchinson, April 10, 1945, Hutchinson Papers.

[30] Grey P. Hulce to Harry F. Byrd, Jan. 10, 1945, copy in Tuck Papers; Wilkinson, *Harry Byrd*, p. 27.

[31] Interview with Tuck.

cism toward Tuck's fitness for the job—was actually typical of the manner in which Byrd operated. Although his potential power was immense, Byrd in fact seldom dictated the choice of candidates; instead he acted only after a careful determination of prevailing sentiment across the state. As one longtime Byrd associate put it, "Harry never bought a ticket before the train was ready to leave the station." [32] Accordingly, Byrd waited for clear-cut evidence of support for Tuck before giving him the nod.

There were two crucial factors which influenced the senator's ultimate decision. First, it became clear that Tuck was the overwhelming choice of the "courthouse crowd," those local officeholders who constituted the backbone of the Byrd organization. The city treasurer of Richmond, for example, informed Byrd, "I have talked to practically all of the fellows in the Treasurer's Association, and I have yet to find a single one who is not favorable to Bill in preference to any man who could be picked." It was similarly reported to Byrd's liaison, Combs, that "the clerks of the state would back Bill Tuck to the man if he is a candidate," and that the same would be true of most other county officials. In recognition of such support, Wysor advised Byrd that he could ill afford not to endorse Tuck. "It begins to look very much now that any other course will upset a great many of our people," he wrote in late March, "and there is no telling just what the reaction would be." [33]

The second important influence on Byrd was that Tuck was known to have the steadfast backing of Governor Darden, under whom he had labored patiently and effectively for four years. By 1945 Darden himself was no mean political power in Virginia, and Byrd was understandably loath to risk a division within the organization between his own loyalists and the combined forces of Darden and Tuck. Consequently, Byrd journeyed to Richmond to confer with Darden at the Governor's Mansion. "We must have sat and talked and walked around for two hours or more," Darden later recalled. "What it boiled down to was this: He was uneasy about Bill. And I told Harry that, no matter how he felt, I just had to be for Bill. . . . There is little doubt

[32] Richmond *Times-Dispatch*, Sept. 28, 1975.

[33] Grey P. Hulce to Byrd, Jan. 10, 1945, copy in Tuck Papers; E. F. Hargis to Combs, Nov. 27, 1944, copy in Hutchinson Papers; Wysor to Byrd, Mar. 30, 1945, Byrd Papers.

that if I had given any ground, Harry would have gone on to take the organization on a move to set Bill aside. I think the thing that gave him pause, and had a sizeable influence on the final decision, was my unwillingness to negotiate about anybody else."[34] The meeting with Darden convinced Byrd that he had little choice if the organization was to be spared a ruinous schism; prudently, he acquiesced in Tuck's candidacy.

Realizing that a major hurdle had been cleared, Darden telephoned his lieutenant governor, then at his South Boston home, shortly after the meeting with Byrd ended. Tuck recalled that he had quickly recognized the vibrant voice as that of Colgate Darden. "Will-yum," asked Darden, "how are you feeling?" "Not so good," Tuck replied. "Well, you're going to feel better," Darden told his political ally. "I think Harry's going to be for you."[35]

Unquestionably, Tuck had good reason to feel better, because he then knew that the endorsement which had been denied him in 1941 and which proved so elusive in 1945 had finally been secured. Given the sway which Harry Byrd held over the Virginia electorate at that time, the senator's coveted nod meant that Bill Tuck's election to the governorship was a near certainty.

There were some political observers who saw an omen of impending trouble for the organization in Byrd's failure to give Tuck his outright support more quickly. Tuck himself later noted that "Senator Byrd wasn't exactly zealous for me. He wanted somebody who would be a good governor, and he wasn't real sure I would be." Looking forward to the Democratic primary election in August, the Richmond *Times-Dispatch* suggested that "the length of time the machine has required to get squared away for this contest is excellent evidence . . . that it is not as serenely confident as of yore. We may be on the verge of important developments."[36]

A more realistic appraisal of conditions in Virginia in the summer of 1945 would have revealed that the time was unpropitious for a challenge to the organization. For one thing, with the war still raging

[34] Richmond *Times-Dispatch*, Sept. 28, 1975.
[35] Ibid.
[36] Interview with Tuck; Richmond *Times-Dispatch*, Oct. 3, 1967, and Mar. 16, 1945.

against Japan, most Virginians were far more interested in casualty lists from the Pacific than in campaign rhetoric. Antiorganization leader Martin Hutchinson assessed the situation despairingly, but aptly, commenting to an associate that "the people have little interest in the election . . . because the war is on, and many people are quite busy with war work, and are disturbed because of the war."[37]

The apathetic condition of Virginia voters was owing not only to the war itself but also to political developments in the state during the war years. The popular administration of Colgate Darden had strengthened the Byrd faction, while at the same time opponents of the organization drifted fecklessly. Enfeebled since the demise of Jim Price, the liberal element lacked cohesion, and with the exception of erstwhile Price ally Hutchinson, they generally lacked leadership. Foes of the organization thus faced the gubernatorial campaign of 1945 deeply despondent. State Senator Robinette, whose judgments were usually morose, accurately expressed the doleful state of the antiorganization forces. "As to the politics in this state," he wrote,

I have been forced to conclude that liberal leadership in Virginia is dead. There was not a semblance of life of such leadership in the Assembly at our recent session. A few men who feel that there should be some sort of liberal leadership in the state were wandering in a maze of doubt and indecision, and utterly hopeless of the future. Heretofore there were a few souls in the Assembly who were willing to discuss plans for the future of liberalism here, but these souls had grown timid, and now life is evidently extinct and political courage a mere memory. One of the senators that I had thought of as a liberal openly stated that he was going to support Bill Tuck.[38]

In their plight the antis had difficulty securing a suitable candidate to oppose Tuck in the August primary. The two prospects who were considered to have the best chance of giving Tuck a serious run were former House Speaker Ashton Dovell of Williamsburg and state Senator William N. Neff of Abingdon. Both men previously had tenuous ties to the organization but were sufficiently independent to attract the support of most antis. The two gave evidence of interest in making the contest, but ultimately both timorously declined to do so—Dovell preferring to run (unsuccessfully, as it turned out) for the

[37] Hutchinson to C. S. McNulty, July 5, 1945, Hutchinson Papers.
[38] Robinette to Martin A. Hutchinson, Mar. 30, 1945, ibid.

Third District seat in Congress, Neff choosing to remain in the state Senate.[39]

With neither Dovell nor Neff willing to offer, the Richmond newspapers began a campaign to produce other candidates. The *News Leader*, edited by the venerable Douglas Southall Freeman, puffed the candidacy of Freeman's fellow historian, Washington and Lee University President Francis Pendleton Gaines, who, though reported to be interested in the governorship, declined to pursue it actively. *Times-Dispatch* editor Virginius Dabney shared Freeman's desire to have opposition to Tuck in the primary, but privately he despaired of achieving it. "I am certainly sorry that matters have turned out thus," he wrote. "The courthouse rings are lining up behind Tuck and I do not know if it is possible now to do anything about it."[40] All the while, Tuck and the organization leaders were naturally hoping that there would be no opposition. "There is no doubt about the fact that Tuck is the popular choice of the people for governor," wrote E. R. Combs to one newspaper editor, "and since there can be no doubt about his qualifications, why should anyone insist upon a fight in the primary?"[41]

Eventually opposition did arise in the person of Moss Plunkett, the Roanoke attorney whom Tuck had defeated for lieutenant governor in the 1941 primary. A veteran supporter of liberal causes and a frequent candidate for public office, Plunkett was best known for his leadership of the Virginia Electoral Reform League, an organization designed to agitate for repeal of the poll tax. Although he was a sincere candidate with a serious reform program, Plunkett was regarded contemptuously by most organization men, who tended to dismiss his candidacy as mildly annoying but harmless. As one Newport News attorney wrote Tuck, "I noticed from yesterday's paper that you at last have opposi-

---

[39] Richmond *Times-Dispatch*, Dec. 10, 1944; Hutchinson to E. D. Lucas, Dec. 14, 1944, Neff to Hutchinson, Jan. 29, 1945, Hutchinson Papers; Wolfe, "Virginia in World War II," pp. 68–69.

[40] Beecher Stallard to Tuck, April 6, 1945, R. Hill Fleet to Tuck, April 10, 1945, Tuck Papers; Dabney to Elizabeth W. Steptoe, April 12, 1945, Dabney Papers. Dabney later recalled that at the time he did not feel that Tuck "had much in the way of qualifications," but that he subsequently formed a much more favorable opinion of him (Dabney to author, Mar. 4, 1977).

[41] Combs to Charles J. Harkrader, April 20, 1945, Tuck Papers.

tion. You will, of course, welcome opposition from Plunkett. He is crazy, and as wild as a March hare." Much of the state press, which had called for competition, tended to belittle Plunkett and to scoff at his chances of victory. One of his hometown papers, the Roanoke *Times*, was indicative of the press reaction when it cast him as a rather bizarre radical who was "achieving something of a record as a perennial candidate. . . . We take it for granted that he will offer against U.S. Senator Harry F. Byrd next year, and perhaps against President Harry S. Truman in 1948." Even one of Plunkett's supporters noted that the press seemed to regard his candidacy "almost as a joke in the face of the Byrd machine."[42]

Certainly organization leaders were not much worried. Shortly after Plunkett's entrance into the race, Combs wrote Tuck, "I congratulate you on your opposition." Congressman Robertson assessed the challenger with heavy-handed sarcasm. "On Saturday," he told Tuck,

Moss Plunkett, whom you so decisively defeated four years ago, made the naive announcement that he had never had any personal ambition to hold public office but would announce for governor as a favor to the people of Virginia. On at least four different occasions he has offered to make a similar sacrifice of his own best interest in behalf of the general welfare, and in August of this year the voters will tell him the same thing that they have told him each time before and possibly in a way that will make a lasting impression.

Tuck himself was unimpressed by Plunkett's candidacy. Referring to a recent local election in Roanoke, he replied to Robertson, "Sinclair Brown beat old Moss over five to one, but apparently he thrives on defeat." To Byrd, Tuck frankly admitted, "I do not consider Plunkett serious opposition."[43]

Though derisively dismissed by the organization, Plunkett proceeded to mount a strident, aggressive campaign focusing on traditional antiorganization concerns. There was an immediate need, he

[42] Letter to Tuck, April 23, 1945, ibid. Roanoke *Times*, April 22, 1945; C. S. McNulty to Martin A. Hutchinson, May 9, 1945, Hutchinson Papers.

[43] Combs to Tuck, May 10, 1945, Robertson to Tuck, April 23, 1945, Tuck to Robertson, April 28, 1945, Tuck to Byrd, April 25, 1945, Tuck Papers. In later years Tuck spoke fondly of some of his former adversaries, but it was clear that he neither liked nor respected Plunkett, whom he regarded as undignified and erratic (interview with Tuck).

said, for improvement in the state's health, welfare, and educational provisions. Crying that "poll tax and democracy cannot live in the same state," he demanded the removal of suffrage restrictions. Constantly pervading Plunkett's speeches was the charge that the state's ills were traceable to the Machiavellian operations of an evil machine run by Senator Byrd, a "boss who pulls the potent power strings from his throne room in Washington."[44]

For his part, Tuck initially followed Combs's advice to "completely ignore the candidacy of Plunkett and await developments."[45] Such strategy seemed politically sound, since engaging in open debate might have aided the lesser-known Plunkett, but soon Tuck's reticence brought down upon him a barrage of newspaper criticism. One Roanoke paper described the lieutenant governor as "statuesque in his silence," while another noted that he had "remained as silent as the Sphinx, and apparently it is his intention to keep silent right up to the primary, depending on the state Democratic machine to bring him victory at the polls."[46] The Norfolk *Virginian-Pilot* claimed that even if such a feat were possible, the candidate had an obligation to make known his position on the issues. "Self-respect," chided the paper, "rules out a sliding into the governorship with lips sealed." The Richmond *Times-Dispatch*, cool toward Tuck's candidacy from the outset, categorized his efforts as a "supergumshoe campaign" and asserted that "the reverberating silence which issues from his political camp is nothing short of thunderous. . . . We have seen some uncommunicative candidates for governor in our time, but if any ever equalled William M. Tuck in this respect, the fact has escaped us." In private the editor of that paper was indignant. "Mr. Tuck is breaking all records for silence," he complained. "I do not think he is going to say another word until the primary. It is ridiculous."[47]

Tuck was not surprised by the press reaction, since early in the campaign he had been warned by some of his advisers that, as he put it, "the newspapers all over the state are going to lambast me as no man

[44] Norfolk *Journal and Guide*, July 21, 1945; Richmond *Times-Dispatch*, July 7, 1945; Shackleford, "The 'Liberal' Movement in Virginia," p. 12.

[45] Combs to Tuck, May 10, 1945, Tuck Papers.

[46] Quoted in Richmond *Times-Dispatch*, July 20, 1945.

[47] Norfolk *Virginian-Pilot*, July 12, 1945; Richmond *Times-Dispatch*, July 5, 1945; Dabney to Elizabeth W. Steptoe, July 5, 1945, Dabney Papers.

ever has been before." But, even though he was prepared for it, the criticism gave him some anxiety as the primary approached. "I am acting as if it is not disturbing me in the slightest," he wrote to a friend, "but to be absolutely honest and truthful it does disturb me some. I would be much happier if I felt they would try to be fair."[48]

With only three weeks remaining until election day, Tuck suddenly increased the tempo of his campaign. Since the change occurred immediately after a clandestine gathering of organization leaders, including Byrd and Combs, at the western Virginia retreat of Mountain Lake, there was speculation that Tuck had been directed by the "brain trust" to campaign more vigorously. Tuck adamantly denied the charge, but some remained skeptical, with the Richmond *Times-Dispatch* noting a "remarkable bouleversement" in Tuck's campaign once the "invigorating air of Mountain Lake galvanized him into action."[49]

Whatever the stimulus, Tuck endeavored during the final weeks of the campaign to parry the accusations made by his opponent. Concerning the low level of state services, he promised to work for improved health care, highways, and public schools, insofar as a balanced budget would permit. On the question of poll tax repeal, Plunkett's chief issue, Tuck was somewhat evasive. Preferring not to advocate the tax directly, yet personally opposed to its abolition, Tuck expediently took the position that the matter be submitted to a popular referendum. As to Plunkett's castigation of the Byrd organization, Tuck hardly needed to make any rebuttal. Even though many of Plunkett's claims were at least partly justifiable, the shrill, carping manner in which they were delivered diminished their effect. Most Virginia voters simply did not believe that they were living under "Tory rule" and "machine terror" as Plunkett charged, and the belligerent tone of his rhetoric may have tended to alienate some who otherwise might have been inclined to support him.[50]

Since both his political philosophy and his personal deportment made him repugnant to organization adherents, Plunkett could expect

[48] Tuck to W. H. Cardwell, Mar. 16, 1945, Tuck to Dr. James K. Hall, July 16, 1945, Tuck Papers.

[49] Interview with Tuck; Richmond *Times-Dispatch*, July 23, 1945.

[50] Norfolk *Virginian-Pilot*, July 12, 1945; Richmond *Times-Dispatch*, Aug. 2, 1945; Shackelford, "The 'Liberal' Movement in Virginia," p. 15.

to gain substantial support only from the usual anti-Byrd bloc, composed mainly of blacks, organized labor, and "liberal" Democrats. Black Virginians, given their accustomed antipathy to the organization, would probably have supported Plunkett by default, and his advocacy of poll tax repeal made him especially attractive. The most respected black newspaper in the state, the Norfolk *Journal and Guide*, praised Plunkett as a "strong anti-machine Democrat" whose campaign against Tuck was "tearing the hide off the Democratic Party and its candidate." The blacks' problem (and Plunkett's) was simply that they did not then possess significant voting strength. Of the approximately 366,000 blacks of voting age in Virginia in 1945, only about 38,000 were registered to vote, and perhaps no more than half of that number actually voted. Thus it was of dubious political advantage to court the black vote, since such action might well alienate enough Negrophobes to offset the black votes gained.[51]

Organized labor, a perennial foe of the organization, generally backed Plunkett, but the voting strength of the unions, like that of blacks, was quite limited. In 1945 the CIO had approximately 40,000 members in Virginia, with a voting strength estimated at from 10,000 to 15,000; the AFL was somewhat larger, though probably not in excess of 65,000 members.[52] In addition there was a sprinkling of unaffiliated local unions of indeterminable membership throughout the state. Organized labor was simply not a base upon which a viable candidacy could be constructed in the Virginia of the 1940s.

In contrast to Plunkett, Tuck did not actively solicit union votes. Campaigning in the textile center of Danville, he commended the "fine spirit of Virginia labor" and pledged his best efforts toward maintaining good labor-management relations, but beyond such pleasing generalities he would not venture. In truth, Tuck probably viewed open union support (a remote possibility, to be sure) with abhorrence, feeling that his interests would actually be better served by labor endorsement of his opponent. Upon learning of one such en-

[51] Norfolk *Journal and Guide*, July 14, 1945; Andrew Buni, *The Negro in Virginia Politics, 1902–1965* (Charlottesville: University Press of Virginia, 1967), pp. 142, 146.

[52] These estimates are based on Key, *Southern Politics*, p. 32; Wilkinson, *Harry Byrd*, p. 56; and telephone interview with Brewster Snow, secretary-treasurer of the Virginia AFL-CIO, April 5, 1968.

dorsement of Plunkett, one state official suggested to Tuck that "this just brings them out in the open, and to my mind it will react favorably to you." Even though organized labor had not yet acquired the stigma which it was to gain later as a result of postwar strikes, the prevailing attitude in fundamentally conservative, agricultural Virginia was such that labor union support was, in the words of columnist Charles McDowell, "something you traditionally try to keep quiet or disown."[53]

Plunkett's campaign depended on strong support from the liberal wing of the Democratic party, but somewhat surprisingly, many of the antiorganization leaders were lukewarm toward his candidacy. Though they agreed with his principles, they recognized that his chances were virtually nil. As one active anti put it, "Moss Plunkett is a crusader, and while no one finds fault with what he stands for, except the machine politicians, yet frankly many of those who should warm up to him do not seem to do so." The problem was largely one of style—no small matter in a state where the way in which a politician spoke was often as important as what he said. "Plunkett's brand of leadership," wrote one student of the period, "was that of a highlander, and the real and imaginary gentlemen of the lowlands did not like his style. [His] zeal was interpreted as erratic by conservative Virginians." To be sure, Bill Tuck's deportment also varied from the prescribed sedate pattern; but whereas Tuck's behavior was adapted to conservative ends, Plunkett's was directed toward reform. One contemporary anti complained that in Virginia "the word 'liberal' is an epithet, a synonym for 'crackpot.'"[54] Unfortunately for Moss Plunkett's gubernatorial aspirations, his program and his behavior led all too easily to such a categorization.

With Plunkett thus handicapped, the main concern of the organization on the eve of the election was the apparent lethargy of the electorate. "I am worried about the apathy and indifference in the campaign up to this point," Congressman Smith informed Tuck, adding, "I don't think you should feel particularly bad about it because

[53] Richmond *Times-Dispatch*, Aug. 2, 1945; Johns Hopkins Hall to Tuck, June 20, 1945, Tuck Papers; Richmond *Times-Dispatch*, Oct. 24, 1968.

[54] C. S. McNulty to Martin A. Hutchinson, April 23, 1945, Hutchinson Papers; Shackelford, "The 'Liberal' Movement in Virginia," p. 12; Washington *Post*, June 12, 1957, p. A–15.

I think it arises from a feeling amongst our friends that Plunkett is not a real contender. On the other hand, they fail to recognize that Plunkett might, in the last few days, arouse the organized labor elements and the general crew of antis, all of whom added together could, if gotten to the polls, mean a good many votes." Tuck was of a similar opinion. Although admitting that he felt confident, he wrote a friend: "There are quite a number of elements opposing me, such as organized labor, the Negro organizations and the disgruntled elements also. These will go out to the polls, and unless my friends . . . go out in large numbers, the results may be disappointing."[55]

The anxiety expressed by Smith and Tuck was needless because, even though the vote was light, the results were overwhelmingly in favor of the organization. On August 7—a day on which the big news concerned the dropping of the atomic bomb on Hiroshima—Bill Tuck defeated Moss Plunkett by a vote of 97,304 to 41,484. Plunkett managed to carry only two counties out of one hundred, and three cities out of twenty-four; all were located in his native southwest Virginia region. Tuck, by contrast, amassed huge margins in many areas of the state, with his greatest support coming in his rural Fifth District, which voted for him by a ratio of roughly six to one. As expected, the antiorganization challenger fared best in the urban and more industrialized areas; in Richmond he lost to Tuck by less than 1,000 votes.[56]

The total vote was extremely low, even for Virginia. Several factors were involved, aside from the suffrage restrictions inherent in the organic law of the state. For one thing the distractions of the war undoubtedly diminished interest in politics; also, the weakness of Plunkett's candidacy, which made an organization triumph seem inevitable, led to voter indifference. For whatever causes, the total number of voters amounted to a minuscule 7.8 percent of the adult population of the state—the lowest percentage ever in a Virginia gubernatorial primary.[57]

Having won the Democratic primary, Tuck might reasonably have

[55] Smith to Tuck, July 31, 1945, Tuck to P. B. Watt, Aug. 2, 1945, Tuck Papers.

[56] Virginia, *Statement of the Vote for Governor and Lieutenant Governor, Democratic Primary Election, Tuesday, August 7, 1945* (Richmond: Division of Purchase and Printing, 1945), p. 3.

[57] Washington *Post*, June 10, 1957, p. A-14. For statistics on voting percentage in gubernatorial primaries since 1905, see Richmond *Times-Dispatch*, Mar. 31, 1946.

felt that his ascension to the governorship was assured, since no Republican had been elected governor of Virginia since the 1880s. Even though the Republican candidate in the general election, state Senator Floyd S. Landreth of Galax, was acknowledged as an astute politician within his own southwest Virginia bailiwick, his lack of statewide recognition, coupled with the overall weakness of his party statewide, seemed to preclude any chance of Republican success in 1945.

The campaign, however, was unexpectedly enlivened by the emergence of a minor scandal stemming from the Democratic primary race for lieutenant governor. Three men were involved in the contest: Delegate L. Preston (Pat) Collins of Marion, state Senator Charles R. Fenwick of Arlington, both Byrd loyalists, and antiorganization state Senator Leonard Muse of Roanoke. In the absence of direction from Senator Byrd,[58] organization regulars divided their support almost evenly between Collins and Fenwick; indeed, final returns showed Fenwick the winner by a mere 572 votes out of the more than 135,000 total votes cast. The organization, its poise already threatened by the uncharacteristic internal discord,[59] was further shaken when Collins successfully contested the election on the grounds of voting malpractices in the southwest Virginia county of Wise, which Fenwick had carried by the well-nigh incredible margin of 3,307 to 122. The voiding of the Wise vote by a Richmond circuit court reversed the outcome, giving the victory to Collins.[60]

The whole affair was unseemly, even for southwest Virginia, where a certain amount of election chicanery was traditional.[61] Organization leaders, who boasted of Virginia's freedom from political corruption,

[58] Although both Collins and Fenwick sought Byrd's endorsement, the senator refused to take sides. "I maintained a strict neutrality," he later wrote to one of his associates. "A great many people asked me how to vote and I declined to tell them" (Byrd to G. Fred Switzer, Aug. 9, 1945, G. Fred Switzer Papers, University of Virginia Library).

[59] The fear was that the Collins-Fenwick split would result in the election of Muse as lieutenant governor, from which position he might vault into the governorship four years thence, as had James Price in 1937 (see Watkins Abbitt to Harry Byrd, May 23, 1945, W. L. Prieur, Jr., to Byrd, May 7, 1945, Byrd Papers).

[60] *Statement of the Vote, August 7, 1945*, pp. 2–3; Richmond *Times-Dispatch*, Sept. 5, 1945; Fredericksburg *Free Lance-Star*, Sept. 29, 1945.

[61] See Horn, "Democratic Party in Virginia," pp. 191–265.

were horrified by the Wise County revelations. "What has occurred," Byrd wrote privately, "has cast discredit upon the whole Democratic organization." Ebbie Combs called it "deplorable," and candidate Tuck agreed: "This is just as bad as it can be, and no good can come from it."[62] The immediate worry, of course, was the impact which the scandal might have on the upcoming general election. "I believe we have a very hard fight ahead of us this fall," Byrd warned Tuck. "By this I do not mean there is any danger about your election, but I think it is imperative, not only from your standpoint, but from that of the organization, that you receive a flattering majority. . . . If your majority falls down, the hostile papers will make a great deal out of it. There is no trouble about you, but the lieutenant governorship will give us a great deal of trouble, as it already has."[63]

Byrd was right; the Republicans wasted no time in trying to exploit the issue. Landreth pointed to the Wise incident as evidence of the need for electoral reform, claiming that under existing laws, "the free will of the people cannot be expressed." He even attempted to implicate Tuck directly in the scandal, despite the absence of any evidence to that effect.[64] Tuck's nomination, he asserted, had been "tainted, nobody knows how much, but a-plenty, with irregularities and injustices practiced in the primary." On another occasion he was even more blunt. "If there have been any irregular votes cast anywhere in the state," he declared, "then those votes went to Bill Tuck, every one of them."[65]

Tuck's rebuttal took several tacks. In part he followed the homely advice offered by Congressman Robertson. "If your opponent continues to harp on the subject of fraud," suggested Robertson, "you might remind him of what happened to the billy goat at the Convention of Animals, where a motion was adopted that all animals would vote by lifting their tails. The billy goat lost his vote on the ground

[62] Byrd to Mrs. R. B. Boatwright, Sept. 26, 1945, Combs to Byrd, Aug. 23, 1945, Byrd Papers; Tuck to Combs, Aug. 24, 1945, Tuck Papers.

[63] Byrd to Tuck, Sept. 11, 1945, Tuck Papers.

[64] Tuck, in fact, had played no role in the contest for lieutenant governor. Like Byrd, he scrupulously refrained from making any public endorsement, though he personally favored Collins (interview with Tuck).

[65] Richmond *Times-Dispatch*, Sept. 3, 1945; Harrisonburg *Daily News-Record*, Sept. 11, 1945; Fredericksburg *Free Lance-Star*, Sept. 21, 1945.

that his tail was up before the motion was adopted." [66] In that spirit Tuck called attention to the fact that while Landreth was belaboring recent Democratic malfeasance in Wise, the record of the Republican party in southwest Virginia was hardly spotless—a charge that was difficult for his opponent to deny.

Mainly, however, Tuck responded to Landreth's accusations by claiming that the Wise County affair had been magnified out of proportion because Virginians were generally unaccustomed to any sort of political impropriety. "No such thing, to my knowledge, has ever happened before," he said in a typical speech. "If Virginia were a state where election frauds were frequently committed, then there would be no occasion for surprise. It is not the mere occurrence of an election fraud, but its occurrence in *Virginia*, which is astounding." He insisted further that the guilty parties be brought to "stern and resolute justice" and promised that if elected governor, he would endeavor to tighten the election laws so as to prevent similar irregularities in the future.[67]

In the end the voting scandal proved to have little effect on the outcome of the general election. The simple truth was that Republicanism to many Virginians in 1945 still bore the faint odor of Reconstruction, and more significantly, to most it exuded the stench of Depression; in short, Republicanism was not yet "acceptable" in the Old Dominion. Accordingly, it was not surprising that Tuck easily defeated Landreth. The final vote was 112,355 to 52,386, with Landreth managing to carry only eleven counties and one city, Roanoke. As had been true in the Democratic primary, voter participation was minimal. Out of a potential voting population of 1,790,694, only 168,764 persons (or 9.4 percent of those eligible) voted for governor.[68]

For Bill Tuck, the size of the vote did not diminish the satisfaction of the victory; for him the result meant the culmination of a boyhood dream. The vision of political eminence which had been implanted

[66] Robertson to Tuck, Sept. 26, 1945, Tuck Papers.

[67] Richmond *Times-Dispatch*, Sept. 18, 1945. For evidence that Tuck was serious about electoral reform, see Tuck to Byrd, Sept. 11, 1945, Tuck Papers.

[68] Virginia, *Votes Cast for Governor, Lieutenant Governor, and Attorney General, General Election, November 6, 1945* (Richmond: Division of Purchase and Printing, 1946), pp. 2–3; Richmond *Times-Dispatch*, Nov. 4, 1945.

during his early years and nurtured throughout more than two decades of public life reached fulfillment with his gubernatorial triumph. As his friend Colgate Darden had reached the governorship just as World War II began, so Tuck would arrive just in time to guide the state through the troublesome postwar era. It would be a task not without grave problems.

II *The Gubernatorial Years*

The Vepco Incident

4. *The Governor as "Commander-in-Chief"*

> Strikes which isolate communities or deprive them of light, heat, power, transportation, medical care, and essential foods, are in a class apart, and there can be and should be no doubt that the public interest is paramount.
>
> —*Walter Lippmann (1946)*

> The first and fundamental function of government is to protect the public interest. All of the complicated activities of government have that simple end in view.
>
> —*William M. Tuck (1946)*

The day of William M. Tuck's inauguration, January 16, 1946, dawned clear and bitterly cold over Richmond. Shivering in weather described as the coldest ever for an inaugural parade, some six thousand persons gathered to watch as the official procession made its way to the Capitol. There, at shortly after noon, Tuck was sworn in as the sixty-first governor of the Commonwealth of Virginia. "Words cannot express my gratitude," he began. "There is no higher honor. I do pray I may prove worthy of it."[1]

Taking office at the time he did, Tuck had ample reason for some trepidation. Although the immediate problems of World War II were over, the difficulties of postwar "reconversion" were only beginning: inflation, unemployment, and the readjustment of the wage-price scale. Virginia shared in these national problems and, to a larger extent than many states, also had to face the war-induced demand for greater services such as schools, hospitals, and highways. The war years had

[1] Richmond *News Leader*, Jan. 16, 1946; Virginia, *Inaugural Address of William M. Tuck*, Senate Document No. 2 (Richmond: Division of Purchase and Printing, 1946), p. 3.

The new governor with his predecessor, Colgate Darden, at inaugural
ceremonies in 1946. (Courtesy of the Richmond *Times-Dispatch*)

brought about vast changes in the state, changes which one economist
claimed "would ordinarily have required decades." [2]

Shortly before Tuck entered office, Senator Byrd warned him of
impending trouble. "I think you, the organization and the Democratic
party are faced with four very momentous years," he counseled. "We
must recognize the fact that there is quite an evolution in progress in all
public matters. People are restless and complaining. . . . The whole
world is very unsettled." Bill Tuck did not need to be persuaded that he
would face serious difficulties as postwar governor. Long before the

[2] Lorin Thompson, "Recent and Prospective Population Changes in Virginia,"
University of Virginia News Letter 23 (April 1, 1947). For Virginia within the larger
context of the South, see Joseph J. Spengler, "Demographic and Economic Change in
the South, 1940–1960," in Allan P. Sindler, ed., *Change in the Contemporary South*
(Durham, N.C.: Duke University Press, 1963), pp. 26–63.

inauguration he had expressed his concern to one state senator. "We are going to face terrible problems," he predicted, "and it will take the very best that is in Virginia to solve them. These years ahead of us, I am afraid, in many respects may be worse than the war years."[3]

The first major problems to confront the new governor came from a source which was destined to cause trouble for him intermittently throughout his administration: organized labor. It was an unlikely source of trouble in Virginia, a state whose predominantly rural economy had not been conducive to unionization. The American Federation of Labor had been established in the state since the beginning of the century, and there had been a considerable amount of railroad unionism in certain western areas of the state, but overall the union movement did not show significant gains until the 1930s, when the gaunt hand of the Great Depression pushed insecure workingmen toward unionization. As early as 1898 the state had established a Department of Labor which, despite several attempts to integrate it with other agencies, managed to remain a separate, though rather feckless, branch of the state government.[4]

Such union activity as had occurred in Virginia before the Tuck administration had been generally nonviolent, with the egregious exception of a widely publicized strike of workers at Danville's Riverside and Dan River Cotton Mills in the fall and winter of 1930—31. Suffering from the pinch of the depression, some 4,000 members of the United Textile Workers of America went out on strike against the Danville company in September 1930, shutting down the plant reputed to be the largest cotton factory in the world, and one whose labor relations had been amicable for nearly thirty years. The ensuing dispute attracted nationwide attention by reason of the brief involvement of "outsiders" including Norman Thomas and Sherwood Anderson, the outbreak of sporadic acts of violence, and the activation of the state militia by Governor Pollard in order to quell disturbances and protect the plant. The five-month strike, termed by the secretary of labor "the most outstanding and bitterly-fought strike occurring in the United States during the fiscal year 1931," ended in defeat for the

[3] Byrd to Tuck, Dec. 8, 1945, Tuck to E. Glenn Jordan, Aug. 23, 1945, Tuck Papers.

[4] George H. Haines, "A History of the Virginia State Federation of Labor, 1895—1944" (Ph.D. diss., Clark Univ., 1946), pp. 28, 264—66.

UTWA and, indeed, for the entire textile union organizing campaign in the South.[5] Moreover, the violence (however slight) and the charges of Communist agitation (however exaggerated) which emanated from the strike served to sour many Virginians on the tactics of organized labor.

The Danville strike proved to be but an aberration in the generally quiet development of labor in Virginia; if the growth of unionization was not extensive, it was at least peaceful. By the end of World War II membership in the AFL and CIO combined had reached a total estimated to be in excess of 100,000 workers.[6] During the course of the war union activity in the state, as in the nation, had been relatively calm, with strikes curbed first by voluntary no-strike pledges by the unions and later, in 1943, by congressional passage of the Smith-Connally, or War Labor Disputes, Act. Once the war was over, however, the fragile truce between labor and management was destroyed as the nation's economy struggled to right itself and adapt to peacetime conditions. The abrupt ending of the war meant that the nation's economic plans were, in Eric Goldman's words, "dangerously fuzzy and incomplete."[7] In the chaotic situation which ensued, with wartime restrictions relaxed, labor and management each endeavored (often obstinately) to exact gains, the result being a series of strikes unprecedented in scope in the entire history of American labor. Although the strikes were usually nonviolent, their frequency and dura-

---

[5] Robert Sidney Smith, *The Mill on the Dan* (Durham, N.C.: Duke University Press, 1960), p. 295; Heinemann, "Depression and New Deal in Virginia," pp. 16–17. The work by Smith is an exhaustive scholarly account of the Danville strike; see especially pp. 294–324. An interesting firsthand narrative by an articulate Danville resident is Julian R. Meade, *I Live in Virginia* (New York: Longmans, Green, 1935), pp. 5–75.

[6] Interview with Brewster Snow, secretary-treasurer of the Virginia AFL-CIO, April 5, 1968; *Official Proceedings of the Fifty-First Annual Convention of the Virginia State Federation of Labor* (Richmond, 1947), p. 3; Key, *Southern Politics*, p. 32. Exact statistics on union membership in Virginia before 1950 are virtually impossible to find since the unions themselves apparently kept no accurate lists of members.

[7] Eric Goldman, *The Crucial Decade—And After* (New York: Knopf, 1960), Vintage edition, p. 19. Postwar labor-management relations are examined in detail in Arthur F. McClure, *The Truman Administration and the Problems of Postwar Labor, 1945–1948* (Rutherford, N.J.: Fairleigh Dickinson University Press, 1960).

Tuck as he was often pictured—in a photograph which he hated.
(Courtesy of the Richmond *Times-Dispatch*)

The governor with Churchill and Eisenhower during a 1946 visit to
Richmond by the World War II heroes. (Courtesy of the Richmond
Times-Dispatch)

tion caused increasing numbers of Americans to view unionism with alarm.

Appearing before the Virginia General Assembly for the first time as governor, Tuck reflected the growing wariness toward organized labor as he called upon the legislators to restrict certain types of union activity. Specifically worried by the recent attempt to organize the employees of the city of Richmond, Tuck asked the legislators to prohibit the unionization of public employees. "To permit organized resistance by public servants," Tuck warned,

> necessarily results in strikes. These would cause interruptions and, at times, complete paralysis of necessary governmental activities and functions, thus jeopardizing the safety and welfare of the people. Unionization of the public service also diverts the loyalty, allegiance and obligations of the employee from the people and their government, which are entitled to them, and transfers them to the union. It creates a tendency on the part of the public servant to . . . rely upon the threat of strikes by the union to compel the granting of his demands. Such an intolerable situation is utterly incompatible with sound and orderly government.

To the reverberation of a "solid burst of handclapping," the governor proceeded to ask the General Assembly to adopt a resolution which would make "unionization of employees of the state or any agency or political subdivision thereof to be contrary to and in violation of its public policy."[8]

Tuck's speech brought a quick and generally favorable response. From as far afield as Atlanta came one endorsement; writing to commend Tuck on his plan, the mayor of that city, William Harts-field, bluntly revealed his resentment toward organized labor. "It seems," he fumed, "that the radicals, pinks, Communists, extreme liberals and their fellow-travelers are having a field day in this country, and everywhere people are complaining about cowardly and gutless public officials who are putting up with their crackpot ideas. Unless a line is drawn somewhere . . . I am afraid we are going to lose a lot of our fundamental American liberties by pure default and cowardice."[9]

---

[8] Virginia, *Address of William M. Tuck, Governor, to the General Assembly, Monday, January 21, 1946*, Senate Document No. 16 (Richmond: Division of Purchase and Printing, 1946), p. 9; Richmond *Times-Dispatch*, Jan. 22, 1946.

[9] Hartsfield to Tuck, Jan. 31, 1946, Tuck Executive Papers.

In a somewhat more restrained manner, most of the newspapers in Virginia lauded the governor's proposal. The Staunton *News-Leader* flatly proclaimed that "government cannot live under unionization of its employees," and the *Northern Virginia Daily* of Strasburg agreed. "No government," it asserted, "can afford to incur the risk of inefficiency [or of having] its activities completely throttled by a strike fomented by professional union agitators." Two of the state's largest papers, the Richmond *Times-Dispatch* and the Norfolk *Virginian-Pilot*, generally concurred, with the Richmond paper presciently suggesting that labor's demands were on the verge of precipitating a legislative reaction against the unions: "The effort to organize public employees is one example of the extremes to which the union movement is now going, at great peril to its whole future in this country." [10]

The response of state labor leaders was predictably hostile toward the Tuck proposal. Usually, in addition to condemning the substance of the proposal, labor spokesmen went on to flay the entire Byrd organization. The leader of the attempt to unionize Richmond city employees, Rex Kildow, announced that the workers had decided to join the union "after taking into full consideration the fact that people like Tuck and the men of the Byrd machine are against them." Ernest Pugh, leader of the Virginia CIO, agreed, claiming that "Byrd is jerking the strings by which Tuck dances. . . . Never to my knowledge has any governor of any state ever delivered such a vicious anti-labor message. . . . The CIO . . . feels he is adopting the same tactics that were adopted by Hitler and Mussolini." The Political Action Committee of the CIO voiced its contempt by implying, with customary bombast, that Tuck's stand on unionism emanated from "the theory of Byrdism [which] cuts sharply at the heart of the basic freedoms of all Americans . . . [and which] is substantially that found in *Mein Kampf*. [Byrd's]

---

[10] Staunton *News-Leader*, quoted in Richmond *Times-Dispatch*, Jan. 27, 1946; *Northern Virginia Daily* (Strasburg), quoted in Richmond *Times-Dispatch*, Feb. 10, 1946; Richmond *Times-Dispatch*, Jan. 28, 1946; Norfolk *Virginian-Pilot*, Jan. 22, 1946. A dissenting opinion was expressed by the Newport News *Daily Press*. In an editorial reprinted in the Richmond *Times-Dispatch*, Jan. 27, 1946, the *Daily Press* called Tuck's speech "plain double talk," and warned that "if government forbids collective bargaining with it, it is the first step toward a ban on any collective bargaining. . . . A right is a right, no matter for whom a man works."

plan to capture and rule Virginia is of the same pattern as Adolf Hitler's plot to destroy all democracies, and rule the world."[11]

Such overblown attacks were of doubtful efficacy. One state newspaper suggested that "men can hang themselves with words [and] drown themselves in their own verbiage. Having thus hung themselves and drowned themselves, the CIO-PAC should be thoroughly dead." In his *Times-Dispatch* column, Thomas Lomax Hunter snorted at the "coarse and vulgar blast of abuse" which the union spokesmen had leveled at Tuck and, having assured his readers that many of the CIO leaders were Communists, proceeded to praise the governor's stand. "Governor Tuck, who, fortunately for us, does not look to Washington for any favors, was quick to recognize and set about the scotching of this alien-inspired gang. Its political billingsgate need not too greatly arouse us."[12]

Virginians, however, were becoming "greatly aroused," and the attitude of the General Assembly reflected the public's apprehension toward labor. Tuck's requested resolution was passed in short order. In its final form the resolution made it "contrary to the public policy of Virginia for any state, county, or municipal officer or agent to be vested with or possess any authority to recognize any labor union as a representative of any public officers or employees or to negotiate with any such union or its agents."[13]

The legislature also enacted two laws relating directly to strikes. One statute, which was easily passed, prohibited the resort to violence in picketing and required that all members of a picket line be bona fide employees of the strike-bound company. A second measure, and one which prompted much more controversy, was an attempt to prohibit the state from rehiring, for a period of five years, any state employee who participated in a strike. After a tortuous legislative course, an

[11] Richmond *Times-Dispatch*, Jan. 22, 1946.

[12] Lynchburg *News*, Feb. 2, 1946; Richmond *Times-Dispatch*, Feb. 1, 1946. Hunter for many years wrote a daily potpourri column for the *Times-Dispatch* under the title "The Cavalier." When his column dealt with politics, he almost invariably supported the policies of the Byrd organization. He was, according to one writer, "a countryman who . . . scorned cities, damned the New Deal and suggested that increasing the poll tax and lengthening the hunting season would do wonders for Virginia" (Fishwick, "F.F.V.'s," p. 156).

[13] *Acts and Joint Resolutions of the General Assembly, 1946*, p. 1006.

amended bill was passed, with the period of prohibited employment reduced from five years to one year.[14]

Labor spokesmen in Virginia were incensed at the actions taken by the 1946 session of the General Assembly, claiming that the legislature was hoping in fact to abolish all collective bargaining. The unionists' alarm was largely unwarranted. The labor measures enacted were limited almost exclusively to cases of strikes against the government; there was virtually no substantial diminution of the right of employees of private companies to strike. The distinction between the right to strike held by employees of private industry and that held by public employees was already widely established. It was generally accepted—as evidenced, either explicitly or implicitly, by the provisions of the Wagner Act and certain CIO charters—that government employees did not in fact possess the unmitigated right to strike.[15] Thus, even though the policy established by the General Assembly in 1946 did indicate increased public disaffection toward labor, that policy was neither as novel nor as noxious as its critics claimed.

It was while the 1946 General Assembly was in session that Governor Tuck first became personally involved in a labor dispute. The incident stemmed from a strike by employees of a Hampton Roads ferry company. Until that time it had been the policy of the state to grant franchises to private companies to provide ferry service across certain bodies of water. Ferrying thus formed an integral part of the state highway system and in some cases served as the only means of getting from one point to another without traveling an excessive distance. On February 8, 1946, a work stoppage against the Chesapeake Ferry Company was called by members of the Seafarers' International Union (AFL). The striking workers, including oilers, firemen, and deckhands, demanded a wage increase of ten dollars per month; the company steadfastly refused to meet the union's demand. The result was the disruption of ferry service, and hence of public transportation, in much of the Hampton Roads–Newport News area. Absorbed in the work of the legislative session, Tuck scarcely noticed

[14] Ibid., pp. 391–92, 561.

[15] Joel Seidman, *Union Rights and Union Duties* (New York: Harcourt, Brace, 1943), p. 108; Richmond *Times-Dispatch*, Feb. 5, 1946. See also Harry A. Millis and Emily C. Brown, *From Wagner Act to Taft-Hartley* (Chicago: University of Chicago Press, 1950).

the strike for several days, believing perhaps that this walkout, like three which had preceded it during the previous year, would be settled quickly. When it was not, and the strike moved into its second week, the governor felt that he must act to bring an end to the disruption of the state's highway system.[16]

The president of the ferry company, Arthur Hitch, was summoned to the governor's office. Tuck informed him that the public convenience and safety demanded operation of the ferries, but Hitch pleaded that, though he recognized the inconvenience being caused, he could not operate so long as the workers remained obdurate. Tuck suggested to Hitch that his company's franchise might be in danger and warned, "You'd better get them to work [or] I'm going to do something about it." After consultation with the State Corporation Commission, he again told Hitch that ferry service must be resumed immediately. When Hitch demurred, the governor, his patience at an end, exclaimed, "Well, we're going to run that ferry!"

Tuck began at once to make plans for seizure of the company's facilities. At his behest, Attorney General Abram P. Staples drew up a bill which allowed the state to acquire the ferry system by right of eminent domain. In requesting the legislature to empower him to seize the facilities, Tuck was careful to disclaim any intention of affecting the on-going labor dispute. "The sole purpose," he averred, "is to prevent the people of Virginia from being made the unwilling and unfortunate victims of a controversy in which their interests seem to be totally ignored." The bill, passed by both houses within a matter of hours, was on the governor's desk by evening; the next day he issued an order effecting the takeover of the ferries by the state. Amid mixed reactions from the Virginia press, the state operated the ferry system briefly under the provisions granted by the legislature. Finally, in 1948, the state acquired the Chesapeake Company at a cost of $2,692,977 and incorporated the ferry service into the highway system, thereby abolishing an anachronistic and often troublesome situation.[17]

[16] Interview with Tuck. The account which follows is based on interviews with Tuck and on the Richmond *Times-Dispatch* and Norfolk *Virginian-Pilot*, Feb. 8–22, 1946.

[17] Richmond *Times-Dispatch*, Jan. 11, 1949. The *Times-Dispatch*, Feb. 22, 1946, praised Tuck's action, while the Norfolk *Virginian-Pilot*, Feb. 21, 1946, condemned the move.

Tuck's handling of the ferry strike revealed, early in his administration, his characteristically direct and forthright—his critics would say rash and heavyhanded—method of dealing with the state's problems. It also served as a mild prelude to another labor incident—an incident which was destined to earn for Tuck a widespread and lasting, if not wholly deserved, reputation for being antilabor.

The Virginia Electric and Power Company was a vast system which served over 1,000 Virginia communities by the end of World War II. Its 12,300-mile network of lines provided electrical power to some 1,700,000 persons—well over half of Virginia's total population at that time.[18] On February 27, 1946, Vepco customers were informed that they faced the possibility of a power blackout. Jack G. Holtzclaw, president of the utility company, announced on that date that he had received notice from the International Brotherhood of Electrical Workers (AFL) that the union, comprising over 1,800 Vepco employees, intended to strike on April 1 unless its demand for a wage increase was met.[19]

It was not the first time that the union had threatened to strike, but on each former occasion the impending walkout had been averted. Previous disputes, to be sure, had caused some anxiety. When, earlier in 1946, the IBEW had issued a similar ultimatum, one Norfolk resident grimly predicted that "if electric current and gas are shut off in the homes and stores . . . there will be suffering and even death from it. I'm sure that our government is standing by to take over the hour the union men walk out." The major Norfolk newspaper agreed editorially, expressing its hope that "the aggrieved union will not take its quarrel out on the innocent public's hide. If the union leaders are good judges of the public temper, they will not embark on such a mad enterprise. If they do, some public authority will have to intervene." Overlooking, or discounting, the governor of the state, the editorial suggested that the only public authority with the power to intervene in such an emergency was the president of the United States.[20]

An amicable settlement had ended the earlier dispute short of government intervention, and it is likely that few Virginians suspected

[18] *The Vepcovian* 20 (July 1946): 98.
[19] Richmond *Times-Dispatch*, Feb. 28, 1946.
[20] Norfolk *Virginian-Pilot*, Jan. 16, 22, 1946.

Big Bill and Little John Q.

Big Bill and Little John Q. (Courtesy of the Richmond *Times-Dispatch*)

that such drastic action would ensue from the latest IBEW threat. Least of all, perhaps, did the state's new governor envision the use of force; by his own admission, he had hardly noticed the announcement of the strike when it was first issued.[21] As time passed, however, he became more concerned that no agreement was reached, and with the company adamantly refusing to grant the union's demand for a 17½ cent per hour wage increase, a strike appeared to be inevitable.[22]

[21] Interview with Tuck.

[22] See Richmond *Times-Dispatch*, Mar. 24, 1946, for a detailed statement of the union's contract proposals.

With ten days remaining before the strike deadline, Tuck instructed Commissioner of Labor John Hopkins Hall to invite representatives of both labor and management to his office in the hope that he might encourage a settlement. The company agreed to send representatives, but the union refused on the specious ground that, because Vepco transacted some business in West Virginia and North Carolina, the governors of those states would have to be present also. Since the power company received approximately 92 percent of its revenues from Virginia, the governor was inclined to question the desire of the union to cooperate; in any case, Tuck decided, there was not time to arrange for such a tri-state conference.[23]

Disappointed by what he regarded as the union's recalcitrance, Tuck announced on March 22 that he felt that he "must take full responsibility" in the impending crisis and embarked upon what he acknowledged to be "drastic" and "unprecedented" action. The threatened walkout, he said, would cause "hunger, famine, pestilence and even death" in a society so dependent upon electrical power. "As governor of Virginia," Tuck declared, "I shall not sit idly by and do nothing in the face of such a disaster. If a strike comes, bringing with it these attendant evils, I shall forthwith order these plants, together with all of their properties and equipments, seized by one of the agencies of the Commonwealth, which will be ordered to operate them for the protection and benefit of the people."[24]

The Richmond *Times-Dispatch* welcomed Tuck's edict. Sharing the anxiety expressed by the governor, that paper warned editorially that "a shutdown which would plunge hospitals into darkness, cut off the milk supply from babies, cripple public transportation and shut off light, heat and refrigeration from thousands of homes cannot be countenanced. . . . Governor Tuck's courageous announcement is neither anti-labor nor anti-capital, but pro-public." From Washington came word that Senator Byrd was similarly pleased by Tuck's stand. "You have a fine sense of timing," he wrote, "and it is such things as

[23] Official statement by Tuck, Mar. 22, 1946, Tuck Executive Papers; Virginia, *Opinions of the Attorney General and Report to the Governor of Virginia, from July 1, 1945, to June 30, 1946* (Richmond: Division of Purchase and Printing, 1946), p. 145.

[24] Official statement by Tuck, Mar. 22, 1946, Tuck Executive Papers.

this that are building up for you throughout Virginia a great backlog of confidence and respect." [25]

The problem facing Tuck was that of finding a way to take over the power facilities once that step was deemed necessary. It was suggested that the procedure might be conducted by the State Corporation Commission, under whose aegis Vepco operated. The governor himself, however, remained noncommittal as to his specific plans beyond the terse statement that he believed the situation could be handled. [26]

On March 24 Tuck informed Vepco President Holtzclaw and IBEW representative J. C. McIntosh that electric service must not be interrupted and, in identical telegrams, set noon, March 28, as the deadline for receiving assurances that there would be no cessation of power. "It is not in the public interest for me to wait until we are enveloped by disaster before moving to protect the people," said the governor. [27] On the day before the deadline, Tuck requested the company to inform him whether or not it would willingly surrender its facilities if a state takeover became necessary, and at the same time he asked the IBEW to ascertain if its members would continue to work under the authority of the state in the event of seizure by the Commonwealth. The company expressed acquiescence; the union was "evasive" in its reply which, in the governor's mind, "amounted to a negative answer." [28]

The Vepco management, meanwhile, had agreed to grant the union's demand for a 17½ cent per hour wage increase but would not consent to make the raise retroactive as far back as the union wished. The company was willing to grant retroactive pay amounting to $125 per man, while the union demanded $250. Thus the factions remained at loggerheads as the strike date approached. [29]

Tuck, dismayed by the apparent refusal of the unionists to work under state authority, was clearly becoming more anxious, and his public statements accordingly became more intemperate. He could not believe, he declared, that Virginians would "follow such evil

[25] Richmond *Times-Dispatch*, Mar. 23, 1946; Byrd to Tuck, Mar. 25, 1946, Tuck Papers.

[26] Richmond *Times-Dispatch*, Mar. 24, 1946.

[27] Tuck to J. G. Holtzclaw, Mar. 24, 1946, Tuck Executive Papers.

[28] Tuck to J. C. McIntosh, Mar. 27, 1946, official statement by Tuck, Mar. 28, 1946, ibid.

[29] Richmond *News Leader*, Mar. 30, 1946.

leadership." Union representative McIntosh was quick to respond to Tuck's comment. "So the Governor presumes to call his own people . . . evil-doers while he assumes a righteous and paternalistic attitude toward Vepco whose vast profits are pooled into the monumental accumulation of wealth now controlled by the financial tycoons of Wall Street," McIntosh protested. "The Lord notes even the fall of a sparrow. Apparently Governor Tuck notes only the fall of the profit bird."[30]

The failure of the IBEW to comply with his request for guarantees of continuous service convinced Tuck that a work stoppage on April 1 was inevitable. His patience nearing an end, he imputed the blame largely to a "truculent and irresponsible labor leader" and, on March 28, proclaimed a state of emergency to exist in Virginia. "I champion the right of labor strikes in proper places [and] shall cheerfully as a citizen and an official uphold . . . their God-given privileges and rights," he announced, "but I deny that in this instance a right to strike exists, either morally or under the laws of Virginia." He proceeded to warn that he might invoke extraordinary powers—powers, he said, which "are not personal to me, but belong to the high office with which I have been entrusted by the people."[31]

Throughout the crisis Tuck had publicly maintained an air of complete confidence but had given no indication of what specific course he would take, simply vowing time and again that "the lights in Virginia will not go off." Privately he had been hard at work devising some means by which to back up that pledge. In trying to work out a plan, Tuck met several times in the privacy of the Governor's Mansion with leading state officials including Executive Secretary to the Governor Virgil Carrington (Pat) Jones, Attorney General Abram P. Staples, Secretary of the Commonwealth Jesse Dillon, State Treasurer W. Tayloe Murphy, State Auditor J. Gordon Bennett, Adjutant General S. Gardner Waller, members of the State Corporation Commission, and the ubiquitous Ebbie Combs.[32] The plan which emerged from those meetings appeared to be substantially of the governor's own devising. Indeed, by the account of one who was present, many of

[30] Official statement by Tuck, Mar. 28, 1946, Tuck Executive Papers; Richmond *Times-Dispatch*, Mar. 30, 1946.

[31] Official statement by Tuck, Mar. 28, 1946, Tuck Executive Papers.

[32] Virginia, *Report of the Adjutant General, for the Period January 1, 1946, to December 31, 1946* (Richmond: Division of Purchase and Printing, 1948), p. 35.

Tuck's advisers expressed reservations about the enterprise, but to no avail. "Throughout the discussion that went back and forth across the circle of important state men," recalled Pat Jones, "the Governor seemed to stand alone. Perhaps some of those present agreed with him, but, if so, they kept it to themselves, and what conversation they engaged in was more in the nature of warning the chief executive against his proposed move. No matter how much they cautioned him—and these men were his lieutenants—he gave not the slightest indication that he was backing out."[33]

Infuriated by what he deemed an appalling callousness on the part of the union toward the public, Tuck, in the midst of one meeting with his associates, pounded his fist on the arm of his chair and declared in stentorian tones: "I'll be damned if they're going to cut the lights out in Virginia. This is just as bad as Jesse James or Dillinger. It's just like sticking a gun in your back. And they'll not get by with it as long as I'm governor. It's my duty to protect the safety of the people and I'm going to do it." That same evening, still agitated, Tuck exclaimed to an aide: "They say I can't do it. They say the union has got us bluffed, that there's no way we can keep the lights from going off." Then in an outburst characteristic of Tuck at his angriest (in that his meaning was to be found more in the vehemence of the delivery than in the precision of the vocabulary), the governor roared: "If the union leaders try to cut the lights off in Virginia, I'll salivate them. I'll give them unshirted hell!"[34]

Once the plan for dealing with the strike had been devised, Tuck would not be swayed from putting the stratagem into action, even though some of his associates continued to be skeptical of its merit. Undaunted, the governor asserted privately that he was content to let his whole political career rest on the outcome of his plan.[35] When that

[33] Virgil Carrington Jones, "Behind the Scenes with a Governor" (unpublished MS, 1946, in Jones's files), pp. 93–122. Jones, a journalist and historian, served as the governor's executive secretary and public relations aide during the first six months of the Tuck administration. He was privy to virtually all gubernatorial matters and, for most of his tenure, lived in the Governor's Mansion. As an astute and articulate observer, Jones provides in his account, written in diary form, an invaluable view of the day-to-day activities of the governor and is especially helpful in reconstructing the events surrounding the Vepco strike.

[34] Ibid., pp. 103–4.

[35] Ibid., p. 115. Jones notes that Tuck "announced with finality that he was going

plan was made known, the resulting clamor not only reverberated throughout Virginia but echoed across the entire nation.

The Virginia State Guard was an emergency militia unit which had been formed during World War II. Ordinarily the Guard would have been disbanded at the end of the war, but Governor Darden had extended the service of the outfit until June 30, 1946. This extension of life provided the opportunity for the Guard to perform what its historian has termed "the most dramatic, albeit unorthodox, service of its career." [36]

At precisely nine o'clock on the morning of March 29, uniformed members of the Guard moved throughout the state delivering to Vepco employees notices which read: "You are hereby notified that you have been drafted by the commander-in-chief of the land and naval forces of Virginia, the Honorable William M. Tuck, Governor of Virginia, into the service of the Commonwealth to execute the law which requires the Virginia Electric and Power Company to provide electric service to the people of Virginia customarily served by it." A second order informed the new militiamen that they would be "granted a temporary suspension of . . . active military duties so long as the Virginia Electric and Power Company is conducting operations without interruption by strike." Their inactive status, however, would be immediately revoked in the event of a strike by the IBEW. Thereupon the draftees would become active members of the state militia and would be ordered to assist in operating the electrical plants by performing the same duties which they had previously performed for the company. The new "recruits," lest they take their orders lightly, were informed that they were forthwith "subject to the military law of Virginia, and for disobedience to orders or other offenses against said law . . . are subject to such lawful punishment as a court martial may direct." [37]

---

to stake his whole future on the outcome of this matter." In an interview in the Norfolk *Virginian-Pilot*, June 8, 1969, Tuck recalled that at the time he was determined, as his grandfather had been at the Battle of Gettysburg, to rise or fall on the issue before him.

[36] Marvin W. Schlegel, *Virginia on Guard: Civilian Defense and the State Militia in the Second World War* (Richmond: Virginia State Library, 1949), pp. 35, 210, 247–48.

[37] The draft order and the executive orders are in the Tuck Executive Papers. See also Schlegel, *Virginia on Guard*, p. 248.

Tuck had formulated his startling plan by adroitly combining several gubernatorial powers, at least one of which was rather archaic. Fundamental to all of his actions was the general requirement, included in the state constitution, that the governor be responsible for the execution of the laws. The constitution further decreed specifically that the governor "shall be commander-in-chief of the land and naval forces of the state, [and] have power to embody the militia to repel invasion, suppress insurrection, and enforce the execution of the laws." One of those laws, as contained in section 4066 of the Code of Virginia, stipulated that a public service corporation be required to furnish continuous service to its customers and that service not be withdrawn or interrupted without the consent of the State Corporation Commission.[38]

The proposed Vepco strike then, if carried out, would clearly have resulted in a violation of the state's public utility law. The question facing Tuck was how best to enforce that law. He found an answer in an arcane statute, believed to have been added to the Virginia code as early as 1785, which made all able-bodied male citizens between the ages of sixteen and sixty-five members of the "unorganized militia" and empowered the governor to employ that militia if needed to execute the laws.[39] The code specified, however, that the "unorganized militia" could not be mustered until the regular militia had been summoned to duty. Accordingly, Tuck, on the night of March 28, alerted the Virginia State Guard and ordered its members to stand by at their respective armories.[40] That technicality having been satisfied, the governor proceeded the following morning to invoke the seldom used and largely forgotten statute to enlist the services of Vepco employees.

Tuck's unprecedented use of the draft made headlines across the country. The New York *Times*, for example, blared, "Virginia Gover-

[38] Virginia, *Constitution* (Richmond: Davis Bottom, Superintendent of Public Printing, 1915), Art. 5, sec. 2, p. 34; Virginia, *Code of 1942* (Charlottesville: Michie Company, 1942), sec. 4066, pp. 1418–19. The code states specifically that "it shall be the duty of every public utility to furnish reasonably adequate service."

[39] *Code of 1942*, sec. 2673(1), p. 884; Carter O. Lowance, "William M. Tuck: Attorney, Governor, and Congressman," *Virginia and the Virginia County* 7 (June 1953): 49.

[40] Jones, "Behind the Scenes," p. 113.

nor Drafts Power Workers, Bars Strike," while a Philadelphia *Evening Bulletin* banner read, "Workers Are Drafted to Prevent Strike; Virginia Governor Makes Men Subject to Court Martial."[41] Within Virginia, editorial comment indicated shock but generally lauded the governor's course. And, almost invariably, such comment evinced an undercurrent of resentment toward organized labor in general. "Governor Tuck's prompt, courageous, realistic action prevented economic paralysis of the state," claimed the Richmond *News Leader*. "It must give Virginians and many others over the nation a lift . . . to see one public official courageous enough to risk the wrath of organized labor in order to protect the public interest." The Danville *Bee* concurred, asserting that the governor's action "squarely challenged the philosophy of the labor movement in America."[42]

Spokesmen for organized labor were predictably incensed. "Unless you . . . recall your dictatorial order," one union executive warned Tuck, "every laborer in Virginia will take the necessary steps to make ineffective your dictatorial action." The IBEW local in Tuck's native South Boston declared, "We accept Governor Tuck's action as a notice to labor unions that the Byrd machine is out to destroy organized labor in Virginia." In Norfolk the head of the IBEW local predicted that before organized labor was finished, Tuck "would rather be picking apples in his patron senator's orchard than occupying his hot seat in Richmond."[43]

Most of the IBEW draftees received their induction notices with understandable surprise, but generally without bitterness. Some even managed a semblance of humor. One worker, upon reading his notice, commented wryly, "I don't believe this is legal. The Navy hasn't released me yet. I don't believe I can be in the Army and Navy at the same time." It was suggested to another unionist that he might like to

[41] New York *Times*, Mar. 30, 1946, p. 1; Philadelphia *Evening Bulletin*, Mar. 29, 1946, p. 2–F. See also Baltimore *Evening Sun*, Mar. 29, 1946, p. 1; Washington *Post*, Mar. 30, 1946, p. 1.

[42] Richmond *News Leader*, Mar. 30, 1946; Danville *Bee*, Mar. 30, 1946. See also Charlottesville *Daily Progress*, Mar. 30, 1946; Fredericksburg *Free Lance-Star*, Mar. 30, 1946. For contrasting views, see Newport News *Daily Press*, April 2, 1946; Roanoke *World-News*, April 2, 1946.

[43] Richmond *Times-Dispatch*, Mar. 30, April 13, 1946; Roanoke *World-News*, Mar. 30, 1946.

frame his draft notice since it was signed by Governor Tuck. After a moment's hesitation the worker brightened. "I'll hang it in my privy," he announced.[44]

Although most of the Vepco workers seemed to accept their new status with equanimity, there were others who were enraged by the governor's tactics. The Governor's Mansion received a number of threatening telephone messages. One caller who identified himself as a navy man told Executive Secretary Pat Jones: "I'm just back from Germany where I've been fighting the same kind of dictator that Tuck is trying to be. We got rid of Hitler and we will get rid of Tuck. I'm organizing a gang of sailors now and we're coming down there and clean up the Mansion." Disturbed by that and similar threats, Jones and Superintendent of State Police Major Charles W. Woodson secured, without Tuck's knowledge, plainclothes policemen to provide continuous protection for the governor. Although there were several incidents suspicious enough, in the tense atmosphere that prevailed, to warrant concern among Tuck's aides, no violence occurred.[45]

Among the first and most vehement of those to denounce Tuck's move was the president of the American Federation of Labor, William Green, who claimed that the governor's action amounted to "enslaving labor." When Green telephoned to voice his complaint, Tuck (with tongue thoroughly in cheek) informed the labor leader that, far from being a form of bondage, it was an honor to serve in the historic Virginia militia! "Mr. Green," Tuck remembered saying, "I haven't enslaved any labor. We have down here what's known as the Unorganized State Militia. It's older than the Constitution and the Army of the United States, and it was once commanded by a gentleman by the name of George Washington and at another time by one called Patrick Henry and a little later by a man known as Thomas Jefferson, and unfortunately for me, I'm in command today. . . . You live in Maryland and you don't have a damned thing to do with what I do."[46]

---

[44] Richmond *Times-Dispatch*, Mar. 30, 1946. According to the official report, "Other than a few derisive remarks by some employees, there were no incidents occurring which were worthy of reporting" (*Report of the Adjutant General, 1946*, p. 9).

[45] Jones, "Behind the Scenes," p. 116–18; *Report of the Adjutant General, 1946*, p. 9.

[46] Norfolk *Virginian-Pilot*, June 8, 1969; interviews with Tuck.

Unimpressed, Green proclaimed publicly that he and his union would "never acquiesce in the principle of involuntary servitude" and informed Tuck that he planned to ask President Truman to intervene. "Well, that's just too bad," chortled the *Northern Virginia Daily*. "Mr. Green forgets that he is not playing with poor old union-bossed Uncle Sam when he threatens to cut off the essential light and power of the people of Virginia. He has yet to realize that Richmond is not Washington, and Mr. Tuck is not Mr. Truman."[47]

Within Virginia, labor spokesmen were joined by antiorganization Democrats in condemning Tuck's action. "It is not a very pretty or pleasant picture we have here in Virginia," lamented Martin Hutchinson, "with the state militia billeted in the capital city and supposedly free men being drafted by order of the governor to work for a private corporation." Moss Plunkett, Tuck's erstwhile opponent, was more blunt. "Governor Tuck," he said, "has gone wild." Never one to miss an opportunity to castigate the organization, Plunkett asserted that the affair was "just another case of the Byrd machine ignoring the rights of the people, but this time they have gone too far."[48]

In light of the low estate of the antiorganization forces at the time, and considering the popular animus against organized labor, it is unlikely that Tuck was much distressed by adverse criticism from those quarters. More alarming to him, by his own admission, was a telephone call which he received from Washington. He immediately recognized the "little high-pitched, raspy voice" as that of Senator Byrd. The draft procedure had apparently taken Byrd by surprise, and the senator, always a prudent man, may well have been somewhat stunned. Tuck hastened to assure him that he believed himself to be on firm ground, having been assisted in his legal planning by the respected attorney general, Abe Staples. Byrd then asked what he proposed to do if Truman intervened. "I'm going to tell him," Tuck replied, "that if he lets the situation alone, that I will keep the lights on, but if he takes over, then I'm expecting him to do the job."[49]

One of the most vexing matters confronting Tuck was the problem

[47] "Virginia-Cured Walkout," *Newsweek* 27 (April 8, 1946): 20; interview with Tuck; *Northern Virginia Daily*, Mar. 30, 1946.
[48] Richmond *Times-Dispatch*, April 3, 1946; Roanoke *World-News*, Mar. 30, 1946.
[49] Norfolk *Virginian-Pilot*, June 8, 1969; interview with Tuck.

of operating the Vepco plants if the IBEW militiamen refused to obey the order to work for the state. Although he was confident of compliance, the governor acted sub rosa to guard against the possibility of a walkout by attempting to secure the services of engineering personnel from various municipalities and state colleges. To that end he instructed Director of the Budget John H. Bradford to send telegrams to certain mayors and college administrators asking that every employee "with training in operation of electric power and light systems or steam boilers be ready upon request to give all possible help in maintaining electric power service in Virginia areas threatened with strike of electrical workers."[50] In addition Tuck received voluntary offers of aid from the federal government, through both the army and navy, with the understanding that such assistance, if accepted, would not be publicized.[51]

As the strike deadline approached, Tuck remained outwardly calm. "I am pleased with the progress of our plans," he announced.

Many capable and patriotic Virginians in and out of the union are offering me their services to the end that the power will not be cut off in Virginia. I am not at this time trying to solve any social, economic or labor problem. These problems can be solved in the weeks, months and years that lie ahead. I am simply exercising my duties and the powers of the high office which I hold to see that suffering, death and devastation do not come to Virginia. The lights in Virginia will not go off.[52]

Privately, he was not quite so assured, at one point remarking to several close associates, "This thing has got to hurry up and end or I'll lose my nerve."[53]

---

[50] Jones, "Behind the Scenes," p. 118; letter from Tuck to author, July 26, 1971. Tuck maintained that his draft order provided the IBEW unionists with a welcome means of circumventing the strike. "For the most part," he said, "the men were looking for that umbrella to hide under. Nine-tenths of them didn't want to strike anyway" (interview with Tuck).

[51] This information was related to the author in confidence, orally and in writing, by one who was actively involved in the Vepco incident.

[52] Richmond *Times-Dispatch*, Mar. 30, 1946.

[53] Jones, "Behind the Scenes," p. 115. Some of those present, according to Jones, did not believe that Tuck was worried, but thought, on the contrary, that he was enjoying the episode. "Hell, Bill," Attorney General Staples told him, "you're having the best time you ever had in your life."

Happily for the governor and for the public served by Vepco, a settlement was reached, as Tuck had hoped, before the final part of his plan went into effect, thereby making it unnecessary for the militiamen to go on active duty. Late in the day on March 30 the IBEW agreed to call off the strike and to resume contract negotiations. After some two weeks of bargaining, the union and the management of Vepco settled on a new contract which guaranteed each worker a wage increase of at least 15 cents per hour. In addition, a fund was set up by the company to be used "to eliminate certain inequities or inequalities in its wage structure—a provision which meant increases of 20 to 30 cents an hour for some employees. Relevant to the recent strike threat, the new contract stipulated that "during the course of this agreement and any renewal period there shall be no strikes, sitdowns, slowdowns, walkouts, continuous union meetings or interference with work by the Brotherhood or any group of its members, and the company, on its part, agrees that . . . there shall be no lockouts of its employees."[54]

Even after the dispute reached amicable settlement, resentment of Tuck's maneuver continued to emanate from some quarters. The Norfolk *Virginian-Pilot* decried the "very dubious use of the gubernatorial military powers," and the Newport News *Daily Press* protested that the "totalitarian implications of Mr. Tuck's action, no matter how sincere, are ominous in a democratic state." In the western part of the Commonwealth, an area with antiorganization tendencies, the Roanoke *World-News* expressed "grave doubt of the validity of Governor Tuck's order drafting workers into the unorganized militia."[55]

Labor leaders remained indignant. Representative McIntosh of the IBEW claimed that a settlement would have been reached earlier except for Tuck's "infamous action"—action which "had nothing to do with the final settlement unless it had the effect of convincing the company that its employees intended to fight . . . in the face of the

[54] Richmond *Times-Dispatch*, Mar. 30, April 17, 1946. The settlement removed the necessity of dealing with a number of questions which had never been resolved. For example, what punishment would the IBEW workers have received had they refused to comply with the governor's order? If they had agreed to work as militiamen, what arrangement would have been made for their wages and for the profits accrued by the company while operated by the state?

[55] Norfolk *Virginian-Pilot*, quoted in Richmond *Times-Dispatch*, April 7, 1946; Newport News *Daily Press*, April 2, 1946; Roanoke *World-News*, April 2, 1946.

Governor's illegal use of the state militia." Boyd E. Payton, president of the Virginia CIO Council, discerning a familiar villain, attacked the move as "the most sinister, damnable and unprincipled act to date coming from the high command of 'Byrdism.'"[56]

In the aftermath of the affair several rumors sprang up. One concerned an alleged rift between Tuck and Attorney General Staples. According to the report of a veteran Capitol observer, Staples had cautioned the governor that he did not have the authority to intervene in the dispute, whereupon "the Governor told the Attorney General to find the authority, or the Governor would find another Attorney General!"[57] While the story was illustrative of Tuck's determination, it was not an accurate indication of the relationship between the two men, who were longtime friends. The governor, of course, had no power to remove the elected attorney general, and had no desire to do so anyway. He was dismayed at the insinuation of animosity between Staples and himself, insisting that the attorney general "co-operated with me right along in the power strike—except that he was trying to hold me down." Indeed, it was Staples who provided legal advice throughout the crisis and afterward prepared a thorough defense of the governor's actions.[58]

Even more annoying to Tuck was the report in a Roanoke newspaper that he had misgivings about the propriety of the Vepco draft. "I don't know," he was quoted as saying. "I was probably wrong." He promptly issued a public denial, claiming that the statement attributed to him was "absolutely without any justification" and reiterating his belief that he had acted correctly.[59] In private too he staunchly denied the authenticity of the remark. Writing to Senator Byrd he said flatly, "I made no statement indicating that I had the slightest doubt about the legality of every step I took." Several months afterward, Tuck wrote an article in which he defended his course of action, concluding, "I would

---

[56] Richmond *Times-Dispatch*, Mar. 30, April 17, 1946.

[57] Friddell, *What Is It about Virginia?*, p. 63.

[58] Interview with Tuck. See *Opinions of the Attorney General, 1945–1946*, p. 144; and *Report of the Adjutant General, 1946*, p. 9.

[59] Roanoke *World-News*, April 8, 1946; Richmond *Times-Dispatch*, April 9, 1946. Tuck's executive secretary, who was with him constantly during the affair, noted that he never once heard the governor express reservations about the enterprise (Jones, "Behind the Scenes," pp. 139–40).

welcome a test of my action in any court of competent jurisdiction." The passage of time did not bring any change in his feelings about the matter. "I was a country lawyer," he recalled years later, "and common sense told me you could do anything to protect the people. The supreme law is public safety."[60]

Tuck's confidence notwithstanding, there were obviously questions about the legality of his draft maneuver. The New York *Herald Tribune*, while agreeing with Tuck that the public must be protected, pointedly asserted that "protection cannot be afforded at the expense of greater dangers by twisting laws to serve purposes for which they were never intended."[61] Although Attorney General Staples produced a cogent legal defense, the courts might well have held that the laws had been twisted too much and that the governor's admirable desire to protect the public had been achieved by unconstitutional means.[62] The question, in any case, remained moot since the resolution of the dilemma made litigation unnecessary.

Although there was some doubt as to the legality of the governor's action, there was no doubt as to its popularity. It was believed that the Vepco incident brought into the governor's office the largest number of letters and telegrams ever received on a single subject to that time; of those messages, the vast majority were favorable to Tuck's stand.[63] Frequently the letters included derogatory references to organized labor in general. One state judge, for example, expressed the hope that after the governor's move, "labor in Virginia will understand that it cannot control affairs in this Commonwealth." A Southside resident heartily concurred: "What the nation needs is not only a good 5-cent cigar, but 47 more governors like Governor Tuck, who has the fortitude to stand up for all the people and not only for the barons of organized labor."[64]

---

[60] Tuck to Byrd, April 10, 1946, Tuck Papers; William M. Tuck, "How a Governor Stopped a Threatened Utility Strike," *Public Utilities Fortnightly* 28 (Aug. 29, 1946), p. 267; Norfolk *Virginian-Pilot*, June 8, 1969.

[61] New York *Herald Tribune*, quoted in Danville *Register*, April 4, 1946.

[62] See *Opinions of the Attorney General, 1945–1946*, pp. 144–54.

[63] Jones, "Behind the Scenes," p. 129; Tuck, "How a Governor Stopped a Threatened Utility Strike," p. 274.

[64] Benjamin W. Mears to Tuck, Aug. 8, 1946, Tuck Executive Papers; Richmond *Times-Dispatch*, April 14, 1946.

Columnist Hunter of the Richmond *Times-Dispatch* reflected the prevailing sentiment of many Virginians. Responding to adverse criticism of the governor by some labor leaders, the venerable "Cavalier" asserted that "the plaints and dismal bleatings we hear are not the real voice of Virginia. . . . You see [opposition] in the papers, but you don't meet it on the streets and even less on the farms." The *Northern Virginia Daily* agreed. Having noted that labor and antiorganization spokesmen would "howl from Dan to Beersheba," the *Daily* submitted that "there is no howling in the Virginia countryside, but a deep sense of relief and general approval of the Governor's action. The billingsgate and invective hurled at the state administration by labor bosses grown arrogant through years of indulgence and pampering, merely serve to amuse the residents of the small towns, villages and rural areas of Virginia. They know the AFL has taken a licking and they're glad of it."[65]

Buoyed by general public approval of his course, Tuck might have used his newfound influence in a crusade against organized labor, but he refrained from doing so. Indeed, he expressed concern for the workers. At the conclusion of the strike threat he informed Senator Byrd: "I think unquestionably Virginia will have to pass laws enabling employees of public utilities to settle their disputes before some board which would be fair to them."[66]

Tuck claimed that he would never have considered action as extreme as the draft had he not believed a dire emergency imminent and felt he had no other device to use. Some of the steps which he took, he confided, were "personally distasteful" but necessary.[67] In later years he recalled too that even though he was assured of his course, he was nonetheless somewhat uneasy. "I was nervous," he admitted, "but just like the captain of a ship in a storm, I couldn't let on. You see, when I went in office, some said I was a weak governor and what a terrible pity it was that Mr. Darden had gone. If the lights had been cut off less than two months after he left, that would have ruined me."[68]

[65] Richmond *Times-Dispatch*, April 4, 1946; *Northern Virginia Daily*, April 1, 1946.

[66] Tuck to Byrd, April 2, 1946, Byrd Papers.

[67] Tuck to A. D. Jones, editor of the Greensboro *Record*, Dec. 9, 1946, Tuck Papers.

[68] Norfolk *Virginian-Pilot*, June 8, 1969. In the course of several interviews Tuck

Indeed, disparaging remarks had been made about his competence, and Tuck could hardly have forgotten that Harry Byrd himself had been dubious about his capability to be governor. The Vepco affair changed all of that. Just as the dispute was ending, a Byrd intimate, William T. Reed, Jr., informed the senator, "I heard of a Moss Plunkett supporter this morning who is now all for Bill Tuck, and quite a number of people have remarked to me that he showed considerably more courage than they expected from him." If Byrd still had reservations about the new governor, those doubts were largely dispelled. He personally commended Tuck on his stand and boasted to others that the governor "certainly showed great ability and courage" and that he was "mighty proud of Bill Tuck's action."[69]

There were sound political reasons for Byrd's euphoria, as his chief lieutenant in Richmond, E. R. Combs, quickly recognized. "I am convinced," Combs said, "that Tuck's courageous stand in this matter has helped us tremendously over the state." He pointed out to Byrd that, in addition to a general strengthening of the organization, there could be a direct benefit to him. "If you should have opposition in the primary this year," he wrote the senator, "and your opponent should be so indiscreet as to undertake to make an issue of Tuck's action in this case, I believe it would help you tremendously." Byrd did have opposition in the primary, in the person of Martin Hutchinson, and the labor issue bulked large in the campaign. Attempting to capitalize on reaction to Tuck's draft maneuver, Hutchinson at one point condemned Byrd for sanctioning the governor's "readiness to call out bayonets for the settlement of labor disputes."[70] That and similar comments allowed Byrd to attack Hutchinson, shrewdly if somewhat unfairly, as an avid advocate of unionism. In an atmosphere of increasing hostility toward organized labor, such a tactic greatly aided Byrd in defeating Hutchinson decisively.[71]

---

indicated that he was encouraged to act partly because he thought that failure to do so would increase the belief, prevalent in some quarters, that he was not a worthy successor to Governor Darden.

[69] Reed to Byrd, April 1, 1946, Byrd to Tuck, April 8, 1946, Byrd to Homer L. Ferguson, April 3, 1946, Byrd to Lewis G. Larus, April 1, 1946, Byrd Papers.

[70] Combs to Byrd, April 1, 1946, ibid.; "Radio Address by Martin A. Hutchinson, July 27, 1946," typescript in Hutchinson Papers.

[71] For an account of the Byrd-Hutchinson primary race and for a discussion of the

The Vepco incident meant that jovial Bill Tuck—the whilom "playboy and clown"—had been forced to meet, within three months of his inauguration, a situation described by one newspaperman as the most serious potential disaster for Virginia since the Civil War.[72] The forthright, though unorthodox, manner in which he handled that crisis brought him national attention; in his own state, his action earned him great popular acclaim on the one hand and the undying enmity of labor leaders on the other. By any reckoning, the event was surely one of the most memorable aspects of Tuck's governorship.[73]

The affair had great significance for Tuck's future. It did much to elevate him in Byrd's esteem and consequently to increase his influence within the organization. It also served, probably more than any single action of his career, to enlarge his already substantial popular following. Finally, the successful outcome of the incident helped to allay the fears of those (perhaps including Tuck himself) who were skeptical of the governor's capability. After the Vepco affair there may have been those who doubted Tuck's judgment or his discretion, but none questioned his mettle. "From then on," Tuck recalled, "I was governor!"[74]

---

exploitation of antiunion sentiment by the Byrd organization, see William Bryan Crawley, Jr., "The Governorship of William Munford Tuck, 1946–1950: Virginia Politics in the 'Golden Age' of the Byrd Organization (Ph.D. diss., U.Va., 1974), pp. 321–34.

[72] Wilkinson, *Harry Byrd*, p. 27; Clarke, "A Salute to Bill Tuck," p. 5.

[73] Over a quarter of a century later persons interviewed by the author invariably recalled the Vepco controversy more vividly than anything else about the Tuck years.

[74] Norfolk *Virginian-Pilot*, June 8, 1969.

Legislative Backlash

5. *The Governor (and the Public) vs. the Unions*

> Labor unions have served a useful purpose in our economy and, no doubt, will continue to do so if wise government keeps them within their proper sphere. But if our system of government, with all its blessings, is to survive, the existing economic dictatorship imposed by ruthless union leaders must be curbed.
>
> —*William M. Tuck (1946)*

The Vepco affair in the spring of 1946 was the most significant labor incident to occur in Virginia in the post–World War II era; yet the threatened power strike was but the most conspicuous of many labor disorders visited upon the state during that time. In the months following the end of the war, Virginia, along with the rest of the nation, suffered through a turbulent, strike-riddled period which culminated in a concerted movement to restrict organized labor.[1]

The main factor which led to the development of antilabor animus was the plethora of strikes which enveloped the country after V-J Day. With wartime government controls removed, prices soared; organized labor then demanded, not without reason, that wages be raised commensurately. When management proved balky, as it often did, labor resorted to its most potent weapon, the strike. Work stoppages reached unprecedented levels in 1946 when, during the first two

---

[1] The course of organized labor in the postwar period is described in broad terms in a number of general histories of American labor, including Joseph G. Rayback, *A History of American Labor* (New York: Free Press, 1966), pp. 387–413; Henry Pelling, *American Labor* (Chicago: University of Chicago Press, 1960), pp. 184–209; Foster Rhea Dulles, *Labor in America* (New York: Thomas Y. Crowell, 1949), pp. 354–76; and Philip Taft, *Organized Labor in American History* (New York: Harper and Row, 1946), pp. 563–90.

months of the year, more man-days were lost than had been lost during the whole of World War II.[2]

Among the most serious labor imbroglios of the postwar years was a proposed railroad strike in May 1946 which would have brought all rail traffic in the nation to a halt. With the danger of a tie-up blinding him to the grievances of the railroad workers, President Harry S. Truman prepared a speech for nationwide radio broadcast in which he intemperately expressed his desire to "eliminate" certain leaders and to "hang a few traitors."[3] Although the speech he actually delivered was somewhat more restrained than the original version, Truman made it plain that he would not countenance a work stoppage by the rail unions. On the day of the strike deadline he went before Congress to demand a law which would authorize the president to draft strikers into the armed services if the strike portended a national emergency. Though the draft proposal was branded by the *New Republic* "a terrifying long step on the road to fascism," Truman's message was widely hailed by the public because, as one newspaper pointed out, "he spoke from the heart of the American people."[4]

It seemed to some observers, including syndicated columnist Arthur Krock, that Truman's plan had involved "borrowing from Governor Tuck of Virginia." The similarity between the Truman proposal and Tuck's Vepco maneuver was not merely fortuitous. It was reported that Senator Byrd had visited the president to ask him personally to call for enactment of a law similar to Virginia's. Later on the floor of the Senate, Byrd revealed with considerable satisfaction that Truman had asked his office to supply information about Tuck's draft procedure, presumably to be used as a model for Truman's own proposal. Claiming that "the action taken by Governor Tuck is nearly identical with the action now proposed by the President," Byrd happily announced that he considered it "a compliment to the old state."[5]

[2] Joel Seidman, *American Labor from Defense to Reconversion* (Chicago: University of Chicago Press, 1953), p. 221; U.S. Department of Labor, *Analysis of Work Stoppages, 1966*, Bulletin No. 1573 (Washington, D.C.: U.S. Government Printing Office, 1968), p. 6.

[3] Cabell Phillips, *The Truman Presidency* (New York: Macmillan, 1966), p. 116.

[4] "Truman's Blunder," *New Republic* 114 (June 3, 1946): 787; Philadelphia *Record*, quoted in Bert Cochran, *Harry Truman and the Crisis Presidency* (New York: Funk and Wagnalls, 1973), p. 207.

[5] Arthur Krock, *In the Nation: 1932–1966* (New York: McGraw-Hill, 1966), p.

The threat of the nationwide rail strike, like the threat of the power strike in Virginia, was removed by an eleventh-hour settlement, thereby obviating implementation of the Truman plan. Nevertheless, the House of Representatives proceeded by an overwhelming vote to grant Truman the draft authority which he sought, clearly indicating the indignation felt by many congressmen and by a growing segment of the American public.[6]

Nettlesome as the rail problem was, it did not produce nearly the public outcry that resulted from concurrent strike activity by the United Mine Workers. Forgetting, or disregarding, the wretched mining conditions which the union was attempting to ameliorate, many Americans regarded UMW walkouts as unconscionable, and the leader of that union, John L. Lewis, emerged in the popular mind as the bête noire of industrial reconversion. Seemingly larger-than-life, Lewis easily fitted the villain's role. He was, in one depiction, "a man of ponderous and majestic bearing with a billowing crown of gray hair and dark, baleful eyes peering from under immense eybrows. His scowl had an Olympian ferocity, and his speech the cavernous tone and the measured cadence of a nineteenth-century Thespian."[7] Although he appeared vain and arrogant to his enemies, Lewis was looked to with virtual veneration by his unionists; in gratitude for the undeniable improvements which his leadership had wrought, UMW members accorded Lewis absolute fealty, thus allowing him, according to one account, to "control the flow of the nation's coal supply as easily as manipulating a bathroom faucet."[8]

The heavy dependency of the nation upon coal at the time meant that UMW strikes affected vast numbers of people directly. The walkout in the spring of 1946 necessitated coal rationing in Virginia. Functioning under a 1920 statute, the State Corporation Commission

152; Tris Coffin, "Washington Hangover," *The Nation* 162 (June 8, 1946): 681; *Congressional Record*, 79th Congress, 2d Session, 1946, 92: 5791; Richmond *Times-Dispatch*, May 25, 1946.

[6] The draft bill was never enacted into law because it was blocked in the Senate.

[7] Phillips, *Truman Presidency*, p. 119.

[8] Ibid. In the present discussion it is germane to emphasize that however justifiable the unionists' demands may have been, the strikes led to an angry public reaction. For insight into the living and working conditions of coal miners, see McAlister Coleman, *Men and Coal* (New York: Farrar and Rinehart, 1943); "Coal," *Fortune*, Mar. 1947, pp. 85–99.

apportioned fuel to various industries and organizations commensurate with their importance. The president of the Virginia Electric and Power Company warned that unless industries abided by SCC regulations, they would have no electricity after three weeks. To help conserve the supply, nonessential operations, such as amusement facilities, were denied any electric power.[9]

When it appeared that the state had been saved from a power strike by Vepco workers only to have the source of that power curtailed by a walkout of mineworkers, Virginians were irate. A sign in a bowling alley read: "Daylight Bowling Only by Order of John L. Lewis, Dictator." Recalling the earlier action of Governor Tuck, an American Legion commander asked Tuck to "draft John L. Lewis into the state militia and give him the command, 'about face.'"[10] Such expressions were illustrative of a growing contempt for unions in general and for Lewis in particular. In the course of numerous and noisy disputes, the leonine UMW chief emerged as a tyrannical ogre whose greedy desire to line the pockets of his workers was exceeded only by his contempt for the public welfare. Senator Byrd summed up the popular sentiment when he exclaimed that Lewis was "drunk with power."[11]

Although the rail and coal strikes were the most critical of the postwar labor disputes, they were by no means the only ones. Headlines during 1946 almost daily told of labor disturbances; few homes were not affected in some way by the widespread unrest. Actual food shortages occurred in some areas, especially in the autumn of 1946 when a strike by the cattle producers led to a serious lack of meat. (This strike prompted one Virginia labor official, still bitter at Tuck's handling of the Vepco problem, to wire the governor: "If you again attempt to enslave the workers, don't you think you should take steps

[9] Richmond *Times-Dispatch*, May 8, 1946.

[10] Ibid., May 11, 1946; J. L. Rose to Tuck, May 13, 1946, Tuck Executive Papers. For Tuck's sentiment regarding the strike, see Tuck to Harry S. Truman, May 6, 1946, ibid.

[11] Goldman, *Crucial Decade*, p. 22. Even a friendly account admitted that had a Gallup poll been taken on the subject in the mid–1940s, "Lewis might have received a popular rating only a notch or two above that of Benedict Arnold" (Coleman, *Men and Coal*, p. xi).

to see they get a little meat, else they may not be able to work either as free men or as slaves.")[12]

Many Virginians, already annoyed by inconveniences resulting from the various strikes, were further alienated from organized labor by several factors, including attempts by certain business interests to convey the impression that the disruptions were solely the result of unreasonable demands by the unions.[13] A more important source of friction was created by a major organizing campaign which was begun in the South by both the AFL and the CIO in the spring of 1946. Reflecting a carry-over of wartime jargon, the CIO campaign, the larger of the two, was known popularly as "Operation Dixie."

Southern hostility to organized labor was of such long standing as to be axiomatic. Among southern whites—certainly among those of the upper class—there was a general detestation of what was once termed "that unholy, foreign-born, un-American, despotic thing known as labor unionism."[14] Many factors worked to make the development of organized labor difficult: the paternalism of the millowners often created a certain docility among the workers; the existence of blacks among the labor force militated against white cooperation; illiteracy was a practical barrier to the spread of information. The belief was long prevalent, too, that the industrial development of the South was dependent upon the region's supply of cheap labor, and that such an advantage would be erased by unionism. Less tangible, but nonetheless disadvantageous to union growth, were the traditional religious and social patterns of the South which tended to inculcate a passive acceptance of the status quo. Summing up southern hostility, according to W. J. Cash, was an equation fixed solidly in southern minds: "labor unions + strikers = Communists + atheism + social equality with the Negro."[15]

[12] E. K. King, president of Norfolk Central Labor Union, to Tuck, Oct. 1, 1946, Tuck Executive Papers.

[13] For the role played in this regard by the National Association of Manufacturers in particular, see Millis and Brown, *From Wagner Act to Taft-Hartley*, pp. 281–91; Clark Kerr, "Employer Policies in Industrial Relations," in Colston E. Warne, ed., *Labor in Postwar America* (Brooklyn, N.Y.: Remson Press, 1949), pp. 47–67.

[14] Quoted in George E. Mowry, *Another Look at the Twentieth Century South* (Baton Rouge: Louisiana State University Press, 1973), p. 75.

[15] W. J. Cash, *The Mind of the South* (New York: Random House, 1941), Vintage edition, p. 362. There are several illuminating analyses of the problems confronting

In the face of formidable obstacles, organized labor enthusiastically embarked upon its crusade to bring unionism to the South. Having announced that the CIO would spend $1 million and employ 200 organizers in its "Operation Dixie," CIO President Philip Murray brashly proclaimed on the eve of that operation: "Our efforts in the South will not be confined nor will they stop at the point where economic organization through labor union is achieved. Our efforts will be directed toward political organization likewise. We believe the Congress of Industrial Organizations is the sole hope of the backward Southern states where a few people live well and the overwhelming majority barely subsist." Union officials were cognizant of the obstacles to be faced, but spoke bullishly. "We expect that we may be confronted with opposition in the South," said one of the leading organizers, "but we mean to see this through. We are going to dedicate not a year but as many years as are required until we re-establish the rights of citizenship for the workers in the South."[16]

The spokesman was correct in anticipating resistance. Among the accusations most often hurled at labor organizers was the charge that unionism, especially the CIO brand, was Communist-inspired. In its competition for members, the AFL openly encouraged that notion. "The workers of the South have their choice," warned AFL leader George Meany, "between an organization of trade unions [the AFL] and . . . an organization [the CIO] that has openly followed the Communist line and is following that line today." His point was not lost on the opponents of unionization. As one southern congressman put it, "I warn John L. Lewis and his Communist cohorts that no second-hand 'carpetbag expedition' in the Southland under the banner of Soviet Russia . . . will be tolerated."[17] Such a comment was

---

organized labor in the South, including a detailed study by Bernard M. Cannon, "Social Deterrents to the Unionization of Southern Cotton Textile Mill Workers" (Ph.D. diss., Harvard Univ., 1951). More succinct are Frank T. DeVyver, "The Present Status of Labor Unions in the South—1948," *Southern Economic Journal* 15 (July 1949): 1–22; and F. Ray Marshall, "Impediments to Labor Organization in the South," *South Atlantic Quarterly* 57 (1958): 409–18.

[16] Allan S. Hayward, "We Propose to Unionize Labor in the South," *Labor and Nation* 1 (April-May 1946): 37; George Baldanzi, "The South Is 32 Million Americans," ibid., p. 44.

[17] F. Ray Marshall, *Labor in the South* (Cambridge: Harvard University Press,

illustrative of another argument frequently directed against unions: namely, that they were instigated and directed by "aliens" (meaning nonsoutherners). The leaders of "Operation Dixie" tried to allay xenophobic southern suspicions by scrupulously pointing out that all of their organizers were "either Southerners or long-time residents of the South." Their claims usually fell on deaf ears, however, because, as historian George B. Tindall has accurately observed, even if such organizers "were born and bred in the brier patch, they became 'outside agitators' when they entered a new community."[18]

Later representatives visiting southern towns were sometimes treated as veritable pariahs. In South Boston, Virginia, the hometown of Governor Tuck, an agent for the Textile Workers Union (CIO) was refused service in a restaurant. "We have instructions to just let you sit—you or any other CIO man," explained a waitress. Upon returning to his hotel, the union representative was met by a "South Boston Citizens Committee" whose spokesman warned, "We don't want the CIO in South Boston and if you value your personal safety you'll get out of town before dark."[19] The incident was discredited by some newspapers, by the mayor of the town, and by Tuck himself, who branded the report "a fabrication of the whole cloth."[20] Yet the episode, even if apocryphal, served to indicate a bitter resentment toward the union movement.

The net gains of the much-heralded southern organizing campaign were questionable. The AFL increased its membership in the region, but not so extensively as had been expected. The CIO's "Operation Dixie," despite grandiose hopes and elaborate preparations, ended with that union not having significantly more southern members than

---

1967), p. 247; Mowry, *Another Look at the Twentieth Century South*, p. 83.

[18] Haywood, "We Propose to Unionize Labor," p. 36; George B. Tindall, *The Emergence of the New South* (Baton Rouge: Louisiana State University Press, 1967), p. 524. For an account of difficulties faced by organizers, see Helen Gould, "Union Resistance: Southern Style," *Labor and Nation* 4 (Jan.–Feb. 1948): 8.

[19] Richmond *Times-Dispatch*, Jan. 2, 1947; Boyd E. Payton to Tuck, Jan. 2, 1947, Tuck Executive Papers. The CIO had always been the more hated of the two major unions in Virginia, especially among the rural conservatives, who could accept an organization of skilled workers such as the AFL, but who found it difficult to stomach a union of unskilled factory hands.

[20] Lynchburg *News*, Jan. 3, 1947; Richmond *Times-Dispatch*, Jan. 5, 1947; Tuck to author, May 15, 1968.

when the drive began. In Virginia the CIO increased its membership by some 7,000 within the first ten months of the drive, and by almost 20,000 in the course of the campaign.[21] Important as such gains may have been, they were not totally gratifying in light of the effort and money expended and the public enmity incurred in the process.

The overall result of postwar labor development in Virginia was to bring about a decided reaction against unionism. Even those Virginians who were reckoned among the more liberal tended to become apprehensive. "We are no nearer world peace than we were a quarter of a century ago at the end of World War I, and the domestic situation is even worse," lamented the brother of antiorganization leader Martin Hutchinson. "With the returning veterans looking for jobs, and the racketeering labor unions striking on every hand, you cannot look to a stabilized economy." Richmond editor Virginius Dabney was likewise morose. Concerned at the threat of a second Vepco strike in the fall of 1946, Dabney feared that "merely reasoning with the Vepco workers is going to have no effect at all. They have shown, it seems to me, that they respond only to pressure." But the problem was more general than that, he explained, going on dourly: "Each union seems to be out to get more in its pay envelope than the next one, and the union leaders keep their jobs by showing the rank and file that they know how to bring home the bacon. Given this situation, I am sufficiently pessimistic to think that nothing will have any weight with them except compulsion."[22]

As the end of 1946 approached, growing numbers of Virginians were in agreement with Dabney. Frustrated by recurring strikes across the nation, disturbed by increasing unionism throughout the South, and jarred particularly by the Vepco dispute within the state, such persons were by that time in a mood for restricting what they regarded as the excesses of organized labor.

Bill Tuck was well aware of the public hostility toward labor and, indeed, could scarcely have been otherwise. "Do something about these damned strikes," one letter demanded of the governor, "or let

[21] Marshall, "Impediments to Organization," p. 409; Marshall, *Labor in the South*, pp. 264–65; DeVyver, "Present Status of Labor Unions," pp. 16–22; Richmond *Times-Dispatch*, Oct. 1, 1948.

[22] Curry P. Hutchinson to Martin A. Hutchinson, Nov. 11, 1945, Hutchinson Papers; Dabney to William T. Stevens, Oct. 5, 1946, Dabney Papers.

some other person with a backbone instead of a wishbone take over your duties."[23] Numerous other messages, similar if less crude in tone, urged Tuck to use his office in an attempt to palliate labor-management dissension.

Although the larger problems of organized labor would require attention at the federal level, Tuck hoped to establish legal machinery in Virginia which would, insofar as possible, ease labor disturbances within the state. In the wake of the Vepco dispute he had called upon the Virginia Advisory Legislative Council (VALC) to undertake a study of the state's labor situation, and late the same year, with a new Vepco disagreement smoldering, he reiterated that request.[24] Since the next biennial session of the General Assembly was not to meet until 1948, it appeared that any remedial legislation would have to wait, unless the governor called a special session, as he hinted he might do in order to limit what he termed "the ruthless racketeering labor czars cut in the image of the recently dethroned dictators." Senator Byrd discouraged such a procedure. "I have been thinking a great deal about what action should be taken," he counseled Tuck. "It would seem to me it would be a great mistake to call a special session of the General Assembly unless you had absolute assurance that your legislation could be passed . . . and, judging by the vote on the labor legislation during the last session, this could not be done."[25]

Tuck perhaps sensed more keenly than Byrd the public desire for protective legislation; consequently, he proceeded on December 10, 1946, to summon a special session for the following January. The ostensible purpose of the extra session was to deal, not with labor difficulties, but with acute problems in the state's public school system. Few observers believed, however, that the deliberations of the legislature would be limited to educational matters. "Speculation

[23] Letter to Tuck, April 26, 1946, Tuck Executive Papers. For further expressions of outrage against labor, see letters contained in Boxes 7 and 9 of Tuck Executive Papers.

[24] Richmond *Times-Dispatch*, April 6, Dec. 11, 1946.

[25] Ibid., Nov. 22, 1946; Byrd to Tuck, Oct. 4, 1946, Tuck Papers. Byrd's doubts concerning the efficacy of an extra session appear to have been unwarranted because the labor program of the 1946 session had been passed rather handily, and the public attitude toward labor had worsened steadily since that time. Byrd may have been opposed to calling a special session because he simply did not wish to antagonize labor unduly in a year in which he was to run for reelection.

immediately arose," noted the Richmond *Times-Dispatch*, "that the Assembly may have before it some kind of labor legislation."[26]

The speculation was confirmed when, several days after he had called the extra session, Tuck presented to the VALC the drafts of two bills which had been prepared by Attorney General Staples: one bill was designed to prevent strikes in public utilities; the other was intended to outlaw the closed shop. Though claiming that he did not desire "any hasty, emotional enactments," the governor made it known that he wanted the Advisory Council's recommendation prepared by the time the legislature was to convene. The *Times-Dispatch*, fearing the results of precipitate action, urged that labor legislation not be considered at the special session but be held in abeyance until the regular term in 1948. "We are in danger," warned the paper, "of having inadequate exploration of the problem during the crowded year-end holidays, inadequate hearings on the bills when the Assembly meets, and a hodge-podge on the statute books when the lawmakers adjourn."[27]

If the newspaper thought that labor legislation might be stayed, it badly misinterpreted the temper of the Virginia solons. Coming amidst a period of heightened antilabor sentiment, Tuck's call for regulatory laws met with an enthusiastic reception, not only from the representatives of the organization-dominated rural areas where resentment ran especially strong, but from some antiorganization sources as well. Delegate Robert Whitehead of Nelson County, an able and respected parliamentarian who was often aligned against the organization, summed up the feeling of most of his colleagues when he wrote, prior to the extra session, "I firmly believe that the time has come when the legislative body must take a positive stand in the strike situation."[28]

On January 6, 1947, Tuck addressed the opening meeting of the special session. He began by presenting his public education proposals,[29] but went on to discuss the labor-management problem, which he termed an "exceedingly vexing matter, laden with danger." Having

---

[26] Richmond *Times-Dispatch*, Dec. 11, 1946.

[27] Ibid., Dec. 15, 1946.

[28] Whitehead to Members of Virginia Advisory Legislative Council, Nov. 20, 1946, Whitehead Papers.

[29] This and other aspects of public education during the Tuck administration are discussed in Chapter 8.

noted that he had been able to meet previous labor crises adequately, he admitted that there was "no assurance whatsoever that all the exigencies of the most uncertain future" could be handled successfully. Though he may never have doubted the propriety of his draft maneuver, it was clear that the governor did not relish the possibility of having to resort again to such a cumbersome, if not unconstitutional, means of averting a crippling strike. He therefore prevailed upon the legislature to enact a measure which would facilitate the settlement of future public utilities disputes. Coupled with this request was a call for passage of a "right-to-work" law. Such an enactment, Tuck claimed, was not motivated by a desire to restrict organized labor but was "designed to preserve the liberty of the individual workman" and to "insure that his right to earn a livelihood . . . would not be dependent upon the whims of an arbitrary, unscrupulous or despotic union leadership."[30]

On the same day that Tuck delivered his message, the VALC announced its endorsement of the Tuck proposals; following public hearings in Richmond and Roanoke, the Council voted by a margin of six to three to approve the bills with only minor changes. Not surprisingly, the six affirmative votes were cast by legislators from rural areas, while the three negative votes were cast by representatives from areas of considerable union strength. Even so, those who opposed the bills claimed that their stand was based not so much upon any philosophical reluctance to restrict labor as upon the more practical grounds that there had been insufficient time for study and that state action should await possible legislation at the federal level. "This problem of ending industrial strife will never be solved piecemeal," explained opposing Senator J. Hoge Tyler of Norfolk, "but must be solved on a nationwide scope by calm and considered reasoning."[31]

A public hearing on the labor proposals, conducted before a joint committee of the House and Senate, evoked great interest, attracting a crowd estimated to be the largest ever to attend a hearing at the

[30] *Address of William M. Tuck, Extra Session, 1947*, pp. 6–8.
[31] Richmond *Times-Dispatch*, Jan. 7, 1947. The three legislators in opposition were Delegates John B. Spiers of Radford and Stuart Campbell of Wytheville, both from southwest Virginia where the United Mine Workers organization was influential, and Senator Tyler, from the shipbuilding center of Norfolk where unions were also active.

Capitol. Union spokesmen, as expected, denounced the bills, mount-
ing an attack so vituperative that the Danville *Register* claimed that
"organized labor [came] to the defense of its special rights with all the
fervor of a Moslem summoned to wage holy war." Ernest B. Pugh,
leader of the state CIO, suggested at the hearing that the bills should be
renamed to reflect their true intent: the utilities bill, he said, should
thus be called "a bill to preserve and protect the profits of utility
companies," while the right-to-work bill should be labeled "a bill to
launch Virginia into the union-busting business." The chief IBEW
negotiator during the Vepco dispute, J. C. McIntosh, recurred to that
earlier incident in his condemnation of the utilities bill, declaring that
"all the bayonets in the Virginia militia can't operate utilities."
Emotional pleas were by no means confined to labor leaders; industrial
representatives were likewise outspoken. In rebuttal to union charges,
an attorney for several industries denied that the contemplated legislation in any way "enslaved" labor; rather, he said, there was "nothing
nearer involuntary servitude than the closed shop." One of the more
rousing speeches was delivered by Remmie Arnold, a Petersburg
manufacturer—later to run unsuccessfully for governor—who ended
an impassioned oration by shouting, "Thank God there's no union in
my plant today!"[32]

Outside the legislative halls a spirited campaign was conducted
against the pending bills. The president of the Virginia State Industrial Union Council, Charles C. Webber, went on radio to denounce
the legislation as "not only a flagrant violation of fundamental principles [but] basically wrong and contrary to our constitutional democratic government." Antiorganization politician Howard Carwile
fulminated against the governor's plan, branding it a "crude and
perilous onslaught of Tuck Toryism in the General Assembly of Virginia." Unionists themselves voiced protests in the cotton mill center of Danville as members of the Textile Workers Union paraded in
front of city hall carrying placards reading "Defeat Tuck's Anti-
Labor Bills" and "We Love Our Union and Intend to Keep It."[33]

Strong support for the Tuck program came, predictably, from the

---

[32] Danville *Register*, Jan. 10, 11, 1947; Richmond *Times-Dispatch*, Jan. 10, 1947.
[33] Richmond *Times-Dispatch*, Jan. 2, 13, 1947; Danville *Register*, Jan. 11, 1947.

Chamber of Commerce and the National Association of Manufacturers. The attitude of the Virginia press, on the other hand, was ambivalent; though generally favorable toward the public utilities bill, some newspapers, including the state's two largest dailies, were dubious about the merits of the right-to-work bill. The Richmond *Times-Dispatch* feared that an open shop law would create more problems than it solved, while the Norfolk *Virginian-Pilot* felt that since such a law would apply only to intrastate industries, it would be "a 70 per cent nullity from birth." The Tuck plan, concluded the Norfolk paper, had "sowed seeds of dissension in the field of labor-management relations. The crop is likely to be more weeds than grain."[34]

The public temper, ill-disposed toward labor anyway, was further aggravated by the bombastic and arrogant approach taken by the unions in their fight against the legislation. The basic union tactic consisted of threatening political death to any legislator who voted for the Tuck bills—a threat which, in light of labor's numerical weakness, could hardly have struck terror in the hearts of many assemblymen. As Lloyd M. Robinette, the implacable antiorganization senator from southwest Virginia, regretfully put it, "The labor people in Virginia will not get out their vote. . . . They do a lot of talking, but mighty little voting."[35] The heavy-handed approach was, in fact, counterproductive, serving mainly to augment the opinion that passage of the governor's bills might, in the words of one newspaper, "help to show the obnoxious type of labor leadership that its bulldozing . . . tactics would not be tolerated." Neatly capsulizing the prevailing sentiment among members of the General Assembly was an extemporaneous remark by one prominent legislator. "I am not at all sure that these are good bills," he said, "and in fact, I doubt if they are. But I am so disgusted with the attitude of labor leaders who have been to see me

[34] Dennis John O'Keefe, "Right-to-Work Legislation in Virginia" (M.A. thesis, Univ. of Maryland, 1963), pp. 36, 42; Norfolk *Virginian-Pilot*, Jan. 14, 1947.

[35] Robinette to Martin A. Hutchinson, May 25, 1946, Hutchinson Papers. Certain unions undertook voter registration drives. In Danville the city treasurer and registrar, at the insistence of CIO Director Lewis Conn, kept their offices open long past the usual closing time in order to allow TWUA members to pay their poll taxes and register. "We want these votes in hand by tomorrow," said Conn. "This is just the beginning" (Danville *Register*, Jan. 11, 1947).

about the bills that I'm going to vote for them. These labor leaders made no arguments against the Governor's legislation when they called on me. They merely threatened. 'If you vote for these bills we'll get you at the next election,' they said. That was enough for me. I'm voting for the bills."[36]

The Byrd organization threw its full weight behind the labor proposals. Governor Tuck, in his finest behind-the-scenes style, worked diligently, later recalling that he "saw and talked individually with almost all of the members of the Senate and House of Delegates, urging them to support the legislation." Given the extent of the organization's grip on the legislature at that time, no undue pressure was needed. Lamenting the dominance of the Byrd faction, state Senator Robinette wrote a friend: "You have no conception of the situation existing in the Senate of Virginia today. There is hardly a whisper of liberalism in the whole membership, because they are bound to the chariot wheels of Senator Byrd and his crowd of buccaneers."[37]

When voting time came, a combination of organization influence, general antipathy toward labor, and reaction to the abrasive tactics employed by the unions resulted in the overwhelming passage of Tuck's proposals. The right-to-work bill was approved by a vote of 77 to 20 in the House and by a margin of 32 to 6 in the Senate. As amended and finally approved, the act stated that "the right of persons to work shall not be denied or abridged on account of membership or non-membership in any labor union or labor organization." Any person denied employment under terms of the act was to be entitled to court action to recover "such damages as he may have sustained by reason of such denial or deprivation of employment."[38]

[36] Richmond *Times-Dispatch*, Jan. 12, 1947.

[37] Tuck to author, May 15, 1968; Robinette to E. H. McConnell, Feb. 18, 1947, copy in Hutchinson Papers. There could be little doubt as to what Byrd's own position was. In the Eightieth Congress, which had just convened, Byrd quickly introduced a bill to outlaw the closed shop at the national level (O'Keefe, "Right-to-Work Legislation," p. 41).

[38] *Journal of the House of Delegates, Extra Session, 1947*, p. 101; *Acts and Joint Resolutions, Extra Session, 1947*, p. 12; Richmond *Times-Dispatch*, Jan. 17, 1947. In his detailed study of Virginia's right-to-work law, O'Keefe found that the bill was supported by 97.3 percent of what he termed the "rural bloc" of legislators and by

The public utilities bill, always the more popular of the two, was enacted by an even larger margin; the vote for passage was 90 to 6 in the House and 37 to 1 in the Senate. The new statute provided that no party to a public utilities labor dispute could engage in a lockout or a work stoppage until two conferences had been held for purposes of negotiation; the governor might attempt to act as mediator at the second conference. If either party proved unwilling to submit to arbitration, that party was to notify the governor of its intent to engage in a strike or lockout no less than five weeks before the proposed deadline. If the governor regarded the work stoppage as harmful to the public welfare, he could in the interim prepare to take over the operation of the utility when the strike or lockout occurred. The state, in that event, was to retain 15 percent of the net income of the utility as compensation for its operation of the facilities. Workers were to be hired by the state to fill all jobs vacated by striking employees; those who chose to remain at work under state operation were to be paid the same salary as they had received previously from the company.[39]

The single opponent of the utilities bill was Senator Robinette. "I am a lone wolf in opposition to this measure," he explained. "Labor is being made the whipping boy of this legislation. . . . Labor, whether organized or not, becomes the serf of the Commonwealth under this bill." The work of the 1947 General Assembly left Robinette dejected. "The reactionaries of the Democratic party are riding higher than ever before," he wrote to a friend. "In my judgment the extra session . . . was called really for the purpose of enacting repressive labor legislation and . . . the so-called educational program was a mere front and a smokescreen." Martin Hutchinson, likewise disconsolate, agreed that the basic purpose of the special session had been to "strike at the labor unions" and detected in that action an ulterior political motive. "Byrd and his people know that they have lost the laboring people," he reasoned. "It is my impression that the session was called for the

---

67.9 percent of the "urban bloc." The lowest level of support was registered by the "southwest bloc" which, representing a region of considerable unionism, gave the bill 47.6 percent of its votes (O'Keefe, "Right-to-Work Legislation," pp. 48–50).

[39] *Journal of the House of Delegates, Extra Session,* 1947, p. 116; *Acts and Joint Resolutions, Extra Session,* 1947, pp. 24–29; Richmond *Times-Dispatch,* Jan. 17, 1947.

purpose of hitting at labor and in that way helping advance the national prestige of Byrd, who, of course, has Presidential ambitions."[40]

Whether or not Hutchinson was correct in analyzing the motivation behind the extra session, he was accurate in suggesting the popular appeal of labor restriction at that time. A Gallup poll released only days after enactment of the Virginia statutes revealed that 40 percent of the American public regarded labor disputes as the most critical problem facing the country, as against a mere 13 percent who deemed inflation to be the most important issue. There was widespread belief that labor should be limited in some way; 58 percent of those interviewed thought that strikes in public utilities should be forbidden, while 69 percent believed that government employees should be denied the right to strike. A distinct majority of all persons polled (66 percent) and a sizable minority of unionists themselves (41 percent) favored the principle of the "open shop," while only 19 percent of the unionists advocated the "closed shop."[41]

The reaction of the state press indicated that Virginians shared fully in the prevailing national mood and were thus gratified by passage of the Tuck program. "The General Assembly has executed beyond all question the will of the majority," crowed the Richmond *News Leader*. "Conservative, individualistic Virginia has seen in the great strikes of 1946, particularly the closing of the coal mines, the threat of labor tyranny, and she has acted unhesitatingly in the spirit of her motto, *Sic Semper Tyrannis*." The success of Tuck's plan, said the *Northern Virginia Daily*, could be "attributed mainly to two causes—the unusual popularity of the Governor both in and out of the Assembly, and the fact that public sentiment in the state strongly favored this legislation." The relatively prolabor Norfolk *Virginian-Pilot* agreed, pointing out that the legislation was "aided by the national climate—a weather situation conditioned by the Lewis excesses of the past two years and by the recent general strikes."[42]

[40] Richmond *Times-Dispatch*, Jan. 17, 1947; Robinette to E. H. McConnell, Jan. 28, 1947, copy, Hutchinson to McConnell, Jan. 9, 1947, Hutchinson Papers.

[41] Richmond *Times-Dispatch*, Jan. 19, 31, April 6, 1947. The Richmond *News Leader*, Jan. 7, 1947, estimated that fully 75 percent of the Virginia people favored some degree of limitation upon organized labor.

[42] Richmond *News Leader*, Jan. 17, 1947; *Northern Virginia Daily*, Jan. 20, 1947;

Though they bemoaned the new labor laws in public and in private, even antiorganization leaders were forced to admit that given the temper of the times, restrictive legislation was perhaps inevitable, and surely popular, in Virginia. Curry P. Hutchinson put the matter succinctly in a letter written to his brother, Martin, shortly after the extra session had adjourned. "The CIO is very much in disrepute at present throughout the nation and especially here in the South," he said. "Their unions are not democratic. The leaders carry the poor devils around in their vest pockets and they tell them what they must do and what they must not do. . . . The Tuck extra session to curb labor meets with the approval of rural Virginia and there is where the machine's strength lies."[43]

To say that the Tuck labor legislation was popular was not necessarily to say that it would prove constitutional or workable. Indeed, there were those who claimed that the right-to-work law would either be struck down by the courts or be rendered useless by enactment of federal legislation and that the public utilities law would not be effective in actual practice.[44]

From the moment of its promulgation, the right-to-work bill was attacked more stridently by critics than was the companion bill, and even those who approved of its intent were skeptical of its viability. However, at the very time when the open shop measure was being debated, a movement was underway in Congress to enact new federal labor legislation which would result in sanctioning the Virginia statute. The Seventy-ninth Congress had devoted much time to various proposals designed to limit union activity, and the most serious measure, the Case bill, was prevented from becoming law only by a narrow vote in favor of sustaining President Truman's veto of the bill. The Eightieth Congress, convening in January 1947, took up with gusto right where the previous session had left off. An avalanche of antilabor legislation began when, on the first day alone, seventeen bills relating to unions were introduced in the House of Representatives;

Norfolk *Virginian-Pilot*, Jan. 15, 1947. See also Lynchburg *News*, Jan. 15, 1947; Staunton *News-Leader*, Jan. 21, 1947.

[43] Curry P. Hutchinson to Martin A. Hutchinson, Feb. 13, 1947, Hutchinson Papers.

[44] Norfolk *Virginian-Pilot*, Jan. 14, 1947; Danville *Register*, Jan. 10, 1947; Staunton *News-Leader*, Jan. 16, 1947.

during the following week fifteen such bills were put before the Senate. By the end of February no less than sixty-five bills had been introduced in the two houses combined.[45]

The measure which was the most sweeping, attracted the widest support, and drew the most bitter attacks from organized labor, was, of course, the proposal popularly known as the Taft-Hartley bill. Union spokesmen denounced the measure vehemently, placing the blame for its inception, not without some justification, on pressure from interest groups such as the National Association of Manufacturers. Utilizing full-page newspaper advertisements, organized labor waged an energetic campaign against the Taft-Hartley proposal. "Let's face it!" warned one AFL ad. "There are employers who don't like labor unions. Their mouthpiece is the NAM. . . . First 'bust' the unions—then 'bust' the country—just as they did in 1929. That's the vicious strategy behind the NAM-inspired SLAVE LABOR BILL." Correct though the unions were in indicting organizations such as the NAM for encouraging enactment of restrictive legislation, the fact remained that, as one historian has said, the Taft-Hartley bill "could not have been passed without an enormous change in the climate of public opinion in the period, and the attitude of the unions . . . did not help matters." The proposal, according to Walter Lippmann, was a "spectacular demonstration of the depth and extent of the reaction against organized labor."[46]

In June 1947, over the veto of President Truman, Congress passed the Labor-Management Relations, or Taft-Hartley, Act. A comprehensive revision of the Wagner Act, the new law contained many provisions, but one of the most salient features, and the one perhaps most detested by labor leaders, was the section which outlawed the closed shop. Although the legality of the union shop was sustained, Section 14(b) specifically guaranteed the priority of state laws over the federal law in that matter, thereby draping the mantle of approval over Virginia's right-to-work law.[47]

While the open shop legislation was being underwritten by congres-

[45] McClure, *Truman Administration and Problems of Postwar Labor*, pp. 124–35, 166–68.

[46] Richmond *Times-Dispatch*, May 15, 1947; Pelling, *American Labor*, p. 191; Richmond *News Leader*, April 21, 1947.

[47] The major provisions of the act are summarized in R. Alton Lee, *Truman and*

sional action, the state's new public utilities law was being put to the test of practical operation. Designed primarily to deal with power company disputes, the statute was used initially in connection with a nationwide telephone strike which began on April 7, 1947. The work stoppage idled some 325,000 members of the National Federation of Telephone Workers across the country, but in Virginia, in compliance with the public utilities law, employees of the Chesapeake and Potomac Telephone Company remained on the job. Notices posted on bulletin boards at C&P plants around the state tersely announced: "April 7. You cannot strike on this date due to Virginia law."[48]

When President Truman intimated that the federal government might take over the operation of the nation's telephone system if the strike continued, Governor Tuck requested that Virginia be exempted from any federal action. Pointing out to the president that the state had legal machinery which would preclude a disruption of service, Tuck assured Truman that "the workers and management of our companies are cooperating with the Virginia government. We have the friendship of both." The general chairman of the Virginia Federation of Telephone Workers did not, however, sound particularly friendly; Alfred V. Atkinson immediately followed up Tuck's message with his own request that Truman not exclude Virginia from federal action. In the meantime, he said, the VFTW would "abide by whatever laws the state has enacted, disregarding our personal views and feelings and regardless of how despotic the laws may be."[49]

After negotiations as prescribed by the utilities law had failed to produce an agreement, the telephone union informed Tuck that it intended to engage in a strike five weeks later. Exasperated, the governor accused the union of bargaining in bad faith. "It is my opinion," he wrote Atkinson, "that the union, though complying with the letter of the law, has violated the spirit of this act . . . and that you, as the leader of the Virginia union, have shown far greater concern for the desires and whims of the National Federation of Telephone Workers than for the welfare of the Virginia members of your union."

Taft-Hartley (Lexington: University of Kentucky Press, 1966), pp. 75–77. For a more exhaustive analysis, see Millis and Brown, *From Wagner Act to Taft-Hartley*, pp. 395–609.

[48] Richmond *Times-Dispatch*, April 6, 8, 1947.

[49] Ibid., April 6, 7, 1957.

Atkinson replied in kind, terming the governor's charge "a flagrant and gross misstatement of fact . . . designed to influence public opinion"—an action which caused his "olfactory nerves to detect an offensive odor permeating the spring air." [50]

Once Tuck learned of the union's decision to go on strike, he officially announced that the state would seize the telephone facilities when the strike occurred. Questionnaires were then sent to all company employees to ascertain their willingness to continue to work in the event of a takeover by the Commonwealth. The results indicated that 3,465 workers, or 76.6 percent of those polled, would accept employment under state auspices. [51] The response, said the Richmond *Times-Dispatch*, was "most gratifying to everyone, except of course, the bitterly disappointed union leadership." [52]

Union leaders were indeed bitter. "Mr. Tuck," blustered J. C. McIntosh, "seems to be far more interested in firmly establishing himself as the 'coupon clippers' cutie' than he is in seeing the workers of the state obtain fair play." Labor's wrath was intensified when Tuck hinted publicly that "those who refuse to work for the Commonwealth may find themselves out of employment for a long time." The thinly veiled threat was assailed as "a new low in strike-busting" by union spokesmen who attributed it to the antilabor policy of the "lustful Byrd-Tuck machine." [53] Despite the war of verbiage, the telephone controversy was settled amicably, without resort to seizure of the facilities by the state; on May 15, the VFTW accepted a new contract offered by the company, thus ending the strike threat for most of Virginia. [54]

Yet in the Eastern Shore counties of Northampton and Accomack the possibility of a walkout remained, since the workers in that area belonged to the Maryland Telephone Traffic Union instead of the

[50] Tuck to Atkinson, April 12, 1947, Atkinson to Tuck, April 14, 1947, Tuck Executive Papers.

[51] Fred A. Saunders (State Corporation Commission) to Tuck, April 28, 1947, ibid.

[52] Richmond *Times-Dispatch*, May 3, 1947.

[53] Ibid., April 15, 1947; Norfolk *Virginian-Pilot*, April 28, May 3, 1947. The public utilities statute specified that "the status of no person as an employee of the utility shall be affected by either his acceptance of employment by the state or by his refusal of such employment" (*Acts and Joint Resolutions, Extra Session, 1947*, p. 28).

[54] Richmond *Times-Dispatch*, May 16, 1947.

VFTW. When the Maryland strike deadline arrived on May 20, the state of Virginia assumed operation of the affected facilities, thereby putting the takeover provision of the public utilities statute into operation for the first time. However, since all of the workers involved had already agreed to work under the aegis of the state, the "seizure" was merely nominal, amounting to nothing more than the posting of signs in company offices announcing that the Commonwealth had taken over. Four days later a new union contract was signed and the state willingly ended its venture into the telephone business.[55]

The affair was not without its lighter moments. In later years Tuck recalled that at one point during the controversy, he decided to place a call himself (as he often did) rather than through a secretary. When he asked for the desired number, the operator—unaware of the caller's identity, and obviously upset over being prohibited from joining the national strike—replied tartly, "Owing to the unfairness of Governor Tuck, I am forced to accept this call!"[56]

In actuality the "takeover" had been very brief and largely theoretical. The result left Tuck exuberant. "Contrary to the predictions of some, and the wishes of a few, the Virginia utilities law has worked," he gloated. "Some of the union leaders have been very loud and vituperative because of this curtailment of their customary power. . . . Such was to be expected from these disappointed moguls, but all others are happy and satisfied."[57]

Within six months of its enactment, the Tuck labor program had proved its viability, either by actual test or by federal legislative sanction. The governor's labor problems, however, were by no means over. Most bothersome during the last two years of his administration were troubles emanating from the activities of the United Mine Workers both at the national level and within the state.

Southwest Virginia, where coal mining was a major occupation and

[55] Ibid., May 20–26, 1947.

[56] Interview with Tuck.

[57] Richmond *Times-Dispatch*, May 26, 1947. The *Times-Dispatch* lauded the public utilities law as having prevented the disruption of telephone service in the state but deflated its praise by suggesting that "no one has determined the extent to which those who voted to work for the Commonwealth were motivated by 'loyalty' and how many were motivated by fear that if they declined to do so, they would lose their jobs."

the UMW was firmly established, had long been regarded as a region somehow set apart from the rest of Virginia—from the "real" Virginia. Poorer than the rest of the state, having far fewer blacks, tending toward political heresy (i.e., opposition to the organization, or even Republicanism), the southwest appeared to be something of an aberration, especially to the residents of the Piedmont and Tidewater regions. In the highlands there remained traces of the rough-and-tumble frontier spirit, discernible in the conduct of affairs both political and personal. As Guy Friddell put it, "The shade of Daniel Boone lingers there."[58]

In the volatile atmosphere of the late 1940s, the frontier spirit of the southwest manifested itself in sporadic outbreaks of violence stemming from controversies between union and nonunion workers. During the first four months of 1948 there occurred several incidents in which union members attempted to disrupt the operation of nonunion mines, intimidated nonunion workers, and destroyed the property of a nonunion company. On April 21 a serious incident took place in Buchanan County when a group of striking union miners, estimated to number around 200, invaded the nonunion strip mine of the Gilliam and Hodges Construction Company and attempted to halt its operation. In the ensuing confrontation several coal trucks were overturned, some property destroyed, and several persons injured; among those hurt was one of the owners, R. L. Gilliam, who suffered a broken jaw and other injuries requiring surgery and lengthy hospitalization.[59]

The coal-mining region of Virginia was unique in that it was the only area of the state where organized labor exerted dominant political influence, thus sometimes allowing unionists to act with virtual impunity. An investigation of the Buchanan County affair at the instigation of Governor Tuck revealed that local law enforcement officials, including the sheriff and Commonwealth's attorney, had made little effort to bring the assailants to book. The sheriff, it was discovered, had actually opposed the work of the state police and had even offered to

---

[58] Friddell, *What Is It about Virginia?*, p. 39; Jean Gottman, *Virginia in Our Century* (Charlottesville: University Press of Virginia, 1969), pp. 380–98; Wilkinson, *Harry Byrd*, pp. 73–76.

[59] Richmond *Times-Dispatch*, Feb. 20, April 23, 1948; Roanoke *World-News*, April 24, 1948; Fredericksburg *Free Lance-Star*, April 23, 1948.

provide for the bailment of one of those arrested.[60] When such knowledge convinced the governor that there was slight hope for securing justice through local authorities, he resorted to a bold and highly unusual maneuver. Asserting that he would not have acted "except by the force of impelling circumstances of a most extraordinary nature," Tuck on June 11 instructed the attorney general of Virginia, J. Lindsay Almond, to intervene and carry out criminal prosecutions against the union miners in the Buchanan County Circuit Court. While acknowledging the rights of workers to join unions of their own volition, Tuck condemned the coercion, intimidation, and violence in Buchanan County as "a deplorable form of gangsterism which will not be tolerated in Virginia."[61]

Attorney General Almond, utilizing the state's antilynching law in novel fashion, arranged for the indictment of no less than 178 UMW miners on the grounds that they had broken the mob violence provision of that statute. On the eve of the trial, to the loud protests of local officials, Tuck ordered 86 state troopers into the county as a precautionary measure. At the trial itself, which was believed to have involved the largest number of defendants in the state's history, 97 of the accused pleaded guilty and prosecution of the others was dropped. In ordering five-year suspended sentences for each of those convicted, Judge Frank W. Smith took the opportunity to chastise the county officials for failing to perform their duties, thereby implicitly condoning the governor's intervention.[62]

The Virginia press generally applauded Tuck's action. The Richmond *Times-Dispatch* commended his willingness to face criticism from southwest Virginia localities and asserted that the result of the trial "abundantly vindicated" his stand. From closer to the scene of the

[60] Richmond *Times-Dispatch*, April 25, 1948.

[61] Tuck to Almond, June 11, 1948, Tuck Executive Papers. In 1947 Tuck had appointed his original attorney general, Abe Staples, to fill a vacancy on the state Supreme Court, and had chosen Harvey B. Apperson to replace him. Apperson, however, died the next year, whereupon Tuck appointed Almond to become his third attorney general in as many years.

[62] Richmond *Times-Dispatch*, July 19–21, 1948. Almond did not contest the suspension of the prison terms, saying, "I am unwilling now to believe that these men are essentially vicious at heart. . . . The Governor of Virginia and the office of the attorney general have not been vindictive in this case and are not so now" (Roanoke *World-News*, July 21, 1948).

trouble the Roanoke *World-News* called the trial "a heartening triumph for justice and the Commonwealth's anti-lynch statute" and lavished praise upon the governor: "The name of Virginia is not going to be sullied by mob violence, whether it be racially inspired or due to excesses of labor leadership. Once more the people of Virginia are beholden to Governor Tuck for courageous determination to perform his duties to the limit."[63]

Attorney General Almond was gratified by the outcome of the affair. In the rather expansive rhetoric that characterized his writing and speaking, he proclaimed,

Nothing that has ever happened in my life has given me more inspiration or produced a deeper sense of gratification than the response of the people of Virginia to Governor Tuck's determined, wholesome and unwavering courage with respect to upholding the peace and dignity of the Commonwealth. I am happy to have had a small part in assisting him in keeping untarnished the escutcheon of Virginia, and in serving unmistakable notice upon law violators that the control of local law enforcement officers will give them no immunity in cases of violence in violation of the laws of Virginia.

Tuck was similarly pleased, and expressed his elation to Almond. "You are a wizard," he wrote. "I think the case came out one hundred per cent perfect, and I congratulate you. My judgment is [that] you will have no further serious trouble in southwest Virginia or anywhere else during my term or yours."[64]

The governor was overly optimistic. Although there were no more incidents of the magnitude of the Buchanan fray, minor skirmishes cropped up periodically; in fact, only days after the Buchanan trial, a truck carrying nonunion men was ambushed by CIO members in Page County, and in a related incident, two nonunionists were attacked as they entered a Luray restaurant. However, the greatest labor problem which confronted Tuck during his last year as governor did not involve any particular local disturbance but arose from a general strike of the United Mine Workers. When, in the spring of 1949, a walkout by the UMW left Virginia facing a fuel shortage, Tuck announced that he was considering activation of the Virginia Emergency Fuel Commission,

[63] Richmond *Times-Dispatch*, July 22, 1948; Roanoke *World-News*, July 23, 1948.
[64] Almond to Ben Lacy, July 29, 1948, Tuck to Almond, July 21, 1948, Tuck Executive Papers.

an agency which had been dormant since 1946. "In this way," he said, "the people of Virginia will be freed from the fear of this constant threat from labor union czars, who have fed on the meat of federal legislation and grown corpulent on the government's baby-sitter formulas." The ending of the spring strike obviated activation of the Fuel Commission, but when another walkout in September raised that possibility once again, Tuck assured Virginians that he would not kowtow to John L. Lewis. "There may be mollycoddling of these labor leaders in Washington," he stormed, "but there will be no mollycoddling in Virginia. . . . I intend to leave the state Capitol in January and I don't intend to leave it cold." [65]

Following up his promise, Tuck ordered the Fuel Commission into operation and requested its chairman, Highway Commissioner James A. Anderson, to "acquire by contract, purchase or condemnation the output of every strip coal mine in the state and see to it that . . . all are kept in operation, either under their present owners or under the Fuel Commission." Satisfied that his plan would produce enough coal for the state's needs, Tuck confidently announced that the fires in Virginia's homes and industries would be kept burning. "This will be done," he vowed, turning his scorn upon Lewis, "despite the threats of this twentieth century synthetic Samson, who is blind and insensible to any public obligation, who cares nought for the rights of any man, and whose principal interest in labor and the working man is to convert them into a suction pump for diverting into his own control the fruits of other men's honest toil and sweat." [66]

The Fuel Commission succeeded in producing sufficiently large quantities of coal. During its first month of operation approximately 370,000 tons were mined, an increase of roughly 400 percent over normal nonunion output. In the face of some union reprisals and scattered incidents of rowdyism, production eventually increased to a yield of some 110,000 tons per week, making the Fuel Commission the largest producer of soft coal east of the Mississippi. With considerable pride Tuck pointed out that Virginia had thus shown the Ameri-

[65] Richmond *Times-Dispatch*, July 23, 1948, April 4, Sept. 20, 1949. The fall 1949 strike idled the state's 14,000 unionized soft coal miners and resulted in the layoff of an estimated 1,500 to 2,000 workers on Virginia's coal-carrying railroads.

[66] Ibid., Sept. 29, 1949; *Address of William M. Tuck, October 21, 1949*, copy in Tuck Executive Papers.

can public that it was "neither necessary nor expedient to become mendicants at the door of a ruthless labor union dictator."[67]

When Lewis announced the end of the UMW walkout on December 1, 1949, Virginia had still not suffered a fuel shortage. In later years Tuck insisted that "if the strike had lasted a hundred years, we'd have had coal."[68] Whatever the long-run effectiveness of the Fuel Commission might have been, Tuck had gained for the time being, through his activation of the agency, the gratitude of most Virginians, at the expense of increased union hostility (if, in fact, any further exacerbation of labor sentiment were possible). True to his jaunty pledge, Tuck did not "leave the Capitol cold."

In his study of recent Virginia politics, J. Harvie Wilkinson asserted that "Bill Tuck is best remembered for his big stick with labor"—a statement surely beyond cavil.[69] From the beginning of his administration until the very end, Tuck found himself plagued by sundry labor disorders. In meeting those problems—threatening to draft strikers, overseeing the passage of restrictive legislation, sparring verbally with union leaders—Tuck attracted the wrath of organized labor; at the same time, and for the same reasons, he won the plaudits of an angry antilabor public.

It was understandable that union spokesmen denounced Tuck and his labor policy; his four years in office witnessed an unprecedented amount of activity in the area of labor relations, and most of that activity was directed toward restricting unionism. Placed within the national context, however, the Tuck program did not stand apart as especially vicious or repressive. That Virginia was well within the national mainstream was illustrated by the spate of restrictive labor legislation enacted contemporaneously by other states. By the end of 1947, twelve states in addition to Virginia had outlawed the closed shop, ten had limited strikes in public utilities, seven had forbidden strikes by public employees, and twelve had banned mass picketing. Furthermore, despite the protests of labor spokesmen, the courts generally approved such legislation; by the time Tuck left office in

[67] McDowell, "Bill Tuck," p. 17; *Address of William M. Tuck, October 21, 1949*, copy in Tuck Executive Papers; Richmond *Times-Dispatch*, Sept. 29, Oct. 29, 1949.

[68] Richmond *Times-Dispatch*, Dec. 2, 1949; interview with Tuck.

[69] Wilkinson, *Harry Byrd*, p. 55.

1950, the major labor enactments of his administration had been upheld explicitly by the Virginia Supreme Court of Appeals or inferentially by decisions of the United States Supreme Court.[70]

There were important political ramifications of Tuck's actions vis-à-vis labor. Antiorganization leaders were hopeful that the governor's stance would appear so extreme that a substantial number of moderates would be forced into their camp, and it is possible that the organization was eventually weakened by its antagonism of labor. According to one student of the period, the "intransigent positions" which the Byrd faction took toward labor "helped to build up an urban-based opposition to the organization which killed it."[71] Damaging though it may have been in the long run, when the state became more urban and industrialized, the Tuck labor program had few immediate deleterious political effects; indeed, just the opposite was true. As the several statewide campaigns of the Tuck years demonstrated, antilabor sentiment formed a vast reservoir which could be, and was, tapped to great advantage by the candidates of the Byrd organization.

In sum, Tuck's policy toward labor accorded well with the mood of the state at the time, a mood which pervaded all of the rural South and much of the entire nation. Regardless of how justifiable the actions of organized labor may have been during the postwar era, the American public had simply come to believe that, as one newspaper put it, "labor had gotten too big for its breeches."[72] The Tuck labor program was to a large extent the logical outgrowth of that feeling. The acclaim which the governor received for his handling of labor was owing mainly to the existence of a truculent antilabor atmosphere which allowed Tuck to lead Virginians in the direction most of them already wanted to go.

As Tuck's personal popularity grew, so too did the strength of the Byrd organization. By the midpoint of the Tuck governorship the organization had established unprecedented control over the political affairs of Virginia. The governorship, both United States Senate seats,

[70] Millis and Brown, *From Wagner Act to Taft-Hartley*, pp. 326–32; Albion Guilford Taylor, *Labor and the Supreme Court* (Ann Arbor, Mich.: Braun-Brumfield, 1961), pp. 151–62; O'Keefe, "Right-to-Work Legislation," pp. 71–81.

[71] Wolfe, "Virginia in World War II," p. 224. Representative of antiorganization sentiment is Martin A. Hutchinson to Charles H. Morris, April 7, 1947, Hutchinson Papers.

[72] Richmond *Times-Dispatch*, Jan. 21, 1947.

and all of the congressional seats save one—the Ninth District seat held by independent-minded John Flannagan—were in the hands of Byrd adherents; the General Assembly was packed with organization regulars. It was then, at the very peak of its power, that the organization committed a rare political error in the form of the so-called Tuck anti-Truman bill—a controversial measure which betokened a growing alienation between the Byrd organization and the national Democratic party and portended trouble within the organization itself.

Harbinger of Southern Revolt
6. *The "Anti-Truman Bill"*

> I have never voted nothing but a Democratic ticket in my life but as Truman wants to put the Negro race equal with us I know that is not right, so who are you going to put up that I can vote for?
>
> —*Virginia voter to Tuck (1948)*

> I am greatly disturbed myself . . . [but] we have been Democrats too long to get out of the party, even though we cannot embrace everything for which the present party leaders stand.
>
> —*Tuck's reply*

The ascendance of Harry S. Truman to the presidency in April 1945 was cause for concern in many quarters, representing as it did the replacement of the near-legendary Roosevelt by a virtual unknown who seemed to be little more than a middling political hack. Below the Mason-Dixon line, however, Truman possessed one estimable virtue: he was, by birth, a southerner. In commenting on the new president's qualifications, the Richmond *Times-Dispatch* praised Truman's "sturdy honesty, courage and determination" and added reassuringly: "He sounds practically like a Virginian. Perhaps the fact that he is the son of a Confederate soldier accounts for this. At all events, it is good to be able to hail his accent, as well as his delivery and his ideas." [1]

The known facts about Truman, such as they were, seemed to warrant southern optimism. On economics and race, two key issues, he seemed safe. During his chairmanship of a special Senate committee to investigate the defense program, Truman had ferreted out numerous cases of government waste and extravagance, much to the delight of conservatives like his Senate colleague Harry Byrd. With regard to the race issue, Truman was deemed enlightened for his time and place, but was quoted as saying publicly: "I wish to make it clear that I am not

[1] Richmond *Times-Dispatch*, April 17, 1945.

appealing for social equality of the Negro. The Negro himself knows
better than that, and the highest types of Negro leaders say quite
frankly that they prefer the society of their own people. Negroes want
justice, not social relations." Overall, Truman's record as a senator was
so acceptable to southern Democrats that they actively maneuvered at
the 1944 national convention to have him replace Henry Wallace as the
party's vice-presidential candidate. When that deed was accomplished,
many southern leaders were gratified. Indicative of the southern attitude was the comment of Alabama Governor Chauncey Sparks, who
happily announced that "in the matter of race relations Senator Truman
told me he is the son of an unreconstructed rebel mother. I think the
South has won a victory." [2]

. By that time, resentment against Roosevelt was running high
among southern conservatives, who sensed that they were losing their
traditional influence within the party. As Virginia's then-Governor
Colgate Darden expressed it, "The Southern Democrat group is now at
the mercy of the Democratic political machines in the Northern cities,
who, trading on the strength of the Democratic label in the South,
simply ignore us." [3] The most visible sign of southern disaffection came
in 1944 when a movement developed to draft Senator Harry F. Byrd for
president. The senator himself did not appear to encourage the effort,
although one observer claimed that Byrd "was not altogether idle" in
his own behalf. At the Democratic national convention Byrd's nomination prevented Roosevelt from being chosen without some semblance
of opposition. The senator commented privately that he was "very
regretful" that his name had been placed before the convention, but
whatever his personal feelings, the act did symbolize a growing
southern disenchantment with the direction being taken by the national Democratic party. [4]

So it was that the succession of Harry Truman was greeted with some
enthusiasm by those who hoped that his leadership would bring a more
conservative ambience to the party and restore the South to an influen-

[2] William C. Berman, *The Politics of Civil Rights in the Truman Administration*
(Columbus: Ohio State University Press, 1970), pp. 12, 21.

[3] Darden to Harry F. Byrd, May 20, 1944, Byrd Papers.

[4] Stetson Kennedy, *Southern Exposure* (Garden City, N.Y.: Doubleday, 1946), p.
134; Byrd to Colgate Darden, July 28, 1944, Byrd Papers. See also Forrest Davis,
"The Fourth Term's Hair Shirt," *Saturday Evening Post* 216 (April 8, 1944): 9–11.

tial position in party councils. Indicative of the renewed hope was the fact that shortly after Truman took office, Senator Byrd visited the While House, where he had not been during Roosevelt's last years. "I came to congratulate President Truman on the fine record he is making," Byrd explained. "He is off to a good start and I want to pledge him my support." [5]

Well over a year later Governor Tuck publicly praised Truman in a resolution before the Virginia state Democratic convention. Even as late as March 1947, Tuck expressed his approval of the Truman administration in a letter to the chairman of the Democratic National Committee. "I assure you of my sincere desire to cooperate in every way possible for the success of our Democratic ticket in the 1948 election," he wrote. "From what I can hear in talking with the people generally, President Truman has gained considerable [sic] in strength." [6]

The rapprochement between Harry Truman and the Democratic organization in Virginia was destined to be of short duration. The estrangement resulted from a mélange of factors, including, to some extent, Truman's handling of foreign policy. Although many southern legislators were conspicuously avid "Cold Warriors" in the late 1940s, Harry Byrd, with his eye ever on the balance sheets, found the cost of containment too high; accordingly, he questioned the European aid program from the outset and voted against the cornerstone of that program, the Marshall Plan. [7]

More significant in the turn against Truman was his stand on organized labor. There were times, as in the threatened railroad strike of 1946, when the president assumed a position sufficiently stern to satisfy the most adamant antiunion elements. On balance, however, Truman seemed friendly to labor, as evidenced by his vetoes of the Case bill in 1946 and the Taft-Hartley bill in 1947. Not only did the vetoes run counter to the prevailing attitudes in Virginia at the time, but they were widely interpreted as being motivated by the political desire to

[5] Roanoke *Times*, April 22, 1945, clipping in Hutchinson Papers.

[6] Richmond *Times-Dispatch*, Sept. 6, 1946; Tuck to Robert E. Hannegan, Mar. 4, 1947, Tuck Executive Papers.

[7] For southern attitudes toward Truman's foreign policy, see Alfred O. Hero, *The Southerner and World Affairs* (Baton Rouge: Louisiana State University Press, 1965), pp. 6–7, and Charles O. Lerche, *The Uncertain South* (Chicago: Quadrangle Books, 1964), pp. 58–59.

capture labor votes. Referring to his veto of the Case bill, for example, a Richmond newspaper claimed that "Mr. Truman did what any President of a small capacity and calculating mind would have done," and added, "A politician of his stamp . . . had rather be President than right."[8]

While Truman's foreign policy and his attitude toward labor created considerable discontent, the factor which was far and away the most important in the southern, and Virginian, disaffection was his stand on civil rights. It was Truman's misfortune to reach the presidency at a time of growing racial animosity. Southern whites were alarmed by repeated federal attacks on the Jim Crow system. In 1941 Congress had affronted segregationist sensibilities by establishing a temporary Fair Employment Practices Commission; by 1945 the Supreme Court had abolished the "white primary," had outlawed segregation in interstate transportation, and had taken initial (if timorous) steps toward requiring racial equality in public education. Already edgy southern whites were made more uneasy by black activists who, though hardly radical according to later standards, were becoming more vocal and more insistent in their demands. Surveying the situation in a widely circulated article entitled "Nearer and Nearer the Precipice," Richmond editor Virginius Dabney commented ominously on racial conditions in the mid-1940s: "Because of the prevailing interracial tension on many fronts, growing out of the current agitation by both Negroes and whites, . . . the country is sitting on a volcano."[9]

The state of Virginia, typically southern in many ways, did not usually share in the rabid forms of racism which plagued the lower South. Lynching, for example, had virtually disappeared since the enactment of an antilynching statute in the 1920s. There were other signs of racial moderation. The Richmond *Times-Dispatch* in late 1943 launched a vigorous campaign to have segregation abolished in public

[8] Richmond *News Leader*, June 12, 1946, quoted in James R. Roebuck, Jr., "Virginia in the Election of 1948" (M.A. thesis, U.Va., 1969), p. 5.

[9] Dabney, "Nearer and Nearer the Precipice," *The Atlantic* 171 (Jan. 1943): 99. For a discussion of judicial decisions affecting segregation, see Richard Bardolph, ed., *The Civil Rights Record* (New York: Thomas Y. Crowell, 1970), pp. 271–72, 283–86; and Carl B. Swisher, "The Supreme Court in the South," in Taylor Cole and John Hallowell, eds., *The Southern Political Scene, 1938–1948* (Gainesville: University of Florida Press, 1948), pp. 292–99.

transportation, and the proposal received what its chief advocate termed "a much more favorable response than was anticipated from everybody, except the politicians."[10] By the late 1940s bills were being introduced in the General Assembly which would have greatly restricted the application of Jim Crowism; though none of the measures approached passage, the very fact that they were considered by the legislature was taken as an encouraging sign by the black community.[11] Indeed, some Virginia blacks acknowledged that they were usually treated relatively well, prompting them, according to one account, to "take pride in being Virginians and look down at lesser peoples."[12]

For the most part, Virginia politics lacked the overt racial appeals which so often afflicted other southern states. Though subtler influences, such as the poll tax, constituted discrimination in fact against blacks, outright demagoguery was rare. V. O. Key, Jr., found the explanation in the state's genteel political tradition. "In a word," he wrote, "politics in Virginia is reserved for those who can qualify as gentlemen. Rabble-rousing and Negro-baiting capacities, which in Georgia or Mississippi would be a great political asset, simply mark a person as one not to the manner born." Nevertheless, Virginia was affected by the general deterioration of racial feelings which occurred in the postwar era. "The social friction created in Virginia by the Second World War worsened race relations," concluded one student of the period. "Stresses of wartime change prompted members of each race to think and to say the most extreme ill of one another."[13]

In such a volatile racial atmosphere, conservative Virginians held out the hope that Harry Truman, as a southern president, would act to defuse the civil rights bomb. Their disillusionment began almost immediately when, in June 1945, Truman issued the first of many calls

[10] Virginius Dabney to Cornelius Wickersham, Jan. 5, 1947, Dabney Papers.

[11] Richmond *Afro-American*, Feb. 28, 1948; Richmond *Times-Dispatch*, Feb. 25, 1948. The bills were sponsored by Richmond Delegate W. H. C. Murray, who was not a member of the Byrd organization.

[12] Key, *Southern Politics*, p. 35.

[13] Ibid., p. 26; Wolfe, "Virginia in World War II," pp. 197–211. A discussion of rising racial conflict in the South during the period is William H. Leary, "Race Relations in Turmoil: Southern Liberals and World War II" (M.A. thesis, U.Va. 1967).

for the establishment of a permanent Fair Employment Practices Commission to replace the temporary wartime agency which was about to expire.[14] The president could hardly have calculated a move more certain to inflame southern passions, since the FEPC had become the focal point of the civil rights crusade. In his inaugural address, Governor Tuck inveighed against the existing FEPC and decried its continuation. Claiming that the agency had the power to determine and to coerce hiring and firing of employees, he scored the FEPC as a symptom of the larger disease of federalism: "One does not have to be a constitutional lawyer to perceive that this invasion of a private individual's right to select his own employees . . . is but the first step in the complete destruction of all his personal liberties."[15] Undaunted by such attacks, Truman persisted, despite the fact that in one analyst's estimation, the issue had become "so hot that no congressman from [the South] could have voted for permanent FEPC legislation and won re-election to public office."[16]

Truman further rattled the conservatives late in 1946 when he issued an executive order creating a presidential civil rights committee broadly charged with investigating existing conditions and making recommendations concerning the improvement and protection of civil rights. The committee's findings were made public in October 1947; in an impressively documented volume entitled *To Secure These Rights*, the president's panel called for an extensive program of federal action which probably exceeded anything that Truman had envisioned. In addition to further discomfiting southern conservatives, the report had the effect of putting the president in a dilemma. As one historian

[14] Robert A. Garson, "The Alienation of the South: A Crisis for Harry S. Truman and the Democratic Party, 1945–1948," *Missouri Historical Review* 64 (July 1970): 448–71.

[15] *Inaugural Address of William M. Tuck*, p. 5. Tuck apprised Senator Byrd that he had received more congratulatory messages on his condemnation of FEPC than on any part of his inaugural address and informed the senator, "I hope that the Southern senators will do whatever may be necessary to defeat this vicious legislation" (Richmond *Times-Dispatch*, Feb. 2, 1946).

[16] Louis Kesselman, *The Social Politics of FEPC* (Chapel Hill: University of North Carolina Press, 1948), p. 169. Virginia newspaper opposition to FEPC is evidenced in the Richmond *Times-Dispatch*, Feb. 3, 1946; a favorable view is contained in the Richmond *Afro-American*, Sept. 15, 1945.

described it, "The choice was either to side with the urban liberals by sending the report, or a part of it, to Congress, or support the South by ignoring its recommendations entirely. Either decision would be irrevocable and would profoundly affect his 1948 Presidential aspirations." [17]

While Truman pondered what direction to take, he received from his trusted special counsel, Clark Clifford, a lengthy memorandum in which the political prospects for the 1948 election year were analyzed. In a crucial passage Clifford predicted that "as always, the South can be considered safely Democratic, and in formulating national policy, it can be safely ignored." That opinion, which proved to be inaccurate, may not have been the critical factor in Truman's decision, but the direction which he eventually took did reveal an utter disregard for the sensibilities of white southerners. On February 2, 1948, he presented to Congress, in the form of a special message, the most sweeping civil rights program ever proposed by an American president to that time. Among other suggestions he specifically asked Congress to establish a permanent Commission on Civil Rights and a Civil Rights Division in the Department of Justice; to strengthen existing civil rights statutes; to provide federal protection against lynching; to protect more adequately the right to vote; and to establish a permanent FEPC. [18]

Although the message contained little that had not been advocated before, it precipitated what one southern journalist called "the loudest political pyrotechnics since 1860." [19] The southern outrage seems to have been more intense because the proponent of the message was a native son who, ipso facto, could not have believed in what he was espousing. "We respected Roosevelt for standing for the civil rights

[17] Berman, *Politics of Civil Rights*, p. 72. The committee's recommendations are set forth in *To Secure These Rights* (New York: Simon and Schuster, 1947), pp. 139–73.

[18] Irwin Ross, *The Loneliest Campaign: The Truman Victory of 1948* (New York: New American Library, 1968), p. 22; Berman, *Politics of Civil Rights*, p. 84.

[19] Ralph McGill, "Will the South Ditch Truman?" *Saturday Evening Post* 120 (May 22, 1948): 17. McGill pointed out that southerners greatly exaggerated the extent of Truman's program, with rumors flying that the president had come out in favor of compulsory race mixing at dances, intermarriage, etc. In actual fact, McGill claimed, the civil rights recommendations were so mild that it was "highly probable that had not the South reacted immediately and with such violence, Negro leaders and organizations would have protested the proposals as weak and mealy-mouthed."

stuff," went a typical southern response, "because we think he actually believed it. But Truman's just pulling a cheap political maneuver."[20]

Whatever the cause of their disapprobation, southerners attacked the proposals in a near-maniacal frenzy, uttering imprecations "as fervid as the shouts at a backwoods camp meeting," according to the Associated Press. A Georgia congressman railed that the Truman program sounded "like the platform of the Communist party," and the Speaker of the Mississippi House of Representatives branded it "damnable, Communistic, unconstitutional, anti-American, anti-Southern." Mississippi Senator James Eastland, employing an oft-used word, claimed that such actions as Truman proposed would "mongrelize" the South. The possibility of a southern bolt from the Democratic party was broached by Representative L. Mendel Rivers of South Carolina, who fulminated that "one of these days the so-called leaders are going to find out the so-called solid South is not as solid as some of the heads of our so-called leaders."[21]

In comparison to such comments—which, in one estimation, made it seem "as if another Sherman had been discovered marching toward the sea"—the initial reaction in Virginia was mild.[22] Governor Tuck reserved comment, noting that he had not had sufficient time to study the proposals. He consented to serve on a committee of the Southern Governors' Conference to study the Truman program but indicated that although he was in sympathy with the basic views of the other southern governors, he might not agree with their methods of counterattack. Senator Byrd, after several weeks of silence, spoke out against the Truman plan at the annual Jefferson-Jackson Day dinner; referring to "inquisitional" agencies such as the FEPC, he darkly hinted that the proposed civil rights package "could very conceivably lead to dictatorship."[23]

The Richmond *Times-Dispatch*, which itself took a moderate stand

[20] Joseph E. Finley, "A Yankee Looks at the Dixie Revolt," *Nation* 167 (July 3, 1948): 18.

[21] Richmond *Times-Dispatch*, Feb. 4, 5, 1948; "War between Democrats," *Newsweek* 31 (Feb. 16, 1948): 24–26. A survey of southern reactions is contained in Monroe Billington, "Civil Rights, President Truman, and the South," *Journal of Negro History* 58 (April 1973): 127–39.

[22] Phillips, *Truman Presidency*, p. 206.

[23] Richmond *Times-Dispatch*, Feb. 4, 20, 1948.

on the matter, commended Tuck and Byrd for their "firm, yet dignified" responses. "Virginians should be thankful," said the paper, "that they have such levelheaded and courageous leaders to speak for them in the councils of the nation at this critical juncture." The *Times-Dispatch* was unaware that at the very time when the laudatory editorial appeared, a bold plan was being devised by the Byrd organization which would thrust Virginia into the very forefront of the anti-Truman crusade.[24]

On February 26, 1948, Governor Tuck made his third appearance of the session before the General Assembly. Since it was highly unusual for a governor to deliver more than one personal message per session, news of the extraordinary appearance brought a huge crowd to the House gallery. If the audience, which spilled into the Capitol corridors, expected fireworks, they were not disappointed, as the governor treated them to a sample of Tuck oratory at its most fulminant. Having recited the terms of the Truman civil rights program, Tuck warned:

If such legislation is enacted, it will constitute a precedent which will bring about the final and complete destruction of the autonomy of not only the Southern states, but of all the states of the American union. Precedents are dangerous. These proposals, if adopted, will open wide the door for the establishment of a totalitarian form of government in this country. . . . This is sufficient power to create in America the counterpart of a Hitler or Stalin. The hordes of police officers set up under the proposed FEPC could easily be converted into a huge gestapo by expanding the scope of their field.

Such potential horrors had come about, claimed the governor, because the Democratic party at the national level had ceased to be responsive to southern desires. "No insult to this region was considered too vile," he roared. "The electoral vote of the South has been counted by the Democratic Presidents even before it was cast." As a result, "the people of the Southern states have been placed upon the sacrificial altar to appease racial and other minority fringe groups in states having a large number of electoral votes."

Tuck's charge that the national Democratic party took the South for granted was not new, and as the Clifford memorandum indicated, it

[24] Ibid., Feb. 24, 1948; Harry F. Byrd to E. R. Combs, Feb. 21, 1948, Byrd Papers.

was not untrue. However, the plan which he proposed to correct that situation was indeed novel. What Tuck requested was a revision of the state's election laws which, in its original form, would have permitted a state party convention or a party committee to decide for whom the state's electoral votes would be cast, even after the election had been held. It would also have kept the names of presidential candidates off the ballot entirely (only the names of the parties and their electors would appear) and would have ordinarily limited the parties on the ballot to those which had been listed on the last presidential ballot (thereby eliminating Henry Wallace's nascent Progressive party). An exception was that a party could appear on the ballot if it had polled more than 10 percent of the vote in any general election in Virginia within the previous five years.[25]

The Tuck message brought a quick and hearty endorsement from the Washington office of Senator Harry Byrd. Declaring that the governor had used "no weasel words," Byrd acclaimed the speech as "historic and of deep significance."[26] Other organization leaders, including notably Congressman Howard Smith and Lieutenant Governor L. Preston Collins, voiced similar approval. Such endorsements were exceedingly rare. The immediate responses to the Tuck proposal were almost uniformly hostile; as the Richmond *Times-Dispatch* noted, "There was such an uproar from every direction as has seldom erupted in modern times." Even some of the organization's putative members in good standing, among them Congressman J. Vaughan Gary, Porter Hardy, and J. Lindsay Almond, expressed varying degrees of disapproval. State Democratic Chairman and Mayor of Richmond Horace Edwards revealed that he had no prior knowledge of the governor's proposal and doubted that it was either "practicable or desirable."[27] United States Senator A. Willis Robertson (who had been elected in 1946 to fill the vacancy created by the death of the aged Carter Glass) issued a cautious public statement conveying agreement with Tuck's objective, but in private he wrote to Richmond editor Douglas Southall Freeman, "When I subsequently became acquainted with the

[25] Virginia, *Address of William M. Tuck, Governor, to the General Assembly, Thursday, February 26, 1948*, House Document No. 22 (Richmond: Division of Purchase and Printing, 1948), pp. 3–6; Richmond *Times-Dispatch*, Feb. 27, 1948.

[26] New York *Times*, Feb. 27, 1948.

[27] Richmond *Times-Dispatch*, Feb. 27, 28, Mar. 2, 1948.

details of the . . . Tuck bill I did not approve of them and made my disapproval known in places where it would do the most good."[28]

While the issue bid fair to disrupt the organization, criticism cascaded down from all sides. The bill was vehemently denounced by spokesmen from the NAACP, the Virginia League of Women Voters, the academic community, and organized labor. Antiorganization Democrats unleashed bitter salvos. Said one, in reference to Tuck's plan, "I would expect something of that nature to come from Gerald L. K. Smith, but not from the governor of Virginia." The whole affair, said another, proved that "Byrd and Tuck and their crew were not any different down in their souls from Bilbo." Martin Hutchinson commented publicly that "had such a proposal been made in the Kremlin of Russia, there would be no occasion for surprise, but here in Virginia, it is indeed shocking."[29]

Opposition emanated from both ends of the political spectrum as state Senator Ted Dalton, the leading Republican spokesman (later to run for governor), and liberal Independent Howard Carwile lent their voices to the rising clamor against the bill. Few critics were more vociferous than Ninth District Congressman John Flannagan, a nonorganization Democrat, who labeled the proposal "a rotten egg" and urged the General Assembly to reject it "with a bang that will be heard around the world." Flannagan's concern was understandable since the "Fighting Ninth," unlike the rest of the state, had a viable two-party system; and as one Democratic leader in the area put it, "The Republicans will make capital game [sic] in the Ninth Congressional District out of the Tuck issue, and that's a matter which I deeply regret."[30]

The wrath of the politicians was more than matched by the state's newspapers, which for the most part differed only in the extent to which they reviled the Tuck bill. The Richmond dailies waxed nearly frenetic in their opposition. "Was there ever anything like it before?" asked the *Times-Dispatch*. "Is this still Virginia? Has the Democratic machine leadership lost its sense of balance in this matter?" The *News*

[28] Quoted in Roebuck, "Virginia in the Presidential Election of 1948," p. 21.
[29] John M. Goldsmith to Francis Pickens Miller, Feb. 27, 1948, Miller Papers; Daniel Weymouth to Martin A. Hutchinson, Feb. 26, 1948, Hutchinson Papers; Richmond *Times-Dispatch*, Feb. 27, 1948; Richmond *News Leader*, Feb. 28, 1948.
[30] Richmond *Times-Dispatch*, Feb. 27, Mar. 1, 2, 5, 1948.

Leader claimed that the real issue was neither Truman nor Wallace: "It is YOU, free Virginians, it is YOU, a thinking, freeborn individual whose rights are being infringed. Rise up and defend YOUR rights." The Richmond *Afro-American* assailed the bill as "asinine and utterly immoral" and asserted that "Governor Tuck proposes the same kind of dictatorship of which he and Senator Harry Byrd accuse the President."[31] One of the most acidulous, and surely most picturesque, of the press critiques was delivered by a small antiorganization paper in southwest Virginia. "Once again," said *The Dickensonian*,

Richmond is echoing with the ululating Rebel yell, and secession is rampant. Not only are Governor Tuck and the august General Assembly seceding from the Democratic party . . . , but from a large number of their own constituents. Now, woah, Bill! Let's think this thing over for a bit. . . . We don't know how the folks down around Richmond feel, Governor, but we do know that the boys back here in the hills are going to vote for the man of their choice come hell and high water. . . . They don't like royal ukases laid down to a subservient General Assembly.[32]

In the face of overwhelmingly hostile criticism, Tuck and organization leaders in the legislature set about to revise the bill. Two changes were made forthwith. The first provided that the instruction of party electors would be solely the responsibility of a party's state convention and could not be delegated to a party committee, as was possible under the original plan. The second broadened the possibilities for parties to get on the Virginia ballot by allowing any party to be listed which had qualified in ten or more states.[33]

The emendations were made with Tuck's full approval and were necessary, said the governor, because the original bill had been "clum-

[31] Ibid., Feb. 28, 1948; Richmond *News Leader*, Feb. 28, 1948; Richmond *Afro-American*, Mar. 6, 1948. The state's second major black paper, the Norfolk *Journal and Guide*, Mar. 13, 1948, castigated the proposal under the banner, "Tuck's Blast on Civil Rights Means Virginia No Better than Mississippi."

[32] *The Dickensonian*, Mar. 5, 1948, copy in Whitehead Papers. The newspaper was edited by an active anti, H. Mayno Sutherland. For other samples of press hostility, see Norfolk *Virginian-Pilot*, Feb. 29, 1948; Charlottesville *Daily Progress*, Feb. 26, 1948; and Lynchburg *News* (normally a pro-organization paper), Feb. 26, 1948. Standing almost alone in defense of the Tuck bill was the Staunton *News-Leader*, Feb. 29, 1948.

[33] Richmond *Times-Dispatch*, Feb. 28, 1948.

sily drafted." The changes failed to mollify most of the plan's detractors. To Martin Hutchinson they meant no more than the "difference between tweedle-dee and tweedle-dum," while to the still irate John Flannagan the amendments seemed "comparable to changing the death penalty from hanging to electrocution: while the method may be more refined and humane, the fact remains that the fellow, under either method, dies. And the fact remains that either under the original proposal made by Governor Tuck or the modified form thereof, democracy in Virginia dies." [34]

As controversy continued to swirl about the bill, a public hearing before a joint committee of the House and Senate was scheduled for March 4 at the Capitol. Each side chose its main advocate carefully. To speak in support of the bill the organization selected Delegate Armistead Boothe of Alexandria, one of the more moderate members of the legislature; to speak in opposition, the antis turned to Francis Pickens Miller, an erudite former member of the General Assembly who was to run for governor in 1949. In an atmosphere fairly crackling with tension, according to press accounts, Boothe defended the measure as "possibly the most liberal voting law in the world today" and urged its passage because "only through legislation can we convince the Democrats in the national party at Washington that we meant what we said." [35] Miller, having been introduced to loud applause by Martin Hutchinson, launched an impassioned rebuttal. "I have more Rebel blood in my veins than anyone in this House," he cried. "The relative for whom I am named was the governor of South Carolina who authorized the shot on Fort Sumter. But, ladies and gentlemen, we are in the Union now . . . and any talk of secession or blackmailing a great national party or moving out of it is too reminiscent for me of the fateful move of 1861." [36]

[34] Interview with Tuck; typescript of statement, undated, in Hutchinson Papers; Richmond *Times-Dispatch*, Feb. 29, 1948.

[35] Richmond *Times-Dispatch*, Mar. 5, 1948. Boothe's role in support of the "anti-Truman bill" appears surprising in light of his subsequent political record. A key figure in the so-called Young Turk rebellion against the old-line organization forces in the 1950s, he broke completely with the organization by challenging Harry F. Byrd, Jr., in 1966 for the Senate seat vacated by the elder Byrd; though losing, he received over 49 percent of the vote (Wilkinson, *Harry Byrd*, pp. 106–10, 333–35).

[36] Richmond *Times-Dispatch*, Mar. 5, 1948.

Fierce floor debates ensued in both chambers as the legislators considered various amendments to the "anti-Truman bill." Among the most outspoken foes of the measure was Delegate Robert Whitehead of Nelson County. Whitehead had begun his political career as a nominal organization man and had supported Tuck for governor in 1945 and Byrd for senator as late as 1946, but in the course of the 1948 legislative session his independence placed him outside the organization. He was, by any reckoning, a formidable adversary, acclaimed as the General Assembly's best speaker and foremost authority on state finances. So great was his reputation as an orator that advance notice of his speeches filled the House gallery with audiences which sometimes included members of the state Senate. "He brought the skill of a prosecutor and the justification of the Scriptures into his arguments," one student recorded, "and he always had a ready supply of homely phrases to catch the ear of the non-lawyer, rural members of the Assembly."[37]

During the 1948 session Whitehead emerged as perhaps the antis' most effective spokesman—"a cocklebur under the saddle of the organization," in the words of a contemporary.[38] Nowhere did Whitehead prove more nettlesome to the Byrd forces than in his opposition to the proposed ballot bill. Privately he averred, "I have the highest regard for Governor Tuck but he has made a mistake in this instance, and I intend to fight this proposal to the end." The fight which he proceeded to wage on the House floor was titanic. On one occasion, disdaining a microphone and speaking in a voice that needed no amplification, he damned the bill as "not legal, not honorable, and neither fair nor wise." Moreover, he exclaimed, it was "the Negro question" which had precipitated the issue, the claims of organization spokesmen to the contrary notwithstanding. "This is the truth: Negroes in Virginia have not received their just deserts," he shouted. "Has reason fled the temple in this hysteria spreading over the country?

---

[37] Shackleford, "The 'Liberal' Movement in Virginia Politics," p. 50. Whitehead was voted the "most valuable" member of the House of Delegates by Capitol newsmen, one of whom described him as "a man who stands on his hind legs and hollers once he has made up his mind on an issue." The consensus was that Whitehead's worst fault was a tendency to overkill by talking too much (Richmond *Times-Dispatch*, Mar. 7, 1948).

[38] Richmond *Times-Dispatch*, Mar. 7, 1948.

Has the General Assembly assumed the position of the Ku Klux Klan, to march under a ballot contrary to our basic law?"[39]

As the bill was being debated, Governor Tuck was subjected to relentless newspaper criticism and to charges that he was engaging in legislative arm-twisting. Delegate Whitehead, for one, claimed that he had "never known so much pressure to be exerted by the executive branch" and asserted that "one by one, and two by two, members of the legislature have been called to the Governor's office and pleaded with to save him." Throughout, Tuck remained outwardly calm; but, in fact, he was growing exasperated, as evidenced by a letter written to a friend in New Orleans. Explaining the status of his pending bill, he fumed that "the papers, the Communists, Jews, Negroes, and so-called liberal Democrats, as well as the Republicans, are giving us a hard fight, but I hope that we will succeed in passing it through the General Assembly. . . . We are in this fight to the end."[40]

Tuck need not have been worried about the eventual passage of his election bill, since the organization was securely enough in control of the legislature to enact the measures even if some of its members wavered. The measure was finally passed during the last week of the session by a vote of 74 to 25 in the House and 29 to 10 in the Senate. The opposition comprised all the Republican legislators, together with Democrats mainly from the larger urban areas and southwest Virginia, the traditional areas of antiorganization sentiment. Though the vote was not close, antiorganization leaders considered the outcome heartening in light of the heavily pro-Byrd composition of the General Assembly.[41]

The election law as finally enacted was quite different from the bill as originally proposed. Under the new law the names of the presidential and vice-presidential candidates, as well as the party labels, were to be printed on the ballot. Furthermore, any new party could qualify for a place on the ballot simply by means of a petition signed by 1,000

[39] Whitehead to T. B. Harvey, Mar. 6, 1948, Whitehead Papers; Richmond *Times-Dispatch*, Mar. 10, 1948.

[40] Richmond *Times-Dispatch*, Mar. 10, 1948; Tuck to John P. Wilkerson, Mar. 4, 1948, Tuck Papers.

[41] *Journal of the House of Delegates*, 1948, p. 1025; *Journal of the Senate*, 1948, p. 952. Antiorganization feeling is revealed in Martin A. Hutchinson to Marion Ramsay, Mar. 11, 1948, Hutchinson Papers.

registered voters. The most important part of the law retained the right of the state party to instruct its electors for someone other than the nominee of the national party. However, in a significant revision of earlier forms of the bill, any such instructions, if they were to be made at all, would have to be made by the state convention at least sixty days prior to election day. If the state party failed to reconvene after the national party's nominee had been chosen, or if it chose no alternative nominee at this second meeting, the Virginia electors would be committed automatically to the national ticket. If the state convention did meet again and select its own candidate, the national ticket could qualify for the Virginia ballot merely by certification of national party officials.[42]

It was ironic, as journalist Guy Friddell commented, that "what started out . . . as the anti-Truman bill to keep the man from Missouri off the ballot, wound up by letting nearly anybody get on it"; and, indeed, the final product did represent one of the most liberal election laws in the nation.[43] Yet, many of the state's newspapers and most of the antiorganization Democrats remained implacable in their opposition. The press criticism, notably that of the Richmond papers, particularly rankled the organization leadership. "In all my experience," Byrd complained, "I have never seen such vindictive, deliberate and wilful misrepresentation of the facts as has occurred to this bill. As a newspaper man, I well know that . . . there are many people who may not agree with the editor but whose minds will be formed unconsciously and will accept constantly recurring statements as being the truth."[44]

Byrd and Tuck agreed that the continuing outcry from the press necessitated some public defense.[45] Accordingly, a few days after the adjournment of the General Assembly, Tuck went on statewide radio to explain the work of the recent legislature and, specifically, to try to allay criticism of the election law—a law which he claimed would

[42] *Acts of Assembly,* 1948, pp. 704–6.

[43] Friddell, *What Is It about Virginia?*, p. 64; Latimer, "Virginia Politics," pp. 29–30.

[44] Byrd to Tuck, Mar. 16, 1948, Tuck Papers.

[45] Byrd suggested to the governor that "there is quite a lot of clarification that we must undertake," and Tuck concurred: "I intend to continue to hammer away on this" (Byrd to Tuck, Mar. 16, 1948, Tuck to Byrd, Mar. 19, 1948, ibid.).

"provide the plainest, simplest and most easily understood ballot in Virginia history." Much of the address, as it turned out, amounted to a broadside against the Truman civil rights program that had prompted the election law revision. In the impassioned, magniloquent phrases for which he was noted, the governor lambasted the national Democratic party. "Should we sit quietly by while a monstrous juggernaut, such as the FEPC, is foisted upon us by vote-hunting elements in all our national parties?" Tuck demanded rhetorically. He, for one, would not: "I shall follow a positive course, now, as the battle is joined, and this course will be pressed despite the blasts of New Deal flugelmen and political thimbleriggers whose principal interest in government is to leech from it the profits of political office. I seek no company with such lickspits and apostates of fundamental democracy who would destroy the principles which have made us strong and great."[46]

Antiorganization spokesmen, like the press, continued to heap abuse on the "anti-Truman" plan, with Lloyd Robinette, for example, claiming that it constituted the "assassination of the Democratic party in Virginia."[47] There were some liberal Democrats, however, who saw a silver lining to the cloud: the unpopularity of the legislation might force a significant number of moderate Democrats away from the Byrd crowd and into the antis' camp. The prospect was so appealing to one anti that while the bill was still pending, he advised Martin Hutchinson: "Don't fight Tuck's proposals too hard. I want the Assembly to adopt them so that we can go to the mat with them for what they did—not what they just tried to do." Hutchinson agreed that it did afford a "golden opportunity," and James P. Hart, another leading anti, concurred: "It is my considered opinion," he wrote, "that we have the opportunity in Virginia (thanks to the Tuck bill) to break the Southern revolt and force the reactionaries out of the Democratic party."[48] The Richmond *Times-Dispatch* echoed the theory that the

[46] Richmond *Times-Dispatch*, Mar. 19, 1948. Tuck had a penchant for the obscure word. It is probable that few of his listeners knew that a "flugelman" was, historically, a soldier placed in the front of a formation as the guide for the rest of the company, or that a "thimblerigger" was a cheater or swindler in games of chance. But they no doubt got his message.

[47] Ibid., Mar. 14, 1948.

[48] H. M. Sutherland to Hutchinson, Mar. 9, 1948, Hutchinson to Sutherland, Mar. 1, 1948, Hutchinson Papers; Hart to Hutchinson, Mar. 26, 1948, copy in Miller Papers.

organization had acted contrary to its own best interests, suggesting that the Byrd lieutenants "might be astonished to learn how many of their once-ardent supporters . . . are saying that this latest performance is too raw for them to swallow." One journalist surmised that "probably no other single action by the machine . . . galvanized the people into such instant and fiery resentment." Even certain organization leaders referred to the affair as a "spectacle" and admitted that it had left many of the faithful "considerably disturbed."[49]

The controversial measures prompted curiosity as to the real source and the real purpose of the legislation. Bill Tuck was more independent in his actions than most organization governors, as attested by his bold stand in the Vepco crisis and by his forthright approach to a tax increase.[50] It was with some justification that he was enraged by accusations that he was simply a myrmidon of Harry Byrd. However, in the matter of the "anti-Truman bill," it is apparent that Byrd was closely involved with its promulgation. Tuck insisted that he "didn't get any dictation from Washington," and the senator himself avowed that he had not seen the proposal before it was submitted to the legislature.[51] Yet, whether or not he had actually seen the draft of the bill, Byrd surely knew of its content and, indeed, seems to have initiated it. In a letter to Ebbie Combs on February 21, five days before Tuck presented the election bill to the General Assembly, Byrd said that he had talked with "quite a number of senators and congressmen in Washington and they think this message from Bill will have a tremendous effect and should be given the fullest national publicity. . . . Please keep closely in touch with it, as this action should be taken, certainly not later than the middle of the week."[52]

In the face of the vociferous outcry against the bill, Tuck made no effort to disclaim responsibility for it; rather, he steadfastly defended the measure. He freely admitted that the bill as originally drawn was a mistake; but after the emendations had been made, it was, he contended, a beneficial and "liberalized" election law. "The newspapers

---

[49] Richmond *Times-Dispatch*, Feb. 28, 1948; Phillips, "New Rumblings in the Old Dominion," p. 35; W. L. Prieur to Harry F. Byrd, April 7, 1948, copy in Tuck Papers; G. Fred Switzer to Burr Harrison, Mar. 16, 1948, copy in Byrd Papers.

[50] See Chapters 4 and 8.

[51] Interview with Tuck; Washington *Post*, Mar. 13, 1948, p. 9.

[52] Byrd to Combs, Feb. 21, 1948, Byrd Papers.

gave me hell," he later recalled, "but it wasn't as bad as they said it was."[53]

Opponents of the bill at the time claimed to perceive ulterior motives in the plan. Some felt that it was designed to promote Byrd's presidential aspirations. "If Harry Byrd wants the Democratic nomination for President," said Earle Lutz, the executive director of the state Republican party, "he should have the courage to announce his candidacy rather than use Governor Tuck's clumsy method." Others believed that the purpose was to set up machinery through which votes could be siphoned off from Truman to the advantage of a third-party candidate, a maneuver which would in effect aid the Republicans.[54]

Tuck professed to have no such specific schemes in mind. "It was just my idea," he later said, "to allow the Democratic party of Virginia to be able to say who the official nominee of the Democratic party of Virginia was. It wasn't my idea to keep anybody's name off the ballot."[55] Yet, whatever his proximal objective, Tuck did have a definite ultimate goal, even if the method of achieving it remained somewhat unclear. He explained it when, in defending the "anti-Truman" measure, he admitted, "This program was designed for one purpose only and that was to enable the people of Virginia to avoid insofar as possible the consequences of the iniquitous civil rights program as proposed by President Truman."[56] The success or failure of the strategy of Tuck and the Byrd organization would be determined as the presidential election of 1948 unfolded.

[53] Interview with Tuck.

[54] Richmond *Times-Dispatch*, Mar. 1, 1948; Frank D. Floyd to Martin A. Hutchinson, Mar. 1, 1948, Hutchinson Papers.

[55] Interview with Tuck. There is unmistakable evidence, however, that Senator Byrd wished to keep the names of the candidates off the ballot (confidential source).

[56] Richmond *Times-Dispatch*, Feb. 29, 1948.

Byrd-Tuck Democrats vs. National Democrats

7. *The Presidential Election of 1948*

The ["anti-Truman"] proposal gave opportunity to all our enemies from every direction to criticise and deliberately misstate facts. I think we all realize that we are in a very critical stage politically, and just what is going to happen is very difficult to forecast.

—Organization leader J. Frank Wysor

Byrd and Tuck have handed our side the state a good deal sooner than we could have taken it ourselves.

—Antiorganization leader George G. Martin

The Tuck "anti-Truman bill" was the first legislative action taken by any state in response to the Truman administration's civil rights program, and was widely interpreted as the precursor of a full-scale southern revolt. The New York *Times* construed the plan as an "indication that the solid Democratic South, its long-smouldering resentment of the national party organization whipped into flame by the President's civil rights message, wants the door left open for a walkout at the national convention if the turn of events calls for it." The *Times* was correct in its inference that the maneuver was motivated by a desire to initiate a movement which would resuscitate the South's influence within the Democratic party. "I hope the other Southern states will go along . . . in our effort to secure at least a measure of justice to the South," E. R. Combs confided to Senator Byrd. "If the Southern states will stick together and stand up for the things which we cannot surrender, we will be able to make our voice heard in the councils of the party, and those in high positions in the party will find that they cannot take us for granted any longer."[1]

---

[1] New York *Times*, Feb. 25, 1948, p. 15. Similar views were expressed by the

The response of southern political leaders to the Virginia plan was mixed. Liberal Florida Senator Claude Pepper denounced the ballot bill as a "brazen scheme," while Governors Millard Caldwell of Florida, R. Gregg Cherry of North Carolina, W. Preston Lane of Maryland, and Governor-elect Earl Long of Louisiana expressed varying degrees of approval. The heartiest response came from Arkansas Governor Ben Laney, who informed Tuck, "I appreciate what you are doing in Virginia about the whole matter. It appears now that we are very well prepared to battle this thing to the last ditch. Of course, we have a few weak-kneed brethren." Within a matter of days several southern states had initiated action emulating that proposed by Governor Tuck.[2]

There was little hint as to how Tuck and the Byrd organization intended to follow up the state's new election law once it was enacted. The governor did not appear eager to take an active part in a concerted southern attack on Truman. Although he voiced agreement with their general purpose, he declined to join a delegation of southern governors who met with Democratic National Committee Chairman J. Howard McGrath for the purpose of protesting the Truman civil rights program. Yet he continued to berate that program—calling it a "civil wrongs" program—and pledged that he would "co-operate, as my recent action demonstrates, . . . in resisting to the last this unwarranted invasion of the rights of the people."[3]

An interesting sidelight to the Tuck-Truman controversy occurred on April 2, 1948, when the two adversaries were brought face-to-face in Williamsburg to receive honorary degrees from the College of William and Mary. It was not the first meeting between the two; they had been introduced some nine months earlier when both had attended the investiture of Colgate Darden as president of the University of Virginia. At that time relations between them were friendly. Afterward Tuck complimented the president on his speech and noted that he

---

Washington *Post*, Feb. 28, 1948, and in "Southern Explosion," *Time* 51 (Mar. 8, 1948): 20. Combs to Byrd, Mar. 30, 1948, Byrd Papers.

[2] Laney to Tuck, Mar. 10, 1948, Tuck Executive Papers. For responses of other governors, see letters in Tuck Executive Papers and New York *Times*, Feb. 28, 1948. Helen Fuller, "The Fourth Party," *New Republic* 68 (Mar. 15, 1948): 9; "Southern Explosion," p. 20.

[3] Richmond *Times-Dispatch*, Feb. 23, Mar. 14, 1948.

Tuck with his sometime adversary, President Truman, in Charlottesville, 1947. (Courtesy of the Richmond *Times-Dispatch*)

had made a "most wonderful impression upon all our people and me." Truman, in a handwritten note, expressed equal pleasure. "I can't tell you what a grand time everybody had in Charlottesville," he wrote Tuck. "I think it was the most successful weekend we have spent." [4] (Later Tuck recalled that his initial impression of Truman was generally favorable, although he—himself no stranger to the salty phrase—had been somewhat surprised by the crudity of the president's language.) [5]

By the time of the Williamsburg meeting, feelings between the two were considerably less amicable. Truman's response to the "anti-Truman bill" had been surprisingly mild, even conciliatory. He claimed that he had been "too darned busy" to pay much attention to such political matters but, with reference to the Virginia action, conceded that each state had the "right to decide how elections should

[4] Tuck to Truman, July 8, 1947, Truman to Tuck, July 12, 1947, Tuck Executive Papers.

[5] Interview with Tuck.

Is This Virginia Democracy? (Courtesy of the Richmond *Times-Dispatch*)

be held within its own borders."[6] Nevertheless, some observers were apprehensive of the Williamsburg confrontation between the governor and the president. The Richmond *Times-Dispatch*, anticipating the meeting, drolly commented that "not since Nathaniel Bacon faced Governor Berkeley, Washington faced Cornwallis, Lee faced McClellan, and 'Choo-Choo Charlie' Justice faced 'Jack' Cloud, have two such notable adversaries met on the Virginia peninsula as will face one

[6] New York *Times*, Mar. 2, 1948, p. 6; Washington *Post*, Mar. 5, 1948, p. 25; "Southern Explosion," p. 21.

another there on April 2." From Washington, Senator Byrd cast a wary eye on the proposed encounter, admitting that he was "wondering how Bill and the President will get along." Tuck, in retrospect, regarded the furor surrounding his meeting with Truman as ludicrous. Some of the people, he recalled, "must have been crazy—thought I was going to shoot him or something."[7]

The meeting, as it turned out, was uneventful, as the governor graciously declined to take the advice of one friend to "kick Truman in the pants . . . when you meet him in Williamsburg." According to the New York *Times*, the ceremony produced no trace of the dispute over Truman's civil rights program, and the relations between the presumable antagonists were cordial. At one point reporters tried to egg the two men, bedecked in their academic regalia, into a dispute. "Oh, I don't guess we'll fight, will we, Governor?" asked Truman; to which Tuck riposted, "Not in these clothes!"[8]

The civility which Tuck evinced at Williamsburg did not mean that his opposition to Truman's politics had softened. Within a week after the meeting took place, Tuck delivered a major attack on the president's civil rights plan. Speaking nationwide over the Mutual Broadcasting System, the governor proclaimed that the "vote-chasing pseudo-liberals who arouse feelings of discontent, distrust and antagonism are the greatest enemies of the Negro. They care nothing for the Negro, North or South, except to use him as a vehicle for their own political preferment." He then issued the South's usual "leave-us-alone, we-know-what's best" appeal:

There is a vast difference between segregation and discrimination. The South contends that segregation promotes racial integrity, not discrimination. I have stated often and I want to repeat now that the individual states are fully competent to solve these matters. Outside interference and dictation will serve only to jeopardize the good relationships that now exist and to make more difficult the solution of the few remaining problems between the races.[9]

[7] Richmond *Times-Dispatch*, Mar. 11, 1948; Byrd to E. R. Combs, April 2, 1948, Byrd Papers; interview with Tuck. Justice and Cloud were college football stars of the period.

[8] John P. Wilkerson to Tuck, Mar. 31, 1948, Tuck Papers; New York *Times*, April 3, 1948, p. 1; Friddell, *What Is It about Virginia?*, p. 64.

[9] Richmond *Times-Dispatch*, April 7, 1948. The speech was the last in a series of

Senator Byrd, "Chief" Ebbie Combs, and Governor Tuck at the 1948 Democratic National Convention in Philadelphia. (Courtesy of the Richmond *Times-Dispatch*)

Such rhetoric suggested that Tuck was ready to plunge headlong into the South's stop-Truman drive. His private statements gave further evidence that he was amenable to that campaign. Writing to Mississippi Governor Fielding Wright, a leader to the attempt to dump Truman, Tuck expressed deep interest in the movement and commented that he believed his views to be "in absolute and complete accord" with Wright's.[10]

However, when on May 10, 1948, dissident southern Democrats assembled in Jackson, Mississippi, to plot a "states' rights" strategy, Tuck was notably absent, as were Byrd and all ranking members of the Virginia organization. The main accomplishment of the Jackson meeting (which constituted the embryo of the Dixiecrat party) was the decision to assemble again in Birmingham if the Democratic national convention in mid-July should choose a candidate or write a platform inimical to southern demands. Tuck's response to news of the actions

three broadcasts made under the auspices of a group of twenty-one southern senators in response to the report of the President's Committee on Civil Rights.

[10] Tuck to Wright, Mar. 24, 1948, Tuck Executive Papers.

taken in Jackson was noncommittal, but the Richmond *Times-Dispatch* believed that he was sympathetic to the decision of the disaffected Democrats. "It appeared a good bet," said the paper, "that if the Philadelphia [national] convention endorsed a Truman-plus-civil-rights platform, some Virginia Democrats would be on hand for the Birmingham convention July 17, and that Governor Tuck would be among them."[11]

Developments during the following weeks cast doubt upon the *Times-Dispatch*'s forecast. Neither Tuck nor any other organization leader took overt steps in support of the anti-Truman revolt; few spoke approvingly about the possibility of repudiating Truman, and some, in off-the-record comments, predicted that most Virginia Democrats would eventually support the national ticket even if it included Truman. Speculation on the eve of the state Democratic convention was that Virginia would not join in the growing southern crusade against Truman, and that the convention itself would be harmonious. "Resentment exists," opined the Richmond *News Leader*, "but outwardly peace will reign."[12]

Any semblance of peace was dispelled almost before the delegates had settled down in Richmond's Mosque auditorium. In the opening address of the convention, State Chairman Horace Edwards startled the assemblage by coming out foursquare against a Virginia bolt at the national convention and, by inference, against the Byrd organization's attitude toward the Truman administration. "We should not, in this childish way, pick up our marbles and go home," admonished Edwards in a rousing flurry of clichés. "Common sense teaches that we gain nothing by jumping from the problematical frying pan into a certain fire." Keynote speaker W. Tayloe Murphy took a decidedly different tack, assailing the national administration and praising the course taken by the "capable and fearless Governor Tuck."[13]

[11] Richmond *Times-Dispatch*, May 12, 1948.
[12] Ibid., May 23, 1948; Richmond *News Leader*, July 2, 1948.
[13] Richmond *Times-Dispatch*, July 3, 1948. Antiorganization Democrats, who might have been expected to applaud Edwards's stand, tended to be skeptical of his sincerity and his motivation. "I trust that independent Democrats will not be fooled by the sudden enthusiasm of Horace Edwards for the preservation of the Democratic party as a national institution," wrote Martin Hutchinson. "He is now a candidate for governor and, of course, wants to get behind him [antiorganization support]"

Love Somebody But I Won't Say Who. (Courtesy of the Richmond *Times-Dispatch*)

With dissension already rife in the cavernous hall, the report of the resolutions committee touched off a full-scale explosion. The report, which had been hammered out during nearly three hours of deliberation, was presented to the convention by Governor Tuck, who had chaired the committee. The package of resolutions contained items condemning the Truman civil rights plan, reaffirming the principle of states' rights, and instructing delegates to the Philadelphia convention

---

(Martin A. Hutchinson to Curry P. Hutchinson, July 8, 1948, Hutchinson Papers). Edwards did, in fact, run for governor (unsuccessfully) in 1949.

to oppose inclusion of a civil rights plank in the national platform and
to vote by the "unit rule." In one surprising resolution, the Virginia
delegation was instructed to support Dwight D. Eisenhower for the
presidential nomination. Most significantly, in accord with the provisions of the new election law, one resolution called for the reconvening
of the state convention if the national convention should nominate a
candidate distasteful to the South.[14]

As soon as he had completed his presentation, Tuck moved adoption
of the resolutions in toto. The convention's permanent chairman, and
the newly elected state Democratic chairman, G. Alvin Massenburg,
called for a voice vote which he decided in the affirmative, despite the
claims of numerous observers that the negative response was equal, or
greater, in volume. The turmoil which ensued was most uncharacteristic of an organization-dominated state convention. Amid angry cries of
dissent, Massenburg recognized two speakers who voiced opposition to
his handling of the resolutions vote, then gaveled the debate to an end.
Some delegates cheered Massenburg's actions, but many booed lustily
and shouted defiance; some stalked out of the auditorium.[15] With such
unseemly discord did the 1948 Democratic state convention come to
an end.

Antiorganization leaders were outraged by the conduct of the convention, especially by the handling of the resolutions vote. Massenburg, in particular, was cited for a "revolting performance" and
condemned for his "arrogant and dictatorial manner."[16] As they often
tried to do, the antis took what satisfaction they could from the
possibility that the intraparty brouhaha would hasten the demise of the
Byrd hegemony. Lloyd Robinette summed it up: "The debacle at
Richmond on July 2, and the reaction brought about by it, have
frightened the Byrd gang, as they were not accustomed to any dissen-

---

[14] Richmond *Times-Dispatch*, July 3, 1948. The bulk of the resolutions committee's work was done by a subcommittee appointed and chaired by Tuck. The
membership of the subcommittee resembled an "honor roll" of organization lieutenants including Byrd "insiders" William T. Reed, Jr., J. Frank Wysor, W. Marshall
King, Collins Denny, Jr., and Harry F. Byrd, Jr.

[15] Ibid., July 3, 4, 1948.

[16] Harrison Mann to Tuck, July 8, 1948, Mann to G. Alvin Massenburg, July 8,
1948, Tuck Executive Papers. Tuck privately defended Massenburg's actions as
"proper, and wholly in order" (Tuck to B. C. Garrett, Jr., July 8, 1948, ibid.).

sion in their own ranks. . . . Massenburg made an ass of himself completely. . . . His ignorant handling of the convention has brought about a split in the organization which I feel will be more or less permanent."[17]

The state's leading newspapers joined the antiorganization spokesmen in decrying the machinations of the convention. To the Richmond *Times-Dispatch* the affair was a "ghastly flop" and a "glaring example of steamroller machine tactics." The Norfolk *Virginian-Pilot* emphasized the adverse effect of the proceedings on the Byrd faction, claiming that "if the Virginia Democratic machine had deliberately set out to sow this confusion and promote this family dissension, it could not have made a better job of it." The Richmond *News Leader* was more precise in its postmortem. "Truth is," said the paper, "the Democratic state machine is in worse general condition than it has been at any time since the unhappy days of 1936–37, when nobody was willing to take the field against Jim Price."[18] Indeed, with the state convention fiasco opening new wounds to exacerbate the scars left by the battle over the "anti-Truman bill," the Byrd organization faced the 1948 presidential campaign with unwonted trepidation.

Antiorganization leaders began early to try to capitalize on the organization's distress. Even before the election bill was introduced, Martin Hutchinson had hinted privately that a challenge to the Byrd forces might be made over the issue of the organization's attitude toward the Democratic nominee for president in the coming campaign; by March he was tentatively advocating that the antis send a separate delegation to the Philadelphia convention.[19]

Following the enactment of the Tuck election law, antiorganization spokesmen raised the issue of the state Democratic party loyalty oath—a pledge which, theoretically, bound all Democratic candidates for office and all members of party committees to support all nominees of the Democratic party in general elections. The question raised by the antis was whether, under terms of the new election law, Virginia

[17] Robinette to Martin A. Hutchinson, July 23, 1948, Hutchinson Papers.

[18] Richmond *Times-Dispatch*, July 4, 1948; Norfolk *Virginian-Pilot*, July 8, 1948; Richmond *News Leader*, July 3, 1948.

[19] Hutchinson to Francis Pickens Miller, Jan. 8, 1948, Hutchinson to James H. Barger, Mar. 16, 1948, Hutchinson to James D. Franklin, Mar. 18, 1948, Hutchinson Papers.

Democrats would be obligated to support the presidential nominee of the national party. The matter of party loyalty was not new in Virginia, having first arisen in 1928 when many Democrats were frightened by the pope and demon rum into voting for Hoover rather than Al Smith. At that time state Attorney General John R. Saunders—displaying a nimble, if not completely logical, legal mind—ruled that the Virginia Democratic loyalty oath applied only to state elections and did not demand party regularity in presidential elections; Saunders's opinion was upheld in 1939 by Attorney General Staples. In April 1948 Attorney General Almond disappointed the antis by reiterating the judgments of his predecessors that the loyalty oath was not, in fact, binding with respect to national elections; hence, Byrd Democrats could support whomever they pleased for president and still remain party members in good standing in Virginia.[20]

Having been thus rebuffed, antiorganization activists decided to take their case to the officials of the national Democratic party. At the opening of the Philadelphia convention in mid-July, a delegation led by Martin Hutchinson, Francis Pickens Miller, and Alexandria attorney Henry Fowler appeared before the credentials committee to request, not that the regular Virginia delegation be unseated, but that all members of the convention be required to sign an oath to support the party's nominees in November. The committee hearing was volatile and produced a particularly bitter exchange between Hutchinson and state Senator M. M. Long, a Byrd partisan who was a member of the credentials committee. Long branded Hutchinson "a disgruntled, disappointed, defeated office-seeker" and charged, "The 'bolt' talk comes only as a straw-man boogeyboo put out by Mr. Hutchinson with an apparent hope of attaining some publicity . . . that might attract some voters to his own threatened 'bolt' in the next Senatorial campaign." Hutchinson retorted that he was "getting tired of these people masquerading as Democrats and using the Democratic party as an escalator to get across the Potomac and vote Republican 65 per cent of the time."[21]

[20] Richmond *Times-Dispatch*, April 26, 1948; Latimer, "Virginia Politics," pp. 30–31.

[21] Richmond *Times-Dispatch*, July 14, 1948. Hutchinson had run unsuccessfully against Byrd for the United States Senate in 1946.

Neither Byrd nor Tuck offered comment on the challenge, beyond the governor's statement that "our credentials speak for themselves." The credentials committee apparently agreed with Tuck, as they turned down the insurgents' request. According to the chairman of the committee, Senator Carl Hatch of New Mexico, "We didn't have the power to require the Virginia delegation to do what Mr. Hutchinson asked us to do." [22] With that decision the Byrd organization won the credentials battle at the very outset of the convention. It was the last victory it was to win in Philadelphia.

The convention opened with a noticeable absence of the hoopla customarily attendant to such events. The Democrats' lack of enthusiasm was understandable. Public dissatisfaction in many areas—the economy, organized labor, foreign affairs—provided the Republicans with inviting and (as the 1946 congressional elections had proved) vulnerable targets. Truman's falling personal popularity added to the disconsolation. "Measured against the towering memories of F.D.R.," wrote one historian, Truman "had always been a puny figure. There was no commanding presence about him. . . . The only emotion he seemed to arouse was ennui." [23] Small wonder it was that the convention manifested, as journalist Alistair Cooke reported, "all the sobriety of a state funeral and the morbid petulance of a suicide pact." One anonymous delegate summed up the general feeling of despair. "There's nothing left for us now," he moaned, "but the consolations of our Gideon Bible." [24]

It is improbable that any delegation entered the convention more downcast than the Byrd-dominated group from Virginia. Organization leaders had hoped earlier in the year that Truman would be removed from contention before the national convention arrived. Both Byrd and E. R. Combs were confident that such would be the case. "I think Truman is certainly losing out," wrote Byrd, "and I cannot see how he can sustain himself. . . . Every day someone comes out against

[22] Ibid., July 12, 1948; Richmond *News Leader*, July 13, 1948.

[23] Ross, *Loneliest Campaign*, p. 4. Reflecting what appeared to be the prevailing sentiment were signs throughout the convention hall reading, "We're Just Mild about Harry" (Robert Bendiner, "Route of the Bourbons," *Nation* 167 [July 24, 1948]: 91). See also William G. Carleton, "The Dilemma of the Democrats," *Virginia Quarterly Review* 24 (Summer 1948): 336–53.

[24] Richmond *Times-Dispatch*, July 13, 1948.

him, or for someone else, but no one comes out for him." Combs agreed: "It is hard to conceive of the Democratic national convention nominating a candidate for President who everybody agrees has not the remotest chance to be elected." As late as July, Governor Tuck expressed his hope that "the Philadelphia Democratic convention will recognize the folly of renominating Truman."[25]

The attempt to stop Truman crystallized in a movement to secure the nomination for Dwight D. Eisenhower. The so-called "Eisencrats" were led by James Roosevelt and included such diverse political types as New York Mayor William O'Dwyer, South Carolina Governor Strom Thurmond, Minneapolis Mayor Hubert Humphrey, and New Jersey's political czar, Frank Hague. Governor Tuck, who had been instrumental in instructing the Virginia delegation for "Ike," was receptive to Roosevelt's plan.[26] When a call went out inviting delegates to a pro-Eisenhower caucus at the Philadelphia convention, Tuck's name was listed among the cosigners. The movement came to naught, however, when Eisenhower, after weeks of disclaiming interest in the nomination, finally issued a firm refusal, and the proposed caucus was canceled.[27]

With their most viable candidate no longer in the running, the southern opponents of Truman scheduled a "Dixie caucus" for July 11, to try to select an alternative. Harry Byrd and E. R. Combs did not attend the caucus, and A. Willis Robertson made only a brief appearance. Tuck, who said he attended "mostly just to listen," was persuaded by other southern leaders to sit on the speaker's platform, but during a fervid oration by South Carolina Governor Strom Thurmond, he absented himself, not to return. He was at some pains afterward to

[25] Byrd to Combs, Mar. 31, 1948, Combs to Byrd, Mar. 23, 1948, Byrd Papers; Tuck to Joseph M. Tusing, July 2, 1948, Tuck Executive Papers.

[26] See James Roosevelt to Tuck, July 3, 6, 1948, Tuck Executive Papers. Martin Hutchinson begged Roosevelt "not to form an alliance of any sort . . . with the enemies of your father whom we loved and admired so much." As he told a friend, "I felt that someone in Virginia ought to let young Roosevelt know with whom he proposed to deal in Virginia" (Richmond *Times-Dispatch*, July 7, 1948; Hutchinson to E. H. McConnell, July 8, 1948, Hutchinson Papers).

[27] The abortive Eisenhower "boom" is discussed in Michael H. Ebner, "The Emergence of Dwight D. Eisenhower as a Presidential Candidate, 1943–1952" (M.A. thesis, U.Va., 1966), pp. 20–33; and in Robert Shogun, "1948 Election," *American Heritage* 19 (June 1968): 30–31.

explain that his early departure was owing to a long-standing dinner engagement and did not imply a rejection of the "Dixie caucus." Nonetheless, his lack of enthusiasm, and that of other Virginia delegates, was apparent.[28]

Since the Virginia caucus was closed to the press, it was not until the nominating speeches were made that the decision of the state's delegation was revealed. At the conclusion of the speech nominating Georgia Senator Richard Russell, Governor Tuck, chairman of the delegation, grabbed the Virginia standard and, amid a flourish of Confederate flags and the strains of "Dixie," led Senator Byrd and the rest of the state contingent around the auditorium. Passing by the still-seated North Carolina delegation, Tuck stopped and cheerfully exhorted Governor Cherry and his fellows to "come on in with the sound doctrine people." Cherry only smiled and shook his head. At another point in the jubilant procession Tuck was reported to have laughed, "If the South goes to hell, we want to go with her!" When the roll-call vote reached Virginia, the governor, who had seconded Russell's nomination, yielded the microphone to Byrd, who announced, "Virginia casts 26 votes for my beloved colleague and desk mate in the United States Senate, Senator Dick Russell."[29]

The demonstration for Russell, futile though it was, marked the only occasion which the Virginia delegates had for celebration. Truman was nominated on the first ballot by a vote of 947½ to 263 over Russell. Adding philosophical insult to tangible injury was the fact that the convention, after a tumultous floor fight, also adopted by a narrow margin a strong civil rights plank for its national platform.[30] The whole affair made an accurate seer of Ebbie Combs, who, just before the opening of the convention, had commented gloomily, "The situation does not look very encouraging to me. I am afraid that the convention will not only nominate candidates wholly unsatisfactory to the South, but that they will include in the platform some or all of the

[28] Richmond *Times-Dispatch*, July 12, 1948.
[29] Ibid.
[30] The struggle over the civil rights plank nearly sundered the convention, and did lead to the walk-out of delegates from Alabama and Mississippi (Shogun, "1948 Election," p. 104; Ross, *Loneliest Campaign*, pp. 120–29). Harry Truman discussed the impact of his civil rights proposals upon the convention in his *Memoirs*, vol. 2, *Years of Trial and Hope* (Garden City, N.Y.: Doubleday, 1956), pp. 179–87.

programs to which the South is bitterly opposed. If both these things are done the Southern Democrats will really be in a bad spot." [31]

The Virginia delegation left Philadelphia dispirited. Byrd referred to it as a "terrible experience," and Combs, who went home early, wrote that "the final session of the convention must have been very humiliating to all Southerners, and I am glad that I personally was not subjected to this severe punishment." The Richmond *Times-Dispatch* in an editorial, "A Gettysburg for Dixie," commended the state delegation for not bolting the convention, but concluded: "All in all, the Virginians and their Southern cohorts who invaded Pennsylvania early this week have sustained a political Gettysburg comparable to that which occurred on the battlefield almost exactly 85 years ago. . . . It was nothing less than complete defeat." Governor Tuck sadly was forced to agree. "We were soundly thrashed," he admitted, "on every issue in the convention." [32]

The series of reversals suffered by the Byrd forces earlier in 1948 meant that the role of the organization in the presidential election took on critical significance. It was quickly apparent that the organization did not intend to give overt support to the States' Rights, or Dixiecrat, party. When the southern dissidents convened in Birmingham in the week following the national Democratic convention, no Virginia politician of stature was present in an official capacity. Richmond attorney Collins Denny, Jr., attended the rump session but insisted that he did not represent Governor Tuck, Virginia Democrats, or "anyone but Collins Denny, Jr." [33] Organization antagonist Lloyd

[31] Combs to Byrd, July 8, 1948, Byrd Papers.

[32] Byrd to Combs, July 19, 1948, Combs to Byrd, July 16, 1948, ibid.; Richmond *Times-Dispatch*, July 15, 1948; Tuck to L. Preston Collins, July 16, 1948, Tuck Executive Papers.

[33] Richmond *Times-Dispatch*, July 17, 1948. Another account noted that the Virginia "delegation" amounted to no more than several University of Virginia students, a woman returning to Virginia from New Orleans, and two passersby. Apparently the convention was filled, as one observer claimed, "by the simple device of accrediting anyone who chose to attend, whether he had a genuine following in his home state or merely happened to be traveling through Birmingham . . . and felt like hearing some Southern-fried oratory" (Roebuck, "Virginia in the Election of 1948," p. 46; *Nation* 167 [July 24, 1948]: 85).

Robinette had a different interpretation. "He claimed he went on his own hook," he said of Denny,

> but this was not true. He was sent as an emissary by the machine in Virginia. He carried tidings of encouragement with assurances that the way for a Dixiecrat ticket would be made easy in the November election in Virginia. There is no doubt in my mind that such a ticket will be in the field in Virginia, and that while no recall of the convention will be made, and this bunch will be clothed with apparent regularity, they will support the Dixiecrat ticket in November. We may just as well get that straight.[34]

If Denny actually represented the Byrd organization, it was a well-kept secret. According to Cabell Phillips, Byrd "not only stayed away but refused to let any of [his] henchmen attend." As to the work of the Dixiecrat convention—which nominated Strom Thurmond for president and Fielding Wright for vice-president—Governor Tuck, who did represent organization thinking, had only a terse "no comment."[35]

The organization's lack of outward enthusiasm for the Dixiecrat movement was by no means tantamount to supporting Truman. The possibility of reconvening the state convention for the purpose of instructing Virginia electors would remain until September, thereby leaving an alternative open. It was the opinion of Martin Hutchinson that the Byrd leadership would "hope for something to happen which will give them justification for the use of the Tuck law." Privately, Governor Tuck made suggestions that indicated the validity of Hutchinson's assumptions. Writing to Lieutenant Governor Pat Collins, Tuck asserted that the nomination of Truman might "serve to impress on the people of Virginia the real meaning of our efforts in the General Assembly last winter and possibly [show] that there was more merit to our position than some at that time realized." To Byrd he was even more explicit. "I have made no public statement or indicated my position," he wrote. "For the present, I believe it best to have nothing to say . . . [but] if the trend continues the way it appears headed now, there might be spontaneous sentiment for a second convention."[36]

34 Robinette to Martin A. Hutchinson, July 19, 1948, Hutchinson Papers.
35 Phillips, *Truman Presidency*, p. 223; Richmond *Times-Dispatch*, July 17, 1948.
36 "Memorandum for Senator Robinette," dated July 19, 1948, copy in Hutchin-

The organization found itself in a quandary, not so much because of ideological as because of practical political problems; that is, the Byrd leadership, in devising its strategy for the presidential campaign, had to consider the potential effect of its actions on the congressional races in the state, since seven of the nine Democratic congressmen faced Republican opposition in November. In addition, Senator Robertson was to be challenged for the seat which he held as the interim successor to the late Carter Glass. In the Democratic primary Robertson easily defeated Roanoke attorney James P. Hart, an inexperienced antiorganization hopeful who in his campaign had made much of Robertson's alleged support of the "anti-Truman" measure—which Hart preferred to call the "freedom-snatching Tuck bill." [37] In the general election Robertson would face a more serious challenge from Robert Woods, a respected Republican who was state chairman of his party.

Such considerations presented the Byrd hierarchy with a perplexing choice as it contemplated the presidential campaign. On the one hand, it was believed that failure to give some support to the Dixiecrats, or at least to ensure that the States' Rights ticket was on the Virginia ballot, would be detrimental to the organization's candidates because, as E. R. Combs put it, "many of our best friends . . . will either vote for the candidates nominated at Birmingham or will refrain from voting at all. The fact that so many Democrats in Virginia probably will refuse to go to the election because they cannot vote for Truman may endanger the election of two or three of our candidates for Congress." Another organization leader reiterated that view. "Robertson and all our candidates for Congress have to be considered," he said. "Generally speaking I think the Southern Ticket on the Virginia ballot will bring out a number of people who will otherwise not come to the polls. In most cases these people will vote for our candidates for Congress." [38]

On the other hand, the failure to endorse the national Democratic

son Papers; Tuck to Collins, July 16, 1948, Tuck Executive Papers; Tuck to Byrd, July 17, 1948, Byrd Papers.

[37] Richmond *Times-Dispatch*, May 11, 1948. The Hart-Robertson contest is discussed in more detail in Crawley, "Governor William Munford Tuck," pp. 418–22.

[38] Combs to Harry F. Byrd, July 24, 1948, J. Frank Wysor to Byrd, July 21, 1948, Byrd Papers.

ticket might result in the loss of support from antiorganization Democrats, some of whom threatened their own "bolt" if the Byrd faction did not come out for the Truman-Barkley ticket. Said Curry P. Hutchinson, "I for one am not going to stand by and see local candidates taken care of and the national ticket slaughtered. We also can split tickets, and the only way to fight the devil is with fire." Lloyd Robinette took the matter directly to the man whose personal stake was probably greatest, Senator Robertson. "I must say to you very frankly," he warned, "that I find many Democrats all over this section who feel that this is a game that two can play at, and many of them are openly expressing themselves that if the leadership of the Democratic party refuses to come out for Truman and Barkley, ... it may mean your defeat in Virginia."[39]

Insofar as the presidential contest alone was concerned, organization leaders knew that the practical effect of supporting Thurmond would be to aid the Republican Thomas E. Dewey. Although Byrd Democrats had little compunction about voting with Republicans in Congress, they were not particularly fond of Dewey, who, on the key issue of civil rights was so acceptable to blacks that he was endorsed by both major Negro newspapers in Virginia.[40]

Also to be taken into account by the organization's brain trust was the fact that many Virginians, rant though they might about the iniquity of the national party, ultimately regarded themselves as loyal Democrats, and as such preferred to support the national ticket. One leading state Democrat, cognizant of that fact, suggested to Byrd that the situation in 1948 was analogous to the 1928 election when many Virginia Democrats found the party's nominee, Al Smith, repugnant, but the organization supported him nevertheless. Byrd rejected such a contention, claiming that "the Democrats of Virginia could make an honorable fight for Smith, because we believed in most of the things for which he stood. The same situation does not exist today." Still, the cautious senator realized that overly aggressive action against Truman was fraught with danger. As one anonymous, but prominent, Demo-

---

[39] Curry P. Hutchinson to Martin A. Hutchinson, Aug. 25, 1948, Robinette to Robertson, Sept. 19, 1948, copy, Hutchinson Papers.

[40] Roebuck, "Virginia in the Election of 1948," p. 60; Shogun, "1948 Election," p. 109.

crat put it, "If they call that convention back into session to nominate another ticket, it will bust the party wide open."[41]

Clearly in a difficult position, the organization finally decided to do what it frequently did: nothing. Ebbie Combs outlined the policy in bold terms to Senator Byrd. "I feel that you, the Governor and other recognized leaders of the organization should probably decline to make a public statement with reference to the national situation," he counseled. "In other words I feel that it might be best for us to try to get through this campaign somewhat as we did in 1944."[42] Generally Combs's advice was followed during the late summer months, as Byrd and most of the high echelon figures in the organization lapsed into a studied "golden silence." The passing of the sixty-day preelection deadline on September 2 meant that the Democratic electors on the Virginia ballot would be pledged automatically to Truman.

Evidence that the Byrd hierarchy intended to pursue a neutral course right up to the election was provided by a meeting of the state Democratic Central Committee on September 25. In a session lasting barely half an hour, the organization-dominated committee merely passed two innocuous resolutions; no mention was made of any presidential candidate. Proponents of Truman and Thurmond each tried to address the committee in an effort to secure official party endorsement but were denied the right to speak by Chairman Massenburg. The pro-Truman group, with Robert Whitehead as its chief spokesman, was outraged. In a statement signed by several notable antis, they denounced Massenburg's actions as being "in keeping with the high-handed manner in which the recent state convention was conducted by this same gentleman" and went on to warn, "If the state Central Committee fails to do its duty by the entire Democratic ticket, they will be held accountable by the Democrats of Virginia."[43]

The actions of the Central Committee—interpreted by the Richmond *Times-Dispatch* as providing a "green light for Virginia bolters"—served to strengthen the long-standing suspicions of antiorganization Democrats that the Byrd leadership intended to do little for

[41] John J. Wicker to Byrd, July 16, 1948, Byrd to E. R. Combs, July 19, 1948, Byrd Papers; Richmond *Times-Dispatch*, July 15, 1948.
[42] Combs to Byrd, Aug. 9, 1948, Byrd Papers.
[43] Richmond *Times-Dispatch*, Sept. 26, 27, 1948.

the national ticket. They further sensed that the issue of supporting Truman might be used as an instrument for realigning the state party. James Hart envisioned such a possibility early when he suggested that "Virginians have a great sense of party regularity . . . toward the national Democratic party. Therefore, I am convinced that if handled properly, a truly Democratic party can be formed in Virginia and we can discredit the Byrd-Tuck-Robertson machine."[44]

Consequently, with less than one month remaining before the general election, a Straight Democratic Ticket Committee was formed. The nucleus of the committee was composed of the leading antiorganization men: Robert Whitehead was chosen as chairman and Martin Hutchinson as campaign chairman. Among the most active workers were such stalwart antis as Francis Pickens Miller, Lloyd Robinette, H. Mayno Sutherland, Joseph Harrison, and E. H. McConnell; Alexandria attorney Henry Fowler served as the primary liaison with Democratic National Chairman J. Howard McGrath. In the short time that remained to them, the Straight Ticket Committee put on an active campaign, sponsoring several rallies, buying time for radio addresses, and sending out numerous letters and brochures. At first the committee was rebuffed in its effort to obtain funds from the national committee, which apparently feared that such aid would offend the Byrd organization, whose support was still desired. Eventually, when it became clear that the Byrd faction was not going to assist Truman's candidacy, the national party headquarters did make a small sum available to the Virginia Straight Ticket Committee.[45]

The Truman boosters declared that the Byrd organization was covertly backing Thurmond. As Martin Hutchinson informed McGrath, "The Dixiecrat organization seems to have plenty of money and it has the silent support of the Byrd-Tuck-Combs machine here in Virginia." It is difficult to ascertain to what extent Hutchinson's claim was valid. The formal States' Rights group in Virginia did not include any prominent organization figures. The chairman of the state party,

[44] Ibid., Sept. 27, 1948; Hart to Martin A. Hutchinson, Mar. 15, 1948, Hutchinson Papers.

[45] Elizabeth C. Williams, "The Anti-Byrd Movement in Virginia, 1948–1949" (M.A. thesis, U.Va., 1969), pp. 21–25; Roebuck, "Virginia in the Election of 1948," pp. 69–72.

Frank P. Burton of Patrick County, and the executive director, Frank Richeson of Richmond, had both been elected to the state Senate in 1947, but neither was an appreciable power within the organization. Most of the leaders of the Dixiecrat party were not from the Southside, the political base of the Byrd hegemony.[46] From all appearances, then, it seems that the organization took no active part in behalf of the State's Righters. According to one student of the movement, "Senator Byrd and Governor Tuck . . . contributed to the ideology but did not become actionists."[47]

Whatever furtive activities they may have been engaged in, no leaders of the Byrd organization openly supported the States' Rights ticket. Senator Byrd remained inscrutable, as he had in 1944 when he prompted the sobriquet, "the Buddha of Berryville."[48] Some ranking organization figures openly endorsed Truman, though usually without much enthusiasm; among them were Third District Congressman J. Vaughan Gary, state Senator John S. Battle, and, significantly, Senator Robertson, whose candidacy for reelection was widely interpreted as a prime factor in preventing an outright organization bolt from the Democratic national ticket. Of all the organization leaders who endorsed Truman, the one who spoke out the most emphatically, and the most colorfully, was Attorney General Almond. In a remarkable speech delivered in Norfolk, he exclaimed: "The only sane and constructive course to follow is to remain in the house of our fathers—even though the roof leaks and there may be bats in the belfry, rats in the pantry, a cockroach waltz in the kitchen, and skunks in the parlor. . . . We cannot take our inheritance and depart into a far country. Where shall we go and to what shall we return?"[49]

[46] Hutchinson to McGrath, Oct. 18, 1948, Hutchinson Papers; Roebuck, "Virginia in the Election of 1948," pp. 55–58. It is Roebuck's thesis that the Byrd forces were restrained from giving more support to the Dixiecrats out of fear that the state Dixiecrat leaders might parlay a good election showing by Thurmond into a rival political machine.

[47] Sarah McCulloh Lemmon, "The Ideology of the 'Dixiecrat' Movement," *Social Forces* 30 (Dec. 1951): 169. Lemmon points out that with the exception of the Crump machine in Louisiana, most state machines did not repudiate the national ticket, mainly for reasons of patronage.

[48] Fishwick, *New Look at the Old Dominion*, p. 251.

[49] Wilkinson, *Harry Byrd*, p. 135.

The organization wheelhorse who came closest to leaving the "house of his fathers" was Bill Tuck. Always a staunch defender of states' rights in theory, Tuck found the Dixiecrat movement even more appealing in the heat of rising racial tensions in his native Southside.[50] When Strom Thurmond appeared in Richmond to speak, he was given an adulatory introduction by the governor. "Mr. Tuck did everything except flatly urge support for Mr. Thurmond," said the *Times-Dispatch*. "The only rational conclusion anybody can draw . . . is that he intends to vote for Thurmond for President. It would seem, furthermore, that he was encouraging others to do likewise." In a subsequent speech, Tuck gave vent to the sort of passions which stoked the Dixiecrat campaign when, discarding his prepared text, he exclaimed, "If the people in New Jersey, or some other place, want to eat with the Negroes, sleep with them, and marry them, it's all right with me, but I don't want anybody coming down here to tell this state how to attend to its business."[51]

On the eve of the election the outcome of the presidential contest in Virginia was still very much in doubt. The States' Rights workers had not succeeded in stirring sufficient enthusiasm for Thurmond to have a chance of carrying the state, but it was believed quite possible that the Dixiecrats would attract enough votes away from Truman to throw the state to Dewey. Still, no Republican candidate since Reconstruction, with the exception of Hoover in 1928, had won the state's electoral vote, and the antiorganization Democrats remained optimistic about Truman's chances. Assaying Virginia, and predicting a close election, political analyst Kenneth Crawford concluded in *Time* magazine that the outcome of the contest might demonstrate that "the state already is less conservative than Byrd, less Southern than Thurmond, and farther from the Civil War than the Daughters of the Confederacy like to think."[52]

The election returns proved Crawford to have been perceptive. Insofar as the congressional races were concerned, the organization's strategy appeared to have been successful, for all Byrd-backed candi-

---

[50] See Roebuck, "Virginia in the Election of 1948," pp. 73–74.

[51] Richmond *Times-Dispatch*, Oct. 11, 16, 1948. Conspicuously present at the Richmond rally was Mrs. Harry F. Byrd.

[52] Kenneth Crawford, "Gone with the Dominion," *Time* 52 (Nov. 1, 1948): 25.

dates were elected. In the most important statewide race, Senator Robertson overwhelmed Republican Robert Woods by a vote of 253,865 to 119,366. However, in the presidential contest, Truman triumphed by amassing 200,786 out of 419,256 popular votes cast, or 47.9 percent of the total vote; Dewey received 41.0 percent, while Thurmond garnered a meager 10.4 percent. Only three congressional districts went for Dewey: the Sixth, Seventh, and Eighth. In the Second District (the Norfolk area) Truman piled up a margin of almost two to one, and in the Fourth District (rural Southside) he held an advantage of approximately five to two.[53] The Dixiecrat vote was surprisingly low but was distributed, as expected, most heavily in the Southside where the concentration of blacks was highest. One deviation from that pattern was the relatively large vote which Thurmond received in the northern Virginia county of Clarke, Senator Byrd's home county. Significantly, the States' Rights ticket polled a majority in only one county, Governor Tuck's home county of Halifax. Though neither Byrd nor Tuck admitted publicly at that time how he voted, it is likely that Byrd voted for Thurmond, and certain that Tuck did so. Indeed, shortly after the election the governor received a letter from Thurmond expressing his "appreciation for all that you did in the Presidential race."[54]

The reasons for Truman's dramatic victory, and for the failure of the Dixiecrat party, have been analyzed extensively; the factors which were at work nationally applied usually to Virginia.[55] In a homely way, Curry P. Hutchinson summed up what was probably the basic reason for the outcome. "I was down at Floyd Court House Monday," he wrote his brother before the election, "and an old farmer and his son told me they were for Truman. The masses of people who have been living well

[53] Virginia, *Statement of the Vote for President and Vice-President, Members of Congress, and United States Senator, General Election, Tuesday, November 2, 1948* (Richmond: Division of Purchase and Printing, 1948), pp. 2–15; Eisenberg, *Virginia Votes*, p. 168; Williams, "Anti-Byrd Movement," pp. 25–26.

[54] Interview with Tuck; Thurmond to Tuck, Nov. 23, 1948, Tuck Executive Papers.

[55] On the Truman "miracle," see Jules Abels, *Out of the Jaws of Victory* (New York: Henry Holt, 1959), pp. 265–303; Ross, *Loneliest Campaign*, pp. 245–71; Phillips, *Truman Presidency*, pp. 247–51; and Cochran, *Harry Truman*, pp. 234–40.

and making money are going to think several times before they vote a Republican ticket."[56]

Antiorganization leaders were, of course, elated by Truman's victory, not only because of that fact per se, but because they viewed it as an important step toward the destruction of the Byrd hegemony. One referred to it as "a complete washout for Tuck," and another spoke of the "unmitigated joy" which he derived from the "defeat that it slapped into Tuck's face, and all of his gang."[57] Robert Whitehead and Martin Hutchinson immediately began to call for a revamping of the state Democratic party, starting with the ouster of Alvin Massenburg as chairman. They also endeavored to use their successful activity on behalf of Truman as a lever to pry national party support away from the Byrd group and to themselves. In that attempt Whitehead prepared a lengthy memorandum on the election for the Democratic National Committee, claiming that the Byrd organization's role constituted "a sorry chapter." Writing to Vice-President-elect Alben Barkley, he was more specific, emphasizing that Byrd himself "did not say a word in behalf of the national ticket" and alleging that "many of his trusted lieutenants were red hot Dixiecrats." Although National Chairman McGrath expressed his gratitude for the work of the Straight Democratic Ticket Committee, there is little evidence that the leaders of the national party ever took concrete steps to aid the antis in their attempt to topple the Byrd faction.[58]

Organization spokesmen, for their part, tried to cast their campaign activities in the best possible light in the aftermath of the election. Massenburg delivered a rambling statement lauding the neutral stand taken by the state Central Committee—a stand chosen because of "an imperative duty to follow a course productive of harmony and the elimination of bitterness and reproach." That explanation did not ring

[56] Curry P. Hutchinson to Martin A. Hutchinson, Aug. 25, 1948, Hutchinson Papers.

[57] W. L. Pearson to Martin A. Hutchinson, Nov. 15, 1948, ibid.; Mayno Sutherland to Robert Whitehead, Nov. 11, 1948, Whitehead Papers.

[58] Whitehead to National Democratic Committee, Nov. 24, 1948, copy in Hutchinson Papers; Whitehead to Alben W. Barkley, Jan. 29, 1949, Whitehead Papers; J. Howard McGrath to Martin A. Hutchinson, Nov. 15, 1948, Hutchinson Papers; Williams, "Anti-Byrd Movement," pp. 27–29.

true to those who had worked for Truman, among them Robert
Whitehead, who assailed Massenburg's statement as "the product of a
laborious effort to create the impression that after all, the Democratic
State Central Committee did a good job. I almost laughed when I read
it." [59]

The fact was that, as Whitehead indicated, the overall effect of the
1948 presidential election could hardly have been interpreted other
than as a setback of sorts for the Byrd forces. Harry Byrd himself
obliquely admitted as much. Offering encouragement to Governor
Tuck shortly after the election, the senator wrote: "You have made one
of the great governors of Virginia and you will go down in history as
such. I am not writing this because you have given any indication that
you feel any criticism, but I have been through it myself, and I know
how easy it is to exaggerate such a situation as now confronts us. . . .
We were placed in a most difficult situation in the last election, and
everything we did was a choice of evils." [60]

In his study of the 1948 election, James Roebuck concluded succinctly that "the Presidential politics of the Virginia Democratic
organization . . . was full of blunders." [61] The outcome of that election
did indeed demonstrate the failure of the organization's plan. Not only
did the stratagem fail to stop Truman even in Virginia, it appeared to
weaken the organization's hold on state politics. From the time that the
"anti-Truman bill" was made public, antiorganization leaders were
hopeful that they would, in the words of one, "be able to harvest a nice
crop of hay out of this mess." Truman's triumph seemed to give
substance to that hope and left the antis in an ebullient mood as they
looked forward to the 1949 gubernatorial election. Francis Pickens
Miller, already an announced antiorganization candidate in that contest, bespoke the optimism of the antis in the afterglow of the Truman
victory. "The question all genuine Virginia Democrats are asking now
is where do we go from here. The answer is, of course," he gloated,

[59] Richmond *Times-Dispatch*, Nov. 4, 1948; Whitehead to Martin A. Hutchinson, Nov. 5, 1948, Whitehead Papers.
[60] Byrd to Tuck, Nov. 17, 1948, Tuck Papers.
[61] Roebuck, "Virginia in the Election of 1948," p. 77.

"that we are going to take over the leadership of the party in Virginia with all that that implies."[62]

It was undeniable that 1948 had not been a good year for the organization: the furor over the "anti-Truman bill," the tumultuous and divisive state convention, the reversals at the Philadelphia national convention, and finally Truman's victory in November—all seemed to diminish the potency of the Byrd hegemony and to give legitimate cause for antiorganization optimism. Still, the Byrd organization was characterized by its resilience, and those who would have written its epitaph were premature in their judgment.

[62] Mayno Sutherland to Martin A. Hutchinson, Feb. 28, 1948, Miller to Robert Whitehead, Nov. 9, 1948, copy, Hutchinson Papers.

State Government
under the Tuck Administration
8. *Making Haste Slowly*

It is a tradition that Virginia's motto "Old Virginny Never Tires"
is to be traced to the fact that Virginia habitually refuses to move
fast enough ever to get tired.

—Educator George H. Denny

They called on me to preach the sermon, and I preached. But
when I passed the collection plate, they began to run out on me.

—William M. Tuck

The longevity of the Byrd organization was traceable in large measure
to its reputation for honesty. In the main, that reputation was a
legitimate one, since state government under the Byrd hegemony was
distinguished by the absence of the more blatant forms of graft and
corruption which often characterized political machines in other states.
When its opponents endeavored to break the organization by the
exposure of scandal, they found little of substance to attack; however,
when they accused the Byrd leadership of niggardliness with respect to
state services, they were on firmer ground. The matter was well
summed up by J. Harvie Wilkinson when he asserted that "although
few Virginians ever questioned the honesty of the organization's management of state funds, many questioned its generosity." [1]

From the time that Harry Byrd had spearheaded the defeat of the
highway bond issue in the 1920s, the "pay-as-you-go" concept had
been a cardinal tenet of the organization. Thus wedded to the balanced
budget, the organization often allowed state services to languish. By
the time that Bill Tuck became governor, the state lagged behind

[1] Wilkinson, *Harry Byrd*, p. 41. The Byrd philosophy of government is set forth
by the patriarch himself in Harry Flood Byrd, "Better Government at Lower Cost,"
Yale Review 22 (Sept. 1932): 66–77.

much of the nation in expenditures for almost every public service—schools, health, welfare—and the situation was worsening as a result of the state's war-induced population growth. Though Tuck was as fully dedicated to the balanced budget as was Byrd, he recognized from the outset of his governorship that improvement was urgently needed in the quality of state services.

Nowhere was the dearth of state support more evident than in the public school system. By virtually every criterion, Virginia's educational system in the mid-1940s was abysmally weak: in the amount of money spent per student, Virginia ranked forty-first among the forty-eight states; in average instructional salaries, thirty-second; in percentage of income spent on education, forty-fourth.[2] Moreover, as one exhaustive statistical study revealed in 1945, the state's effort in the field of education was far below its ability to pay.[3]

Bill Tuck had never been known for his academic attainments. Though keen of mind and sharp of wit, he was not, in the usual sense of the word, scholarly. He was the recipient of four honorary doctorates, but his only earned degree—a law degree from Washington and Lee University—was the capstone of an academic career which, by his own admission, rarely rose above the level of mediocrity. Nonetheless, Tuck appreciated the importance of education. He had grown up in a home where learning was valued; he was sent to private boarding schools; and he had spent his first year out of college as a teacher-principal in a small high school. Whether because of, or in spite of, his own self-proclaimed intellectual shortcomings, he always held men of learning in high esteem. His interest in education was genuine.[4]

During his campaign for governor, Tuck placed high priority on the need to improve the public school system—terming it "our main

[2] Richard A. Meade, "Rank of Virginia in Education," *University of Virginia News Letter* 22 (Oct. 15, 1945).

[3] Mississippi, for example, was last in the nation in money spent for education but was a creditable ninth, far ahead of Virginia, in the percentage of income devoted to education (Roy C. Woods, "Where Does Your State Rank?" *School Board Journal* 110 [April 1945]: 21–22; see also J. L. Blair Buck, *The Development of Public Schools in Virginia, 1607–1952* [Richmond: State Board of Education, 1952]).

[4] Late in his career, somewhat disillusioned with politics, Tuck remarked that he believed the best life would be that of a scholar, devoting oneself to "nothing but history and culture" (interview with Tuck).

problem of state"—and he contined to push toward that goal throughout his administration.[5] He was always careful at the same time,
however, to urge only such improvement as could be done within the
limits of a balanced budget, and rebuked those who advocated deficit
spending for education. "We should be willing to work and supply the
fuel necessary to meet the requirements of our own generation," he
proclaimed, "and not be so profligate as to burn up in the fireplaces of
today the weatherboarding and shingles on the house bequeathed to us
by our forefathers." Having called a special session of the General
Assembly in January 1947 in order to secure additional funds for
education (most of which was earmarked for teachers' salaries), Tuck
grew testy when criticized by some for alleged lack of concern for
teachers. "Too much emphasis," he said, "has been placed upon the
amount of money paid the teachers and too little upon improving the
quality of instruction." In a rather remarkable discourse, he continued:

Ptolemy I was reminded by Euclid that there was no royal road to geometry,
and that applies with equal force to all learning. Learning and wisdom cannot
be bought and sold over the counter as common pieces of merchandise. . . .
[Teachers'] service transcends in importance the ordinary occupation or
profession, and it is more appropriate to compare their labors with those of
the ministry than with those engaged in ordinary pursuits of life. . . . In
abolishing the one-room school, let us not abolish [its] spirit. The one-room
school, with all its handicaps, promoted concepts of character and training
which remain the fundamentals of today.[6]

The Tuck governorship overall witnessed a steady, if unspectacular,
improvement in public education, as attested by various statistics: the
total value of school property almost doubled from 1946 to 1950; the
amount of money allocated to schools for the last biennium of his
governorship (more than $58 million) represented an increase of ap-
proximately $24 million over the amount appropriated four years
earlier; teachers' salaries rose from an annual average of $1,416 in
1945–46 to $2,236 in 1949–50; and the annual per capita expendi-

---

[5] William M. Tuck, "Education, Our Main Problem of State," *Virginia Journal of Education* 38 (May 1945): 378.

[6] Richmond *Times-Dispatch*, Jan. 23, 1947; Virginia, *Address of William M. Tuck, Governor, to the General Assembly, Wednesday, January 14, 1948*, Senate Document No. 1 (Richmond: Division of Purchase and Printing, 1948), p. 8.

ture for each pupil rose from $90 to $133 during the same period.[7]

Yet, despite improvements, serious difficulties remained. One glaring problem was the disparity in the quality of education between rural and urban areas. Since the funding formula required the localities rather than the state to bear the brunt of educational expenses, schools in rural areas generally suffered as a result of inadequate tax bases; rural Dickenson County, for example, spent only $52 for each child in the 1947–48 session, while the wealthier cities of Richmond and Norfolk spent $185 and $188 respectively.[8]

Another problem was the inequality between black and white schools. Like all other southern states, Virginia had operated a segregated school system since the "separate-but-equal" doctrine had been sanctioned by the Supreme Court in the 1896 case of *Plessy* v. *Ferguson*. Although white Virginians claimed (with some justification) that education for blacks was better in the Old Dominion than elsewhere in the South,[9] the inescapable fact was that black schools were inferior to white schools in almost every respect—in the valuation of school property, in the salaries paid to teachers, in the amount spent per pupil. As the Richmond *Times-Dispatch* concluded, "We have seen to it that there was separateness, but we have not seen to it that there is equality."[10]

One potential solution to such problems involved the use of federal funds, since Congress was giving serious consideration to providing aid to state schools during the late 1940s; but the Byrd leadership would have none of that. "All of the states should oppose grants of federal money for education," declared Tuck, "and should demand that the federal government put its own house in order. Every state should be free to educate its own children in its own way without having outside and undesirable ideologies crammed down their throats."[11] The gov-

---

[7] Virginia, *Annual Report of the Superintendent of Public Instruction*, 1946–47 (Richmond: Division of Purchase and Printing, 1947), pp. 253, 263, 311; *Annual Report*, 1949–50, pp. 263, 272, 338.

[8] *Annual Report*, 1947–48, pp. 290–92.

[9] See Ernst W. Swanson and John A. Griffin, eds., *Public Education in the South* (Chapel Hill: University of North Carolina Press, 1955), pp. 64–67.

[10] Richmond *Times-Dispatch*, April 5, 1948.

[11] Ibid., Jan. 24, 1947. For Byrd's similar view, see *Congressional Digest* 28 (Nov. 1949): 273.

ernor's comment was a telling one, in that it revealed the seldom articulated, but nonetheless deep, fear of the federal control which might one day force the end of public school segregation.

The breakdown of segregation did, in fact, become a matter of increasing concern during the Tuck governorship. As early as 1938 the United States Supreme Court, while not overturning the separate-but-equal doctrine, had ruled that real equality of education for blacks must be provided. Some two years later a United States Circuit Court brought the issue home to Virginia by ruling in a Norfolk case that pay scales must be equalized between teachers in white and black public schools. An even more direct blow in behalf of equal education in Virginia came when United States District Court Judge Sterling Hutcheson ruled in 1948 that not only must salaries be equalized, but physical facilities must also be equal for both races—a decision which would necessitate a vast school construction program in the state.[12]

As the demise of the segregated school system impended, Tuck made it plain that he was unalterably opposed to integration. Speaking on one occasion not long after the Hutcheson decision, he discarded his prepared text and ripped into the whole civil rights movement. "I want to tell you right now," he exclaimed, "that if I have the power to stop it, there won't be any mixed schools in Virginia." Privately he reiterated that view in a letter to a constituent. "I am opposed to Negro children and white children attending the same schools," he wrote. "They have tried it here in Virginia, but will never succeed as long as I have anything to do with our public affairs. The better elements of both races do not want this. It is only being pushed on us by the big cities in the North."[13]

It turned out that the school desegregation crisis did not come during the Tuck administration; by grace of some four years, Bill Tuck escaped having to confront as governor the problems which arose from the epochal *Brown* decision. When the great challenge did arrive in 1954, Tuck aligned himself shoulder-to-shoulder with Harry Byrd in an all-out effort to prevent the implementation of that decision.

[12] Bardolph, *Civil Rights Record*, pp. 270–72; *Virginia Journal of Education* 41 (April 1948): 328; Henriques, "John S. Battle," pp. 116–25.

[13] Richmond *Times-Dispatch*, Oct. 16, 1948; Tuck to Mrs. O. G. Yeatts, Sept. 16, 1948, Tuck Executive Papers. Tuck's involvement in the school desegregation and civil rights controversies is discussed more fully in Chapters 10 and 11.

The record of the Tuck governorship in other areas of state service, such as mental and physical health, was much as it was in the area of education: increased expenditures which led to gradual improvement, but which still left many problems unsolved. The greatest progress was in the control of tuberculosis, a disease which for some reason was unusually prevalent in Virginia, especially among blacks; only five states had a higher mortality rate from tuberculosis than did Virginia. At the outset of his administration, Tuck singled out the tuberculosis problem for particular attention, announcing that there was "no reason why the dread white plague may not be eradicated entirely in Virginia." At Tuck's direction, state appropriations for the prevention and treatment of the disease were vastly increased; the $8.5 million allocation by the 1948 General Assembly surpassed by far the sum total of all funds appropriated for tuberculosis control since the inception of the state Health Department some forty years earlier. By the time Tuck left office the waiting lists for admission to sanatoriums had been virtually eliminated, and the death rate from the disease had been reduced appreciably.[14]

The least effective state service rendered by Virginia during the Tuck years was public welfare. The Commonwealth's penuriousness in that field was a reflection of Harry Byrd's abhorrence of anything that smacked ever so slightly of socialism. To Byrd the welfare state was, in his own words, "that state of twilight in which the glow of democratic freedoms is fading beyond the horizon, leaving us to be swallowed in the blackness of socialism, or worse." The senator had no intention of allowing his Virginia to be so swallowed. As J. Harvie Wilkinson put it, " 'Welfare' was always a nasty word in the Byrd vocabulary."[15]

Public assistance was given grudgingly in Virginia. From the time the program was created, the state's welfare rolls were small, the payments minimal. Only four states in 1948 provided general assis-

[14] Richmond *Times-Dispatch*, April 4, 1946, Jan. 11, 1950; *Virginia's Health: Annual Report of the Virginia State Department of Health, 1950* (Richmond: Division of Purchase and Printing, 1950), p. 48; Virginia, *Address of William M. Tuck to the General Assembly, January 11, 1950* (Richmond: Division of Purchase and Printing, 1950), pp. 48–49.

[15] Harry F. Byrd, "The Threat to the American System," in Sheldon Glueck, ed., *The Welfare State and the National Welfare* (Cambridge, Mass.: Addison-Wesley, 1952), p. 76; Wilkinson, *Harry Byrd*, p. 48.

tance to fewer persons relative to total population than did Virginia (214 per 100,000). As governor, Tuck had no great desire to see that state of affairs changed. Although he recommended to the 1948 General Assembly a substantial increase in welfare appropriations, he delivered at the same time a pungent discourse on the potential evils of government aid. "I have a sincere and abiding interest in the proper care of all worthy applicants for assistance," he told the legislators, "but I am convinced there has developed an unwholesome tendency on the part of many of our citizens to look to the government for gratuities all through life. It is incumbent upon our agencies not to become a party to this trend." [16]

Tuck need not have feared that any tendency toward sloth would be abetted during his administration. The welfare appropriations voted by the 1948 General Assembly constituted the largest single increase in the state's history and, by the end of Tuck's governorship, monthly expenditures for welfare were nearly twice what they had been when he took office. Yet, Virginia's welfare program was hardly one to induce massive indolence, as statistics in 1950 revealed that the state's expenditures for public assistance were still among the lowest in the country. [17]

All in all, the development of public services during the Tuck governorship was reminiscent of an adventure experienced by the fictional Alice in Lewis Carroll's *Through the Looking Glass*. After seeming to have run very hard without getting anywhere, Alice was told by the Red Queen that it was necessary in that peculiar land to run as fast as possible just to stay in the same place. In the post–World War II era, with its rapid inflation and ever-accelerating demands for public services, Virginians, paying-as-they-went, could have appreciated how Alice must have felt.

Critics who claimed that the quality of state services in Virginia was too low often placed the blame on the Byrd organization's adherence to the balanced budget philosophy. Such critics were only partially correct, since spending could, of course, have been increased and the balanced budget maintained—provided that the level of taxation was

[16] *The Book of the States, 1948–49* (Chicago: Council of State Governments, 1949), pp. 375–78; *Address of William M. Tuck, January 14, 1948*, pp. 6–7.

[17] *Virginia Public Welfare* 24 (July 1946): 11; ibid., 26 (May 1948): 6; *Welfare Worker* 28 (Mar. 1950), p. 11; *Book of the States, 1952–53*, pp. 321, 328–31.

sufficiently high to secure the requisite revenues. Therein lay the rub: only slightly less sacrosanct than the balanced budget in the organization's scheme of things was the preservation of Virginia's status as a "low-tax state," a condition deemed necessary for the attracting of business to the Commonwealth.

By the mid-1940s, however, the need for various services had burgeoned to such an extent that the state's treasury was simply unequal to the demands placed upon it. Tuck, who had stated during his campaign that he hoped to avoid any tax increase, had scarcely taken office when he realized that certain problems, notably the highway system, needed immediate attention and that increased revenues must be secured. Accordingly, he called upon the 1946 General Assembly for an increase of one cent per gallon in the gasoline tax, the main source from which highway funds were derived. Only after lengthy parliamentary wrangling did the legislature approve the increase, which led to a substantial renovation and expansion of the secondary road system. Tuck was elated by the improvements made possible by the new gasoline tax, a measure which was regarded as his "most conspicuous piece of personally-directed legislation" of the 1946 session. "At last," he crowed, "the people of Virginia are out of the mud!"[18]

Within two years the governor had come to realize that a more sweeping tax increase would be necessary in order to meet the growing demand for state services. Eschewing such innovations as the imposition of a general sales tax or the levying of taxes on selected products such as tobacco, he proposed that existing taxes on corporate and personal incomes be increased. Specifically, he recommended that the net income tax on corporations be raised from 3 to 5 percent and that net income tax rates on individuals be raised from 1½ to 2 percent on incomes under $3,000, from 2½ to 3 percent on incomes between $3,000 and $5,000, and from 3 to 5 percent on incomes in excess of $5,000.[19]

The tax plan touched off a furor. "In a solid phalanx," reported the Norfolk *Virginian-Pilot*, "spokesmen for manufacturing, public

[18] Carter Lowance, "The State Faces Budget Problems," *Commonwealth* 14 (Dec. 1947): 19; Norfolk *Virginian-Pilot*, Mar. 10, 1946; Richmond *Times-Dispatch*, Mar. 15, 1947.

[19] *Address of William M. Tuck, January 14, 1948*, p. 10.

utilities and business generally attacked the Governor's proposal as ranging from burdensome to ruinous." Predictably, the public response was mostly adverse. One angry citizen was moved to put his feelings into doggerel verse which appeared in a Richmond newspaper:

> Any way you take it
> We're out of luck,
> With High-Tax Harry
> And High-Tax Tuck.
>
> We work and we skimp
> But we can't save a buck,
> For High-Tax Harry
> And High-Tax Tuck.
>
> We voted Democratic
> And now we're stuck,
> With High-Tax Harry
> And High-Tax Tuck.[20]

Some of the state's leading newspapers, notably the Richmond dailies, led the criticism of the proposed increase. The balanced budget should be maintained, they said, but it should be done through reduced expenditures rather than increased taxes. "Half-hearted, elastic economy," admonished the *Times-Dispatch*, "is no more a virtue than elastic chastity, or an elastic conscience"; it would thus be better for the legislators to "sharpen their pencils and pare down expenditures, in which case they will not have to chew their pencils quite as hard in an effort to find needed revenues." The *News Leader* echoed that theme, claiming with considerable exaggeration that the Tuck plan amounted to "confiscatory taxation" which would reduce Virginians to the status of "tax slaves." If the proposals were enacted, said the *News Leader*, it would be the "blackest of dates in eight decades of Virginia finance." There were even indications that Senator Byrd was not totally pleased with the Tuck plan. "I am afraid we are getting off on the wrong foot at Richmond," he confided to one friend. "We can't talk economy and fiscal conservatism for 25 years and then expect the people to change around with us in a short time."[21]

[20] Norfolk *Virginian-Pilot*, Feb. 8, 1948; Richmond *Times-Dispatch*, Feb. 17, 1948.

[21] Richmond *Times-Dispatch*, Jan. 15, 1948; Richmond *News Leader*, Jan. 19, 1948; Byrd to J. Frank Wysor, Jan. 21, 1948, Byrd Papers.

Opposition to the proposed increase was so strong that it appeared for a while that the governor's program might be defeated or drastically modified. With the rumor of revolt spreading, Tuck grew apprehensive as the showdown vote approached. At the last moment he sent a note to Delegate E. Blackburn Moore, floor leader of the House, suggesting that passage of the measure seemed doubtful at that juncture. The crafty Moore, who was even then in the process of presenting the bill for a vote, sensed that a delay might be in order, and therefore permitted the Assembly to adjourn for the weekend without calling for a vote.[22]

The hiatus gave Tuck time to put his political talents to work. Fortuitously, the entire General Assembly had been invited to spend the weekend in Williamsburg. The governor had been invited to leave early for the excursion, but, as he told Senator Byrd, he declined in order to "stay here and go down with the General Assembly." It was just the opportunity which Tuck needed, and he made the best of it. Riding with the legislators on a train from Richmond to the restored colonial capital, he assiduously worked his way up and down the aisles—cajoling here, prodding there—trying to muster the votes needed to put over his tax program. He left little to chance. Having learned in the course of the weekend, for example, that one delegate who could be counted on for support, Wrendo M. Godwin of Accomack, might be absent when the critical vote came up, Tuck telephoned to inform Godwin that an airplane was being sent to bring him back to the Capitol. When the startled delegate protested that he feared airplanes and had never flown before, the governor replied jauntily, "Well, Wrendo, you're going to fly today!"[23]

The efficacy of Tuck's maneuvering was attested when his tax package came to a vote during the week following the Williamsburg trip. Both the House and Senate approved the program by comfortable margins, although Tuck noted afterward that opponents of the plan gave him "a right hard fight." In order to secure its passage he claimed that it had been necessary to "talk, eat and practically sleep" with the legislature.[24]

[22] Interview with Tuck.

[23] Tuck to Byrd, Jan. 29, 1948, Tuck Papers; interview with Tuck.

[24] Tuck to J. L. Rollins, Feb. 12, 1948, Tuck Papers; Wilkinson, *Harry Byrd*, p. 41.

Getting Down to the Pinfeathers

Getting Down to Pinfeathers. (Courtesy of the Richmond *Times-Dispatch*)

The Richmond press continued to condemn the tax program, alleging that the Commonwealth had been converted thereby into a "high tax state." The charge was questionable. Undeniably, the amount of revenue collected did rise abruptly following the rate change; still, even after the increase, only eight states ranked lower than Virginia in terms of per capita tax collections. Judged on the basis of tax burden—i.e., the comparison of taxes to income—Virginia stood approximately in the middle of the forty-eight states.[25]

[25] Sara K. Gilliam, *The Trend in Taxes Paid by Virginians, 1940–1950* (Charlottes-

The whole tax affair was vexatious to Tuck. In trying to provide for expanded (and badly needed) state services, he found himself squeezed between two conflicting components of the Byrd organization's philosophy: on the one hand, the pay-as-you-go system had to be maintained; on the other hand, taxes were to be kept low. Thus caught in the middle, the governor was chagrined that certain critics, particularly the Richmond newspapers, did not sympathize with his position. He regarded it as a betrayal when the papers, whose editorials had earlier pleaded for improved state services, pilloried him when he asked for additional revenue with which to fund those improvements. "I regretted to have to recommend [more] taxes," he lamented to an old friend, "but there was widespread demand for improvement in . . . essential services. Many are complaining that I have not asked for enough taxes, and others are complaining that I asked for too much. I have done the very best I could." [26]

Some years removed from the governorship, Tuck retained traces of bitterness but, in a lighter mood, he characteristically expressed his feelings in the form of a story. Opposition to his call for additional taxes reminded him, he said, of the tale of an antiquated Northern Neck tavern which, according to legend, had a room inhabited by ghosts. For years no one had been able to sleep overnight in the haunted room. When at long last an itinerant preacher stayed the whole night through, the incredulous tavern keeper asked him the next morning if anything untoward had happened. "Oh, I saw a few ghosts," came the nonchalant reply. "What'd you do?" asked the host. "Well," explained the traveler, "we sang awhile, we prayed awhile, and we preached awhile. Then I got out the collection plate and they all vanished." [27]

Although the Tuck governorship could not legitimately be termed a "reform" administration, it did include some progressive innovations, such as creation of the State Water Control Board, an agency designed to guard against the pollution of state streams. There were also several

ville: Bureau of Population and Economic Research, 1952), pp. 23, 28, 58, 61; Alan S. Donnahoe, "Measuring the State Tax Burden," *Journal of Political Economy* 55 (June 1947): 243; W. H. White, "Some Aspects of Virginia's Tax Structure," *University of Virginia News Letter* 27 (April 15, 1951); *Book of the States, 1950–51*, pp. 232–33.

[26] Tuck to J. L. Rollins, Jan. 29, 1948, Tuck Papers.

[27] Norfolk *Virginian-Pilot*, June 8, 1969.

salutary prison reforms, including the abolition of corporal punishment—a practice which, Tuck believed, "would give a man of any intelligence a mental wound from which it would be impossible for him to recover."[28]

One of the most ambitious reform attempts of the Tuck years involved an effort to reorganize the state's administrative structure. A thorough reorganization in the 1920s during the governorship of economy-minded Harry Byrd had produced a streamlined government which was widely hailed as a paragon of efficiency. However, in succeeding decades state agencies had proliferated to the extent that by the time of Tuck's inauguration, the size of the state bureaucracy had become the object of considerable criticism. The Richmond *Times-Dispatch* in 1946 embarked upon an editorial crusade for reorganization, charging the present system with "waste, extravagance and inefficiency." Opponents of the Byrd organization loudly agreed, contending that the inordinately large number of state employees was an important factor in the perpetuation of the Byrd regime; they further pointed out that bloated state payrolls revealed the hypocrisy of an organization professedly dedicated to frugality.[29]

Though organization spokesmen issued obligatory denials of the accusations, both Byrd and Tuck privately conceded that some reform was needed.[30] The result was the appointment by the governor of a study commission to consider governmental restructuring. Based on the commission's report, a modified reorganization bill was enacted by the 1948 General Assembly whereby seventy-two existing agencies were consolidated into a more manageable thirty, at an annual saving of approximately $1.5 million. Far from satisfied, the *Times-Dispatch* bluntly labeled the reorganization a "flop."[31] Yet, despite the fact that the number of state employees was not substantially reduced, the revamping did provide more efficient administration. Furthermore,

[28] Interview with Tuck. See Virginia, *Annual Report of the Department of Corrections, 1947–48* (Richmond: Division of Purchase and Printing, 1949), pp. 5–30.

[29] Richmond *Times-Dispatch*, Jan. 23, 1946; Horn, "Democratic Party in Virginia," pp. 333–38; Hall, "James H. Price," pp. 266–71.

[30] Byrd to Combs, Jan. 21, 1946, Byrd Papers; Richmond *Times-Dispatch*, Jan. 22, 1948. See also J. H. Bradford, *State Employment in Relation to Population* (Richmond: Office of the Director of Personnel, 1946).

[31] Richmond *Times-Dispatch*, Mar. 14, 1948.

from a political standpoint, the effort (though by no means a complete success) was advantageous to the Byrd forces since the mere attempt at reform lessened the efficacy of the issue as a campaign weapon by opponents of the organization.

The Tuck administration also witnessed a curious attempt at reform of the state's suffrage laws, including a movement to abolish the poll tax as a prerequisite to voting. Opponents of the organization largely blamed that tax for keeping the electorate at a manageable size—a contention starkly borne out by the facts. For example, whereas 64 percent of the eligible electorate had cast ballots in the pre–poll tax election of 1896, only 26 percent did so in the first election after enactment of the tax; indeed, it was not until the presidential election of 1936 that the total vote in Virginia reached pre–poll tax levels, despite the enfranchisement of women and a 30 percent population increase in the interim.[32]

Opponents of the tax condemned it not only because it diminished voter participation, but because it lent itself to political abuses, notably the block payment of taxes by interested parties. Even though the constitution specified that each prospective voter must personally pay his own tax, the practice of block payment was almost standard procedure in some areas and was often used to good advantage by the Byrd organization. In the congressional elections of 1934, for example, incumbent Fifth District Representative Thomas G. Burch importuned Bill Tuck, then a rising state senator, to "look after getting the taxes of our friends paid in Halifax County" and suggested that "after going over the situation, if you will write me I will be very glad to render any help possible towards getting the taxes paid." Tuck agreed, assuring Burch that he would try to encourage poll tax payment through newspaper publicity and that he would "also request the tax collectors to work along this line, and at last we will go over the list and see that all of our particularly close friends are taken care of." Prior to the deadline for tax payment before another congressional election, Tuck similarly advised Burch that he and his associates

[32] Buni, *Negro in Virginia Politics*, p. 24; Holt, "Virginia Constitutional Convention," p. 96; *Southern Planter* 98 (Dec. 1937): 4, 10; William F. Swindler, *Government by the People: Theory and Practice in Virginia* (Charlottesville: University Press of Virginia, 1969), p. 66.

could use to your advantage around $150 or $200 for this purpose, all of which if not used for said purpose will be returned. We think that a large amount of this will be later collected by the Treasurer or his deputies, and as it is collected the same will be refunded to you. . . . I have requested [a deputy collector] to hold out for us the poll tax tickets of all good Democrats who could be depended upon to support you in the general election in November.[33]

In an organization whose hallmark was a reputation for honesty, the manipulation of the poll tax was an unseemly aberration and was the one practice which, more than any other perhaps, smacked of traditional "machine rule." Anti-Byrd politicians, together with leading state journalists, thus made poll tax abolition a prime goal during the 1930s and 1940s. By the time of Tuck's governorship the agitation had become so strong that the Byrd leadership was forced to consider elimination of the tax, even though both Byrd and Tuck defended it as being, in Tuck's words, "a very proper and legitimate instrument to test the sustained interest of the voter in public affairs."[34] The result was the creation of a suffrage study commission, chaired by Delegate Stuart B. Campbell of Wythe County, which after months of deliberation formally recommended in late 1945 that the tax be abolished. To replace the function of the tax as a means of determining qualified voters, the commission recommended annual registration which could be accomplished in any of three ways: by making application in person before the local board of election; by payment of all state and local taxes (except the real estate tax) before the penalty date; or by voting during the preceding year. Further, in its most controversial recommendation, the commission urged that the suffrage law be amended so as to subject potential voters to "such tests as to literacy and such further requirements as the General Assembly may prescribe."[35]

Since such changes necessitated amendment of the state constitution—a cumbersome process involving approval by two consecutive sessions of the General Assembly, followed by ratification in a popular

[33] Burch to Tuck, April 12, 1934, Tuck to Burch, undated, and April 26, 1938, Tuck Papers.

[34] Tuck to author, Nov. 16, 1973.

[35] Virginia, *Suffrage Laws: Report of the Commission to the Governor and the General Assembly*, Senate Document No. 8 (Richmond: Division of Purchase and Printing, 1946), pp. 7, 11.

referendum—almost four years intervened before the matter was settled. In the meanwhile opposition to the so-called Campbell Amendments developed from diverse sources. On the one hand the amendments were opposed by those who favored retention of the poll tax pure and simple. Among such opponents was, somewhat surprisingly, the eloquent antiorganization Democrat Robert Whitehead, who claimed that he could "see no just reason why a citizen should not be required to make some small contribution to his state in order to exercise the right of suffrage. . . . One should not be permitted to exercise a voice in the control of a corporation if he is not a stockholder thereof. I do not think that $1.50 a year is an unreasonable exaction from a citizen in return for the privilege of voting." Aware that his advocacy of the tax put him at odds with most of his antiorganization cohorts, Whitehead proclaimed defiantly: "I'm a poll tax man and I am not ashamed of it. Let the radical groups in Virginia take that and chew it over all they please."[36]

Most of the opposition, on the other hand, came not from those who, like Whitehead, favored the tax, but from those who wanted the tax abolished but feared that the requirements embodied in the Campbell Amendments would be even more detrimental to voter participation than the tax itself. In short, the harshest critics of the proposed changes were, in many cases, the anti-Byrd politicians who had clamored most vociferously for repeal of the tax. Such opponents were particularly wary of the extensive discretionary power which would be given to the General Assembly in setting prerequisites for voting. As one writer to the Richmond *Times-Dispatch* suggested, it would be risky to give such latitude to "any man who was . . . a party to Tuck's 1948 election bill. [Organization leaders] are asking, 'Can't we trust the legislature of Virginia?' Does the record justify trust? I think not." Another Richmond resident, with a bow to Shakespeare, put the same concern into the form of a "Voter's Soliloquy":

> . . . To end the tax,
> To end? Perchance but to begin.
>   Ay, there's the rub,
> For in that end of tax, what laws may come.

[36] Whitehead to Howard H. Davis, July 15, 1941, Whitehead Papers; Richmond *Times-Dispatch*, Feb. 21, 1946.

State Senator Lloyd Robinette was of the same mind, characterizing the amendments as "ten times more restrictive" than the existing law. If the people were to ratify the changes, he warned, "they will find that in asking for bread they have been given a stone."[37]

While protest against the Campbell Amendments swelled, little was heard from those Byrd partisans who supposedly advocated the revisions. Noting the apathy of the organization, the Richmond *Times-Dispatch* concluded shortly before the referendum that "the outcome may hinge on whether the Byrd-Tuck machine sends 'the word' down the line. . . . If the 'heat' is applied, and the courthouse organizations are thrown into high gear on behalf of the amendments, they may pass. Otherwise, it seems likely that they will be defeated." Finally, a mere two weeks before the referendum, the organization hierarchy bestirred itself, with both Byrd and Tuck issuing public appeals for support of the amendments; the revisions, said the governor, would "constitute a forward step of lasting benefit to the people of Virginia."[38]

The last-minute rallying of organization forces came too late, as the Campbell Amendments were defeated by a decisive vote of 56,687 in favor to 206,542 (or 78.5 percent) in opposition. The amendments did not receive a majority of favorable votes in a single county or city; in some localities the vote ran as high as ten to one against the revisions. Antiorganization leaders were elated by their apparent success. "I think only the 'Ever Faithful' voted for the amendments," one commented. "All who are free men in any sense of the word voted 'nay.' In reality it was as bitter a dose as the Byrd-Tuck Anti-Truman Bill now of such ill fame."[39]

The overwhelming defeat of the Campbell Amendments did seem to constitute, prima facie, a setback for the Byrd organization; yet, from a purely political standpoint, it was far from an unmitigated disaster. There were even those who suggested that the organization's lukewarm support throughout most of the controversy indicated that

[37] Richmond *Times-Dispatch*, Feb. 15, Nov. 4, 1948; Frederick D. Ogden, *The Poll Tax in the South* (University, Ala.: University of Alabama Press, 1958), p. 208.

[38] Richmond *Times-Dispatch*, Oct. 17, 23, 25, 1949.

[39] Heard and Strong, *Southern Primaries and Elections*, p. 206; Ogden, *Poll Tax*, p. 213; Curry P. Hutchinson to Martin A. Hutchinson, Nov. 11, 1949, Hutchinson Papers.

the Byrd leadership actually preferred to see the amendments fail. One student of the period contended that it was "quite possible, indeed likely, that the Byrd organization wished to see the Campbell Amendments defeated and were pleased to sit back and let the liberals work hard to bring about that result."[40] It was, in truth, nearly inconceivable that so potent an organization would have permitted the devastating defeat of any proposition whose passage it sincerely desired. In retrospect the Campbell Amendments emerged as a clever stratagem by which the organization could hardly have lost: the amendments which the organization sponsored were designed so that, if they were approved, considerable control over the electorate would still be possible; if they were defeated, the poll tax would remain—a prospect which was by no means repugnant to many organization leaders. And, whatever the outcome, the organization would at least have given the appearance of acceding to the popular will.

The handling of the poll tax controversy, like the plan for reorganization of the state government, exemplified the adroit political maneuvering of the Byrd forces during the Tuck governorship. Responding when necessary to meet growing criticism, the organization did not necessarily succeed in solving the problems it confronted; but, essential to the maintenance of its supremacy, its actions did succeed in removing such problems from the easy exploitation of its enemies.

In January 1950 Bill Tuck left the governorship to be succeeded by John S. Battle, another Byrd regular, whose elevation to the state's highest office came only after an acrimonious primary election in which he barely staved off the challenge of antiorganization candidate Francis Pickens Miller.[41] Tuck's departure was accompanied by widespread acclaim throughout Virginia. Even his frequent nemesis, the Richmond press, praised his performance. The *Times-Dispatch* hailed him as "a good, an honest, a constructive and a courageous governor,"

---

[40] Henriques, "John S. Battle," p. 157. See also Buni, *Negro in Virginia Politics*, p. 140.

[41] Tuck was only peripherally involved in the 1949 contest. The best of the numerous studies of that campaign are Peter R. Henriques, "The Organization Challenged," *Virginia Magazine of History and Biography* 82 (July 1974): 372–406; and James Robert Sweeney, "Byrd and Anti-Byrd: The Struggle for Political Supremacy in Virginia, 1945–1954" (Ph.D. diss., Univ. of Notre Dame, 1973), pp. 104–52.

and the *News Leader* suggested that "in any list of Virginia's finest governors of this century, Mr. Tuck would rank one-two with Mr. Byrd, and take your choice." A leading Virginia journalist concluded that "though one disagrees with much that he did, even though he made mistakes, the net picture is that of a man who faced up to the issues, worked hard at his job, fought for what he believed, and damned the torpedoes to get things done." Of all the encomiums, the one which was perhaps the most meaningful to Tuck was that which came from a man who at the outset had been dubious of his ability— Harry Flood Byrd. "It was very sad to me when you left the governorship," he wrote Tuck. "You left office with the affection and respect of all the Virginia people. . . . Everywhere I go people have commented on you and your administration. . . . You will stand throughout all history to come as one of Virginia's greatest governors."[42]

The Tuck governorship was indeed a full one, with positive accomplishments in a number of areas. There was, for example, the tax revision which, though controversial, remained the basic revenue system under which the state operated until 1966, when it was supplemented by a general sales tax; there was the administrative reorganization which helped to eliminate some of the bunglesome bureaucratic practices which were hampering state government; and there were significant increases in appropriations for state services, though as one critic commented, such increases often allowed the level of service to rise only "from abysmally low to merely too low."[43]

On the debit side of the ledger there was the "anti-Truman bill," a measure adjudged by one observer to be so offensive that "no man, save under Oriental torture or on deathbed confessional in quest of absolution, probably ever will confess having had a hand in writing it." Tuck sharply dissented from such an indictment of the bill. Although he was capable of admitting his errors—he once said, in a typically earthy metaphor, that some of his mistakes made him feel "like a one-legged man in a tail-kicking contest"—he resolutely defended the "anti-Truman bill." His contention was that, far from keeping anyone's name off the ballot, the measure in its final form actually made it easier

[42] Richmond *Times-Dispatch*, Jan. 12, 1950; Richmond *News Leader*, May 4, 1967; McDowell, "Bill Tuck," p. 8; Byrd to Tuck, Jan. 21, 1950, Byrd Papers.
[43] McDowell, "Bill Tuck," p. 17.

for candidates to get on the ballot.[44] In truth, the much-maligned bill did not substantially alter the electoral process; its promulgation did, however, provide tangible evidence of the Byrd faction's growing alienation from the national Democratic party, and in so doing succeeded in driving the state's liberal Democrats into ever more intransigent opposition to the organization.

The most important events of the Tuck governorship were, by any reckoning, those involving organized labor. The most celebrated incident was the Vepco affair, but of greater significance in the long run was the series of labor laws enacted under Tuck's guidance in 1946 and 1947. Although the legislation provoked angry objections from union leaders at the time, subsequent developments showed the laws to be less detrimental to labor than union spokesmen had predicted.[45] The most controversial of the laws, the Right-to-Work Act of 1947, continued to generate heated debate in subsequent years—so much so that one student of labor law protested that the furor over the act was "all out of proportion to its actual legal effect upon labor relations and the growth or decline of unions."[46] Despite persistent lobbying for its repeal by pro-labor groups, the Right-to-Work Act of 1947 (with minor revisions by the 1954 legislature) remained a cornerstone of Virginia labor law for decades.

Throughout his governorship, Tuck proved to be a captivating figure, even to those who were not predisposed in his favor. There had been other governors—Harry Byrd, for one—who had accomplished more, but none who captured the imagination of the public in the way that Tuck did. His extraordinary appeal was largely attributable to the man's personality and his manner of operation—in short, his style. It

[44] Richmond *Times-Dispatch*, Jan. 8, Jan. 12, 1950; interview with Tuck.

[45] On the effect of the Anti-Picketing Act of 1946, see Arnold Schlossberg, "Current Trends in Labor Law in Virginia," *Virginia Law Review* 41 (June 1956): 691–92, 709; on the Public Utility Labor Relations Act of 1947, see Robert R. France, "Seizure in Emergency Labor Disputes in Virginia," *Industrial and Labor Relations Review* 7 (April 1954): 347–66.

[46] Schlossberg, "Current Trends," p. 709. See also John M. Kuhlman, "Right-to-Work Laws: The Virginia Experience," *Labor Law Journal* 6 (July 1955): 453–61. According to Kuhlman (p. 494): "It is impossible to conclude that the right-to-work law has made a positive contribution to labor-management relations. . . . There is no evidence to indicate that it has reduced the number of strikes, nor has there been a drastic change in hiring practices."

was not so much what Tuck did, as how he did it, that engaged the attention of Virginians. He had no use, he said, for public officials who were always "dying of the can'ts"; he believed in forthright action. His approach, which was decried by some critics as impetuous or ham-fisted (or both), was likened by a more sympathetic observer to "a boisterous summer storm with deafening thunder, blinding lightning, and driving rains from which the land emerged rejuvenated, all sweet, green, smiling and amazed."[47]

Ever the country boy at heart, Tuck remained utterly unaffected by the glamour of high office. It was not unusual for him to answer his own office telephone or to drive his own car, including an old, nondescript one which he kept near the Mansion, the better to sneak away unobtrusively on periodic jaunts into the hinterlands. "Once in a while," he recalled, "just to keep from going crazy, I would slide away for twelve or fourteen hours and go to my cabin [in Halifax], and sit around there and have a drink, and pinch myself and think, 'Hell, I don't reckon I'm governor.'" But such respites never lasted long, he lamented, because soon "they'd be sending state police out there wanting to know where I was, and asking what to do about this or that, and I'd think, 'Just might as well go back.'"[48]

In his official travels throughout the state, Tuck made a habit of dropping in at country stores along the way to visit briefly with the cracker-barrel savants who were always to be found loitering there-abouts. The encounters could be enlightening, and sometimes hum-bling. Tuck relished telling of the time, for example, when at such a stop one of the locals, having noticed the big black car from which Tuck emerged, said to him, "Mister, you must be the highway commis-sioner, or else how would you get the number one license on your car?" Tuck gently replied, "That's the one they save for the governor." Unimpressed, the countryman, to the accompaniment of a spray of tobacco juice, rasped, "I'll betcha, by God, you didn't get it that way."[49]

Even while restricted to the environs of the Capitol, Tuck managed to mingle with the plain people whose company he cherished. He

---

[47] Friddell, *What Is It about Virginia?*, pp. 62, 64.
[48] Norfolk *Virginian-Pilot*, June 8, 1969.
[49] Interview with Tuck; undated press release, Tuck Papers.

Governor and Mrs. Tuck, 1948. (Courtesy of Dementi Studios)

enjoyed walking around downtown Richmond, window-shopping along Broad Street, as might any ordinary citizen. A sunny afternoon sometimes found him relaxing on a bench in Capitol Square, tossing peanuts to the squirrels and swapping stories with sundry passersby. On one such occasion he was joined by two soldiers who happened to be passing through the city. Not recognizing the burly figure as that of Virginia's highest public official, the soldiers inquired where they could get a stiff drink. After chatting with the men for a while, the governor himself provided the desired libations by ushering the astonished strangers into the Mansion as his guests for the cocktail hour. At other times he invited similar newfound friends to join him for an evening of his favorite entertainment—the Old Dominion Barn Dance, a country music hoedown at the WRVA theater located near the Mansion.[50]

Some of Tuck's escapades were of a more antic nature. One night he decided to test the security around the Mansion by stepping out into the yard and firing a pistol in the air. He then held his watch to see how long it would take the Capitol police to reach him. After a considerable time they arrived, thoroughly shaken. "When they finally got here," Tuck said later, "their knees were knocking so, they scared me!"[51] Virginians, surely, had never seen a governor quite like Bill Tuck.

The Tuck governorship, placed within the context of twentieth-century Virginia politics, represented the Byrd organization at the height of its power. The General Assembly during that time was laden with organization regulars; antiorganization forces, for the most part, were simultaneously at a low ebb. Moreover, the increasingly conservative public mood in the postwar era was congenial to the philosophy of Byrdism. The Tuck administration emerged in retrospect as the culmination of the organization's "golden age."

It was, nevertheless, during those years that evidence of future trouble began to appear. The embitterment of organized labor, the alienation of the black community, the estrangement of liberal and moderate Democrats—all of these developments portended the weakening of the Byrd hegemony. The waters of conservation which Tuck had ridden at floodtide were slowly but ineluctably receding as

[50] Wilkinson, *Harry Byrd*, p. 26; McDowell, "Bill Tuck," p. 17.
[51] Friddell, *What Is It about Virginia?*, p. 61.

the governor left office. Never again would the Byrd organization so thoroughly dominate the political life of Virginia. To suggest that signs of decline were discernible, however, is not to imply that the organization's demise was imminent; it was not. That confraternity, with Bill Tuck as its avatar, would last for some years yet. For the time being, it was with an aura of immense prestige that Tuck left the governorship to begin what would turn out to be a temporary retirement.

III   *The Congressional Years*

From Richmond to Washington
9. *A Not-So-Quiet Interlude*

I have no further ambitions of any sort.
> —*William M. Tuck to David K. E. Bruce*
> *(January 1950)*

I am complimented that I should be mentioned for so high a position as congressman. . . . The kind of life and work, I believe, would be appealing to me.
> —*Tuck to his sister (January 1953)*

In January 1950 Bill Tuck returned to his native Halifax to take up the more tranquil life of a Southside Virginia lawyer-planter. Although he was a man of bountiful energy who had wielded his gubernatorial power with gusto, he had found the demands of office increasingly burdensome and so professed relief at returning to private life. "I had such a tumultuous administration," he recalled, "filled with so much acrimony. I eagerly looked forward to the day it would all be over." [1]

Ensconced once again in South Boston, Tuck resumed his legal career, rejoining his former partner, Donald P. Bagwell, and his own stepson, Lester Dillard, in a thriving practice. Unencumbered by the cares of public office for the first time in twenty years, he took pleasure in being with his family, especially since his first grandchild, William Munford Tuck Dillard, had just been born. To all outward appearances the former governor was, as he claimed to be, content in his new role. "I am . . . enjoying as never before the quietude and serenity of this fine old Southside Virginia community," he wrote his friend David Bruce. "It is good to lay down the responsibilities of high public office." [2]

There were indications all along, however, that Tuck's exit from

---

[1] Norfolk *Virginian-Pilot*, June 8, 1969.
[2] Tuck to Bruce, Feb. 22, 1950, Tuck Papers; Lowance, "Tuck," p. 8.

politics would not be permanent. At the time he left the governorship, the Richmond *Times-Dispatch* asserted that "a man with his talent for public office must not retire when in his prime. The record he has made for the past four years should preclude that."[3] At the age of fifty-three, Tuck did have the reasonable expectation of a good many more active years. Though he remained mum as to his future plans, he maintained frequent communication with his Byrd organization associates, particularly with the senator himself, concerning both state and national affairs. He continued to be harshly critical of the Truman administration, writing to Byrd after the outbreak of the Korean War, "What a terrible price we are paying in blood, money and lost liberties for . . . turning over the affairs of this country to the type of people we now have in positions of leadership, who have fouled up both our domestic and foreign situation." On another occasion he told the senator, "People are fast losing faith in Truman, and while the wish may be father to the thought, it looks to me like the people are ready to vote against him, war or no war."[4]

It turned out that Tuck's absence from the state political scene lasted for approximately two years. When he reappeared, it was with the same rambunctiousness that had characterized his earlier career. Invited to deliver the keynote address at the 1952 state Democratic convention in Roanoke, he seized the opportunity to vent his hostility toward the national Democratic party in general and the outgoing Truman administration in particular. Liberally lacing his speech with such epithets as "political rapscallions . . . traducers . . . tormenting minions of vice and venality . . . political vultures," the former governor excoriated what he called "the 'something-for-nothing' boys who would peddle the honor of their government for pap from the public trough." In cadences faithful to the southern tradition of fulsome oratory, he continued his harangue:

I say to the purveyors and practitioners of those spurious doctrines which now threaten to engulf us that we will not be fettered or enchained. We will not

[3] Richmond *Times-Dispatch*, Jan. 12, 1950. One newspaperman wrote Tuck shortly thereafter that the members of the press corps "bemoan the fact that the Tuck Era has ended and news has to be dug up these days, where before you made it. . . . You are already a legend among the newspaper people" (M. W. Armistead III to Tuck, July 24, 1950, Tuck Papers).

[4] Tuck to Byrd, Sept. 9, Sept. 20, 1950, Tuck Papers.

servilely genuflect to "Trumanism" and "Fair Dealism." We will not be suppressed by the iniquitous FEPC acts, the unrestrained tyranny of union bosses, or the wanton profligacy of government wastrels. We will not be driven into the full embrace of socialism. . . . We will not capitulate, nor give quarter, to any foe of Americanism and free institutions, whether he seeks to clothe himself in the raiment of a Democrat or of a Republican.[5]

Incited by Tuck's philippic, the organization-dominated Roanoke convention took steps to "protect" the state party against the possibility of unacceptable developments at the upcoming national convention. Though the despised Truman had removed himself from consideration for renomination, Byrd Democrats feared, with good reason, that the national convention meeting in Chicago might choose an equally repugnant nominee. Consequently, the state convention, at Tuck's insistence, formally avowed its option (as provided for by the "anti-Truman" act of 1948) to reassemble after the Chicago convention in order to select a Virginia Democratic nominee if it so desired. Whether or not the leaders of the state organization planned to utilize that option, they apparently hoped that the potentiality of a "bolt" might provide them with more leverage inside the councils of the national party. Before it adjourned, the Roanoke assemblage indicated its acceptance of Tuck's hard-line approach by electing the former governor as chairman of the state Democratic party.[6]

Only days after the state convention ended, the Virginia delegation headed for Chicago, with Governor Battle, Byrd, Tuck, and E. R. Combs in the vanguard. Realizing that their views were badly out of alignment with those of the national party, the delegates approached the convention in a defensive, combative mood. They were agitated particularly by rumors that some form of loyalty oath would be required of each delegation before it could be seated. On the eve of the convention Tuck let it be known that he would have no part of any such oath. "Virginians have been pretty good custodians of their honor for the past 300 years," he said testily, "and if I wanted to deliver custody

[5] Paul T. David, Malcolm Moos, and Ralph M. Goldman, eds., *Presidential Nominating Politics in 1952—The South* (Baltimore: Johns Hopkins Press, 1954), p. 20; Fredericksburg *Free Lance–Star*, July 17, 1952.

[6] Richmond *Times-Dispatch*, July 18, 1952. Tuck was reluctant to accept the chairmanship and acquiesced only at the insistence of Senator Byrd (see Tuck to Byrd, Mar. 19, 1952, and Byrd to Tuck, Mar. 20, 1952, Byrd Papers).

of my honor to anyone, I wouldn't deliver it to that . . . convention." [7]

When the rumored loyalty pledge became a reality, the Virginia delegation was divided over what action to take. One faction favored a moderate response which would assure the official seating of the group, while another faction, headed by Tuck, opposed any action which might be construed as compromise. "Do it," the former governor warned his colleagues, "and I believe you'll repent in sackcloth and ashes before this convention is over. I hope we will not yield to those who would chastise us." Furthermore, he contended, signing the pledge would constitute a violation of the instructions given to the delegation by the recent state convention. [8]

In an effort to accommodate the Virginians and avoid an unseemly floor fight, the convention agreed to dilute the loyalty pledge requirement by exempting those states whose laws made compliance infeasible, as was allegedly the case in Virginia. Such a concession was insufficient to placate Tuck, who claimed that signing even a pro forma pledge would mean "bowing the knee to Baal." He was unalterably opposed, he said, "to jumping through any . . . hoops provided by such political hoodlums." Byrd shared Tuck's feeling and, in an uncharacteristically brusque outburst, declared, "We are not going to yield one damn inch." [9]

The controversy thus moved to a showdown on the convention floor. The Virginia delegates were permitted to take seats but, even as the presidential nominating commenced, they were ruled unqualified to participate officially in the proceedings. The most dramatic moment came when, during the roll call of states for nominations, Louisiana yielded to Virginia. What then transpired—the so-called "great foot race"—produced immediate, and continuing, debate.

Amidst the clamor arising from the various liberal delegations that were protesting Virginia's right to participate, convention chairman Sam Rayburn recognized Governor Battle, the chairman of the Virginia delegation. It was reported by journalists covering the event that Battle, a moderate within the Virginia group, departed for the speaker's platform with Tuck in hot pursuit. According to one account, the former governor, having been fortified for the evening

[7] Fredericksburg *Free Lance–Star*, July 22, 1952.
[8] Ibid.
[9] Ibid.; Henriques, "Battle," p. 287.

meeting by a few prandial libations, was "in the mood for total revolution" as he hurried for the rostrum, armed with a sizzling speech which he hoped to deliver to the convention. That speech, said one veteran newsman, "would, no doubt, have been another Sumter." Battle, however, arrived at the platform first and delivered a conciliatory address which, even though it did not contain any retraction of Virginia's stand against the loyalty pledge, sufficiently impressed the assemblage to allow Virginia to remain as an active participant, "un-oathed and un-pledged." [10]

There was much speculation as to what the outcome would have been had Tuck delivered the speech which he allegedly carried in his pocket to the rostrum. One journalist who had accompanied Tuck earlier in the evening claimed that during the taxi trip to the convention hall, the former governor had practiced reciting the address. It was, according to that firsthand account, "the greatest undelivered oration ever undelivered. . . . The incomparable William, in that ride to the stockyards, would have reduced William Jennings Bryan to schoolboy forensics." [11] Had the speech been delivered (assuming that it did, in fact, exist), it might well have resulted in the refusal of the convention to permit Virginia any further participation in the proceedings; that, in turn, would likely have precipitated a bolt by Virginia and other southern states. Some writers theorized that expulsion was precisely what the hard-line Byrd faction wanted, since it would have put the onus for a break on the national party rather than the state party. Evidence for such an interpretation could be seen in Byrd's own preconvention comment that "if they want to throw us out, let them. A good many of us would welcome it." At the convention one reporter observed that "Byrd and Tuck were itching for a fight and hoping to be kicked out." [12]

The tale of the "great foot race"—the dignified Battle and the pugnacious Tuck jostling through crowded aisles in a mad dash for the rostrum—quickly became a part of Virginia political folklore, despite the fact that both participants denied the veracity of the story. Battle later recalled that his mind at the time was solely on the task before

---

[10] Henriques, "Battle," pp. 289–90; Friddell, *What Is It about Virginia?*, p. 64; Latimer, "Virginia Politics," p. 49.

[11] Quoted in Henriques, "Battle," p. 290.

[12] Richmond *News Leader*, July 23, 1952; Henriques, "Battle," p. 286.

him and that he was unaware that Tuck had any intention of addressing the convention.[13] Tuck, for his part, disclaimed almost every aspect of the incident. He maintained that, first of all, he never had a prepared speech; the alleged text "just did not exist." His discourse in the taxi was merely what he would have told the convention and, as it turned out, was substantially what Battle said. Furthermore, he did not engage in any "foot race" on the convention floor. Battle, he explained, had been recognized by the chair and was clearly the only person entitled to speak. "I had sense enough to know I couldn't be recognized," Tuck said, "and I didn't want to be." Why, then, did he follow Battle to the podium? According to the former governor, it was not to try to supplant him but "to support him, to sustain him, if he needed it, . . . but he didn't need any help. He made such a fine, wonderful speech, . . . an eloquent speech." He was pleased with the results of the address, he said, because neither he nor Byrd was trying, as some charged, to provoke the convention into throwing them out. "All we were doing," he insisted, "was standing firm on principle."[14]

If the traditional account of the "great foot race" exaggerated Tuck's bellicosity at the Chicago convention, it did indicate accurately his growing alienation from the national Democratic party. Having voted for Georgia Senator Richard Russell on all three ballots which were taken, Tuck was not pleased when the nomination went to Illinois Governor Adlai Stevenson, whom he branded "the Truman candidate." His disenchantment became obvious in late August when he resigned as state party chairman, a position he had held for barely six weeks. He resigned, he said, because he could not support Stevenson until the candidate stated his views more fully on certain issues, and in the meanwhile, he felt he could not function conscientiously as party chairman. (In announcing his decision, he blithely explained that his attitude toward Stevenson was akin to that of the man who, upon reading a tombstone inscription, "Follow Me," scribbled the addendum: "To follow you I'm not content / Until I know which way you went.")[15]

The Stevenson candidacy in Virginia was given enthusiastic support

[13] Henriques, "Battle," p. 290.
[14] Interviews with Tuck.
[15] Fredericksburg *Free Lance–Star*, Aug. 28, 1952.

by the antiorganization Democrats (Martin Hutchinson, Robert Whitehead, Francis Pickens Miller, et al.) and was accorded polite endorsement by some leading organization figures, including Governor Battle, Senator Robertson, and Attorney General Almond. Tuck and Byrd, however, remained uncommitted throughout the summer. Writing to an active member of the powerful "Democrats for Eisenhower" movement, Tuck explained his position: "I have not as yet been able to reach a definite conclusion as to what I should do. I do not see how I can ever endorse the Truman ticket, and hence I may have to adopt a somewhat quiescent role, which . . . is contrary to my nature. . . . I greatly admire you and others who are able to come out and boldly proclaim where you stand." [16]

With some three weeks remaining before the election, Tuck finally determined his position. A conference with Byrd led to the decision that each man would make a statewide radio address, with the senator to speak first. [17] In his address on October 17, Byrd stopped short of endorsing Eisenhower but made it clear that he would not support Stevenson. When Tuck's turn came a week later, he went even further, pointing out that Stevenson was supported by "a motley collection of many of the most evil influences in America," enumerating among them the Americans for Democratic Action and the National Association for the Advancement of Colored People. He had planned to keep silent, he said, "but now that Stevenson has embraced Trumanism, I cannot be true to myself without speaking out firmly. . . . Candor compels me to say that the Eisenhower platform in many vital particulars . . . more nearly conforms to the traditional principles of the Democratic party than does the Truman platform." [18]

The Byrd and Tuck statements delivered the coup de grace to Stevenson's candidacy in Virginia, if any further blow were necessary. By receiving 56.3 percent of the vote to Stevenson's 43.4 percent,

[16] David et al., *Presidential Nominating Politics*, pp. 27–28; Sweeney, "Byrd and Anti-Byrd," pp. 190–91; Tuck to Mrs. Abram P. Staples, Oct. 13, 1952, Abram P. Staples Papers, University of Virginia Library, Charlottesville.

[17] Sweeney, "Byrd and Anti-Byrd," p. 193.

[18] Richmond *Times-Dispatch*, Oct. 23, 1953. It will be recalled that some Virginia Democrats, including then-Governor Tuck, had expressed interest in Eisenhower as a possible Democratic presidential nominee in 1948; see Chapter 7.

Dwight D. Eisenhower became only the second Republican since Reconstruction to carry the Old Dominion.[19] Yet, such was the curious nature of Virginia politics that the Republican victory was interpreted as an indication of the strength of the state Democratic organization, and of the Byrd-Tuck wing in particular.[20] Tuck personally gained stature in Byrd's estimation by standing loyally alongside the senator while some other organization regulars were flirting with Stevenson. From that point onward, few men were closer to Byrd politically than was Bill Tuck.

Tuck's increased visibility during the 1952 presidential campaign stimulated speculation that he might ere long seek elective office again. There were several alternatives. First, although it was virtually unprecedented, there was the possibility of running for a second term as governor in 1953, and some within the organization, in fact, counseled Tuck to keep that option open. There was the chance, too, that the former governor might challenge the incumbent A. Willis Robertson for the United States Senate in 1954. During his tenure in the Senate, Robertson had remained loosely within the Byrd organization, but he had incurred the displeasure of his senior colleague on several occasions by taking a too-liberal stance, as in his support for Truman in 1948 and Stevenson in 1952. Some observers believed that because of such gaffes Byrd would have preferred to have the more dependable Tuck as his fellow senator, provided that the change could be made without sundering the organization. Tuck did briefly consider running against Robertson but was reluctant to do so because, as he explained, even though Robertson's "heart never was right, he usually voted with Byrd"; it would have therefore been difficult to mount a convincing conservative campaign against him.[21]

As it turned out, Tuck offered for neither the governorship nor the Senate, but for the House of Representatives. The Fifth District seat became vacant when, after years of not-so-patient waiting, the incum-

[19] Strangely, Eisenhower failed to carry Tuck's home county of Halifax, where Stevenson received 59.0 percent of the vote (Eisenberg, *Virginia Votes*, pp. 181–84).

[20] It is difficult to gauge the extent of the intra-organization friction produced by the divergent stands of its various members. See David et al., *Presidential Nominating Politics*, p. 28, and Owen Randolph Easley, Jr., "Some Implications of the 1952 Presidential Election in Virginia" (M.A. thesis, Univ. of North Carolina, 1955).

[21] Interview with Tuck.

bent, Thomas B. Stanley, received Byrd's nod for governor to succeed Battle and resigned from Congress in early 1953 in order to make the gubernatorial race.[22] Tuck's name quickly came to the fore as a candidate to replace Stanley, but the former governor himself had reservations. "I am moved by all sorts of considerations," he wrote his sister, noting in particular, "There are financial [aspects] which I must consider, as I would be losing heavily." He went on to admit, though, that he was somewhat intrigued by the possibility and was flattered that, as he put it, "there are so many who would like to have it, but are willing to stand aside in my favor." His sister well understood the lure which the new opportunity presented, writing him:

Neville [another sister] said you ought to stay at home and keep away from all that responsibility. I told her that as long as you had been active in political affairs, even if you shut up your law office and moved out in the country, you would never be content unless you kept up with everything, and for you it would be better if you were in a position where you could help mold . . . right decisions. You are certainly qualified and although you have had Virginia's highest honor, this too is an honor, and if the people see fit to send you, which I know they will, I imagine you will feel that it is a call to duty that you can't ignore.

His sister was right. When the Fifth District Democrats met in Danville on March 7 to choose their candidate, Tuck's was the only name placed in nomination.[23]

The Danville gathering was not, however, totally harmonious. The delegations from the counties of Franklin, Carroll, Grayson, and Wythe, miffed at Tuck's refusal to support Stevenson in the previous presidential election, did not board the Tuck bandwagon. In the western part of the district where they were located, Republicanism was strong, and the success of Democratic candidates always depended on presenting a united front; consequently, they resented Tuck's apostasy in 1952, feeling that he had been largely responsible for Eisenhower's carrying the district. One of the leaders of the anti-Tuck forces explained: "We don't have anything against Bill Tuck. We like

[22] Stanley was elected in November, but only after a spirited challenge by the able Republican state Senator Ted Dalton of Radford.
[23] Tuck to Mrs. M. R. Buckley, Jan. 30, 1953, Mrs. M. R. Buckley to Tuck, Jan. 26, 1953, Tuck Papers; Richmond *Times-Dispatch*, Mar. 8, 1953.

him. But we don't think that any man honored as he has been by his party should bolt that party. . . . If a man bolts to the Republican party, we feel he should go to the Republican party for favors." When the actual balloting took place and it became evident that Tuck would win easily, many of the disaffected delegates walked out of the meeting in protest. In the end Tuck was nominated, receiving 525 out of a possible 761 votes which could have been cast. "I was highly pleased over the convention," he wrote shortly thereafter. "Although I could well do without the job, naturally I did not want to be discredited or repudiated here in my own district. . . . There were a few disgruntled noise-makers from some of the counties [but] the sentiment for me was overwhelming." [24]

Having secured the Democratic nomination without undue effort, Tuck could reasonably anticipate a handy victory in the special election scheduled for April 14. His Republican opponent was a political neophyte named Lorne Ross Campbell, an attorney from the Grayson County town of Independence. Initially it appeared that the unknown Campbell would pose no threat to the wily and experienced Tuck. However, certain circumstances peculiar to the time combined to make the race much closer than it ordinarily would have been. First, there was a good deal of lingering hostility toward Tuck on the part of Stevenson Democrats—a fact clearly underscored by the Danville convention; it remained doubtful whether, or to what extent, such disenchanted Democrats would support their party's nominee. Second, many Fifth District Democrats had broken lifelong voting habits in casting ballots for Eisenhower the previous November; with the taboo against voting Republican thus eliminated, such persons might feel less constrained to vote Democratic in the congressional election.

Campbell's strategy consisted mainly of trying to discredit Tuck within his own party by harping on the former governor's desertion of the Democratic ticket in 1952. "If a man is a States' Rights Democrat on the new of the moon, an Eisenhower Democrat on the full of the moon, and a Virginia Democrat on the wane of the moon," he asked his audiences, "how are we to know what he will be in the dark of the moon?" Tuck, of course, recognized the incongruity of such an appeal

[24] Richmond *Times-Dispatch*, Mar. 8, 1953; Tuck to Mrs. M. R. Buckley, Mar. 11, 1953, Tuck Papers.

and counterattacked accordingly. "My opponent," he said, "boasts of his own party regularity and [yet] appeals to Democrats to abandon their party. In the same breath he credits me with carrying Virginia for Eisenhower and [then] begs to be elected because he will be on the Eisenhower team." Such an approach, he said mischievously, reminded him of a certain shifty Virginia politician of the post-Reconstruction period, of whom it was once said:

> He wandered in and wandered out,
> And left the traveler still in doubt,
> Whether the snake that made the track
> Was going South or coming back.[25]

As the election approached, Tuck and his backers predicted that the outcome would be close—much closer than anyone had guessed at the outset. The race attracted some national attention as the first congressional election after the Eisenhower victory; since the Fifth District, invariably Democratic theretofore in modern presidential elections, had gone for Eisenhower, the Tuck-Campbell contest was anticipated as an indicator of the extent of permanent Republican inroads in the South. In the perspective of state politics, the election was watched as a test of the Byrd organization's ability to cohere in the aftermath of the divisions which had been manifest in the 1952 presidential election.

In the end, Tuck was elected, though the margin of victory was not overwhelming: he received 16,693 votes (57.8 percent) to his opponent's 12,182 (42.2 percent). Campbell managed to carry the normally Republican counties of Carroll, Grayson, and Wythe (all of which had gone heavily for Eisenhower), as well as Henry County, where Tuck was hurt by the labor vote. Had Tuck not carried his own Halifax County by almost 3,000 votes, the outcome would have been close indeed. As it was, it constituted what Tuck himself called the toughest fight of his political life to that time.[26]

Looking back on his unexpectedly narrow victory, Tuck later chuckled over two incidents which had occurred during the campaign.[27] Both took place in the mountainous western region of the

[25] Richmond *Times-Dispatch*, April 12, 1953.

[26] Ibid., April 15, 1953.

[27] These stories, which Tuck frequently repeated, may be found in an extensive interview with Tuck printed on Nov. 2, 1975 (ibid.).

district where resentment was still keen over Tuck's desertion of the Democratic presidential ticket in 1952. In one small town he approached a group of men and introduced himself, hand outstretched, to the first one he reached; the man glowered at Tuck and said, "I wouldn't touch your hand." When the candidate said that he was sorry that the man felt that way, the reply came back, "Well, you ought to have thought about that last fall, before you made that speech [for Eisenhower]." As Tuck made his way through the rest of the group the response was the same until finally two of the men did shake hands with him. "Well," said Tuck expansively, "you seem to be gentlemen." "No, sir," one of them replied, "we're Republicans."

The other episode was similarly illustrative of lingering disaffection toward Tuck in the Blue Ridge region. The candidate entered a country store owned by an antiorganization Democrat, introduced himself, and asked cheerfully how the campaign seemed to be going in that area. The storekeeper, without even looking up from his work behind the counter, replied, "There ain't no interest up here." Hoping to elicit some favorable response, Tuck continued his inquiries, only to receive the same answer every time. Finally the exasperated storekeeper straightened up, looked Tuck in the eye, and said firmly: "There ain't no interest up here, and ain't none of 'em coming out to vote. And I'll tell you this: the more of 'em that stays at home, the better off you're gonna be!"

Tuck could find the incidents amusing since he was now back in public office for the first time in approximately three years. No one was more gratified perhaps than Harry Byrd, who expressed delight that his outspoken conservative ally would be joining him in Washington. "I predict for him another notable record of public service," said the senator, adding, "He will soon be a commanding figure in the House of Representatives."[28]

It turned out that Tuck never quite lived up to Byrd's roseate prediction. Owing to vast political and social changes which were only obscurely foreseen in 1953, Tuck's career in Congress would never acquire the luster which had marked his governorship. Even so, his performance on Capitol Hill soon revealed that he had lost none of his fieriness and that his zest for political combat was as strong as ever.

[28] Ibid., April 15, 1953.

A Most Massive Resister

IO. *The Struggle against School Integration*

> The attitude of Virginians, educated and uneducated, towards the problem of race is basically the same in the day of Harry Byrd as it was in the day of Thomas Jefferson or Robert E. Lee.
>
> *—Francis Butler Simkins*

> No race excels the Negro at being judges of human nature. . . . I have never heard of a Negro being named Abraham Lincoln, Thaddeus Stevens, Lloyd Garrison, Franklin Delano, Harry Truman or Eleanor R., and I never expect to hear one called Earl Warren.
>
> *—William M. Tuck (1954)*

> On this subject [integration], I am not a "gradualist," I am a "neverist."
>
> *—Tuck (1956)*

Bill Tuck had barely settled into his congressional seat when on May 17, 1954, the Supreme Court of the United States announced its decision in the landmark school desegregation case of *Oliver Brown et al.* v. *Board of Education of Topeka, Kansas.* In an opinion which expressed the view of a unanimous Court, Chief Justice Earl Warren asserted that separate school facilities for whites and blacks were "inherently unequal" and thus in violation of the equal protection of the laws guaranteed by the Fourteenth Amendment; racially segregated public schools must therefore be abolished.

Observant Virginians might have seen the *Brown* decision coming, had they wanted to admit to themselves that such a thing could happen. The Court had been chipping away at the "separate-but-equal" doctrine for a number of years in various southern states; during the Tuck governorship Virginia's own system of segregated schools had come under sporadic attack.[1] Even so, when the *Brown* decision was delivered, the people of the Commonwealth were thunderstruck. In upsetting the pattern of legal segregation which had existed for over half a century, the *Brown* decision opened one of the bitterest and most turbulent eras in the history of Virginia politics.

Considering the furor which would eventually ensue, the initial response of Virginia's officialdom to the Court's decree was, for the most part, restrained. Governor Stanley expressed his confidence that the people of the state would "receive the opinion of the Supreme Court calmly" and announced that he contemplated "no precipitate action." Senator Byrd, while describing the decision as a "most serious blow" to states' rights, did not seem overly exercised. The most severe public denunciation came from freshman Congressman Tuck, who claimed that he could not find words to express his "chagrin" over the "acute problem" which had arisen. "The decision," he continued, "imposes upon the good people of America a way of life not envisioned in our Constitution and to which many are unalterably opposed. . . . The abolishment of segregation in our schools will lower the standards of public education, and will tend to mar the cordial and understanding race relations which have existed for so long. . . . I trust that we may find some workable solution to what appears at present to be an insurmountable and intolerable problem."[2]

That Tuck's response was more adamant than that of other state leaders could have been attributed in part to political considerations. Since much of the Fifth District which he represented in Congress lay within the state's Southside—a region comprising a disproportionately large black population, but having few black voters—Tuck recognized the practical necessity of taking a stand which would be palatable to his preponderantly white constituency. His opposition to the *Brown* decision, however, was by no means dictated solely by the exigencies of politics; he profoundly believed that the decision was wrong, and potentially ruinous to his region. "It is not a political matter with me," he told Byrd, "but one of deep concern for the

---

[1] Although the thrust of earlier decisions had been merely to require equality within the principle of separate-but-equal rather than to abolish the principle itself, those decisions were perceived by many, including Tuck, as portending the end of segregated schools. See Chapter 8.

[2] Richmond *Times-Dispatch*, May 18, 1954.

welfare of our people. I would be perfectly willing to scuttle my own political life if that should be necessary to preserve the integrity of both the white and the colored races in Virginia."[3]

The vehemence of Tuck's opposition to desegregation can be understood only against the backdrop of the age in which he grew up. The early twentieth century was a time of intense racial feeling, not just in the South but throughout the nation. It was during those years that social scientists purported to "prove" the innate inferiority of the Negro race; historians pictured blacks as lazy and immature by nature and interpreted Reconstruction as an example of the danger inherent in allowing blacks to participate in the political process. Popular attitudes on race were greatly influenced by the highly acclaimed "epic" motion picture, *The Birth of a Nation*, released in 1915, which demeaned blacks as lustful cretins and, conversely, glorified the Ku Klux Klan as the saviors of southern civilization. Not surprisingly under such conditions, lynchings reached alarming proportions. In sum, the abasement of blacks during Tuck's formative years was thoroughgoing, and, like the vast majority of his southern contemporaries, he emerged from that period with an ingrained belief in black inferiority.

Withal, Tuck was not an unmitigated racist of the ilk frequently spawned under the same conditions in more southerly climes. His theory of race relations was akin to that espoused by Booker T. Washington, whom he admired. As a student at William and Mary, he had heard Washington speak and, as he later recalled, was "much impressed by what he had to say. He was undoubtedly a great American."[4] Particularly attractive to Tuck were Washington's advocacy of self-help for blacks and, even more, his manifest belief in the social separation of the races.

In his political career Tuck disavowed open animosity toward blacks. He took pride in the fact that as governor he had secured state funds for the construction of a memorial to Booker T. Washington on the Virginia farm where the educator was born; had established a day in honor of Joseph Jenkins Roberts, a black Virginia native who became president of Liberia; and had dedicated a monument in Philadelphia to James A. Bland, the black composer who wrote Virginia's state song.

[3] Tuck to Byrd, Sept. 3, 1954, Tuck Papers.
[4] Tuck to Dr. J. K. Hall, Oct. 8, 1945, ibid.

In addition to such largely symbolic acts, he showed concern in more tangible ways by establishing by executive order a state park for blacks and, more importantly, by securing unprecedented appropriations for tuberculosis control, an especially virulent disease among blacks. If Tuck's public record did not establish him as an egalitarian—and surely it did not—it did reveal a certain measure of solicitude within the limits of what was then politically feasible in Virginia. So it was without a hint of conscious dissimulation that Tuck in later life repeatedly denied accusations of bigotry. Regarding himself as enlightened in his racial views, he said (typically), "My relations with the colored race have been good. I harbor no malice or ill will; on the contrary, in my public and private life I have promoted their welfare in an effort to continue the racial understanding and peace we have enjoyed for so many years."[5]

Put most simply, Bill Tuck was a paternalist of the old school. In his personal dealings with blacks he evinced friendliness and some care for their well-being; in his public life he generally stayed within the genteel Virginia tradition, refraining from blatant techniques of race-baiting.[6] On the other hand, there was nothing in his career to suggest that he found existing race relations unjust, and certainly nothing to suggest that he favored any government-instigated alteration of the status quo. So long as the doctrine of "separate-but-equal" prescribed the patterns of interracial behavior, Tuck was content; when that doctrine came under attack, he was jolted into an intransigent defense of the old order.

The basis of Tuck's opposition to the *Brown* decision was clearly racial, but he also rejected that decision on other (though not unrelated) grounds. There was, for example, the matter of states' rights. As a strict constructionist, he put great store in the Tenth Amendment, which reserved to the respective states those powers not delegated by the Constitution to the United States. He maintained that each state had the right to operate its school system as it saw fit, irrespective of the dictate of the Fourteenth Amendment that no state should deny to any

[5] Tuck to J. C. Massey, May 26, 1954, ibid. For Tuck's own account of his dealings with blacks, see the Halifax *Gazette*, Oct. 27, 1955.

[6] The nature of Tuck's personal relationship with certain blacks may be seen in numerous letters in both his personal and executive papers; e.g., Tuck to Clarence Green, Oct. 24, 1947, Tuck Executive Papers.

person the equal protection of the laws (the clause upon which the *Brown* decision was based). In Tuck's view the Supreme Court—"nine reprehensible individuals gasconading in judicial ermine," he called them—had wrongly used the Fourteenth Amendment to vitiate the Tenth, thereby undermining the principle of states' rights. "It transcends the race question," he wrote, "and involves the unlawful taking of our constitutional liberties. There is no end to what the Supreme Court can do under this decision, and we must fight to have it reversed." Privately he expressed bitter contempt for the Court, commenting disdainfully that "a first class Virginia justice of the peace could have reached a more sensible decision and written a better opinion."[7]

Tuck's outrage was all the greater because he believed the desegregation issue to have been instigated by nonsouthern forces who were motivated, not by genuine concern for blacks, but by base political considerations; indeed, Tuck was convinced that blacks themselves—or at least the "better element" among them—did not want integration. Sounding a familiar refrain of southern rhetoric, he said, "We have had trouble only when outsiders who know nothing of the problems of the colored man, and care less, have interfered for the sole purpose of attracting the minority vote in pivotal states to control Senatorial and Presidential elections." On the day after the *Brown* verdict was delivered, he summed up his opinion in a letter to a personal friend. "It was a political, not a judicial, decision," he wrote, "given by a combination of New Dealers, Fair Dealers and Republicans, with reckless disregard for the effect it would have." On other occasions he asserted that the decision resulted from a Communist-inspired effort to weaken the nation by fomenting internal dissension. The whole affair, he told Byrd, amounted to "the worst thing that has ever happened since the foundation of the Republic."[8]

Largely because of the reputation which he had acquired during his governorship for what one writer called "shoot 'em-up conservatism," many Virginians looked to Tuck to lead the fight against desegregation. "I only wish you were at the helm now," wrote one of his

[7] Speech by Tuck, Feb. 11, 1960, Tuck to William O. Story, Jr., Nov. 18, 1954, Tuck to Roscoe Stephenson, June 7, 1954, Tuck Papers.

[8] Tuck to J. C. Massey, May 26, 1954, Tuck to Ida Jane Brawner, May 18, 1954, Tuck to John H. Daniel, June 17, 1955, Tuck to Byrd, November 5, 1954, ibid.

constituents, "as we need you more than when you adjusted the labor situation." A Richmond schoolteacher, urging Tuck into action "for the sake of our state and the Southland," ended by saying, "I would give $1000 of my $2000 old-age savings if Bill Tuck were governor of Virginia today." From throughout the state Tuck was importuned with similar appeals.[9]

There was no reluctance on Tuck's part to speak out. "This is not a kid glove age," he told one Richmond city official, "and in these distressing times, if we do our duty, we all have to speak up openly and frankly and fearlessly." The only question in Tuck's mind was one of tactics—of how the Court's mandate might be most effectively thwarted. Initially he seemed at times to envision some sort of token compliance as the best response. Writing to Georgia Governor Herman Talmadge shortly after the ruling was handed down, he said: "There are some counties and cities in Virginia where we may have integration in compliance with the Supreme Court decision. For instance, we have one large county [Buchanan] where there is not a single Negro family and there are many other counties where there are only a few Negro families." The approach which he seemed to favor was that of local option. As he explained to one member of the legislature, "I am opposed to integration, but if there are any counties in Virginia who want it, . . . then I would say let those counties have it, but those of us who do not want it should not be forced to maintain public schools for the integrationists."[10]

At other times, however, he presaged the hard-line, no-compromise stand which he would later take, suggesting in one letter that evasion of the Court's decree might "require the closing of our public schools and the establishing of private schools." Such action would not be too drastic for him. "Personally," he wrote, "I would prefer to teach my children at home rather than to subject them to such an unspeakable situation."[11]

[9] Wilkinson, *Harry Byrd*, p. 27; letter to Tuck, June 10, 1954, letter to Tuck, May 23, 1954, Tuck Papers. The Tuck Papers contain numerous letters in this vein, many of them openly skeptical of Stanley's fortitude in the face of the crisis.

[10] Tuck to Philip J. Bagley, Oct. 28, 1954, Tuck to Talmadge, May 25, 1954, Tuck to C. William Cleaton, Nov. 23, 1954, Tuck Papers.

[11] Tuck to F. T. Faulconer, June 9, 1954, Tuck to Edmund T. DeJarnette, Oct. 18, 1954, ibid.

In the meanwhile Tuck acquiesed in the relatively moderate approach taken by Governor Stanley, who in August 1954 appointed a commission to study the problem and recommend a course of action.[12] The thirty-two member group (all white) was dominated by rural, black-belt Byrd loyalists and was chaired by state Senator Garland (Peck) Gray, an influential legislator from the Southside's Sussex County, who was on record as being strongly opposed to integration. Tuck made sure that his views were known to the commission. Writing to one of its members, he spelled out his recommendations point-by-point. Essentially, the Tuck plan called for a referendum to be held in each locality. If the people voted for integration, all state funds for public schools in that locality would be withdrawn and tuition grants would be provided by the state to allow individual students in that locality to attend segregated private schools elsewhere. His "major premise," he said, was that the state "should not make provision of any sort, financial or otherwise, for integrated schools." Having delineated his proposed course of action, he went on to deliver a remarkable discourse on the situation confronting the commission as he perceived it:

Nothing in my lifetime, and I doubt at any other time in the history of the Commonwealth, has ever come so close to the hearts of the people because it involves the education of our children and grandchildren, and is an effort on the part of extreme left-wingers to instill into them every imaginable spurious doctrine. . . . I hope that you and your commission will provide the leadership necessary and indispensable in this crisis. I know that there are some members of the commission who favor a foot-dragging, mealy-mouthed, shilly-shally approach. This do-nothing policy will not suffice or satisfy. A firm stand, followed by vigorous action now, will do much to stimulate those . . . who may be on the fence. We know the Virginia Negroes, and if we let them know now that there will be no compromise in this matter, . . . they will take their places among their own race and not make these foolish, Communistically-inspired demands.[13]

[12] The following account draws generally from Benjamin Muse, *Virginia's Massive Resistance* (Bloomington: Indiana University Press, 1961); Robbins L. Gates, *The Making of Massive Resistance* (Chapel Hill: University of North Carolina Press, 1964); and the best and most recent study, James W. Ely, Jr., *The Crisis of Conservative Virginia: The Byrd Organization and the Politics of Massive Resistance* (Knoxville: University of Tennessee Press, 1976).

[13] Tuck to John H. Daniel, June 17, 1955, Tuck Papers.

To his friend, commission chairman Peck Gray, Tuck put the matter bluntly. "It makes me sick," he said, "when I hear these folks talking about delaying. That is like a mongrel requesting the hand of a beautiful young lady in marriage and she said, 'Not now, but come back next year.' We must fight this thing to the bitter end." Later, Tuck wrote Gray again, urging him to "take a strong, firm stand on this issue, and do not veer from it one inch, regardless of whether or not other members of the commission go along with you." [14]

The Gray Commission deliberated for well over a year before delivering its recommendations, leaving some Byrd organization leaders increasingly concerned over the possible political ramifications of the impending report. As the then-Attorney General J. Lindsay Almond warned Byrd early on, "That which we have known and believed in, sometimes called the 'organization,' might well founder in the absence of . . . a courageous and constructive program with reference to this explosive subject." Of particular concern to the Byrd hierarchy was the possibility that failure to take firm control of the integration issue might open the way for a successful challenge to the organization in the next gubernatorial election—either from a Republican (most likely Ted Dalton again) or from an antiorganization Democrat such as, specifically, the redoubtable Robert Whitehead. (Though personally opposed to integration, Whitehead emerged during the controversy as a "moderate" who advocated tolerating some integration rather than close the public schools.) One Byrd adherent pointed out the problem in an anonymous letter to Peck Gray. "It has come to my attention that the organization has not taken a stand in regard to the issue of separation of the races," he wrote, "[and unless it does] the Whitehead group will completely dominate the area when the governor's election comes up two years hence." The issue, he continued, could be "won on one simple basis: that it is morally and spiritually wrong to integrate the races." An elderly former member of the General Assembly put the matter more succinctly in a letter to Tuck. "Are you going to smugly sit and serenely let Robert Whitehead split the organization into smithereens? Are you, Bill?" he asked. "Such delay is quite wonderful

[14] Tuck to Gray, June 14, 1954, Oct. 25, 1955, ibid.

for the anti-machinist but such delay is hell for the segregationist and the organization." [15]

While the Gray Commission deliberated for month after month, opposition to desegregation intensified. The growing antagonism found a vehicle for expression in an organization bearing the unwieldly name of the Defenders of State Sovereignty and Individual Liberties. Though ardently dedicated to preserving segregation, the Defenders were generally more restrained in their methods than were the White Citizens' Councils which sprang up in the deeper South during the same period. Abjuring Klan-type excesses, the Defenders attempted to couch their appeals in such a way as to attract "respectable" citizens. Their success was attested by a rapid rise in membership: within a year of its founding in October 1954, the organization boasted twenty-eight active chapters; a year later there were sixty chapters comprising approximately twelve thousand members. [16] A charter member of the Halifax chapter, Bill Tuck contributed to the Defenders' monthly newsletter and proselytized in the group's behalf, hailing the Defenders as "patriotic in all respects, and in line with our finest American traditions." It was no accident that the largest local chapter was in Halifax. [17]

When the Gray plan was finally announced in early November 1955, the public temper had become substantially more defiant than it had been when the committee began its work the previous summer. Indicative of the hardening of attitudes was a rancorous and emotional speech delivered by Tuck to a Defender-sponsored gathering of some twenty-five hundred persons in Halifax two weeks before the Gray plan was made public. "We have met here tonight," he began, "because of our interest in preserving the purity of our race, as well as our liberty

[15] Almond to Byrd, Aug. 16, 1954, copy, [unsigned] to Gray, Mar. 1, 1955, letter to Tuck, June 7, 1955, ibid. For a discussion of Whitehead's position, see Gates, *Making of Massive Resistance*, pp. 150–53.

[16] Wilkinson, *Harry Byrd*, pp. 120–22; Gates, *Making of Massive Resistance*, pp. 36–38.

[17] Tuck to Tazewell G. Nicholson, Jan. 31, 1956, William E. Maxey, Jr., executive director of the Defenders, to Tuck, Dec. 21, 1955, Tuck Papers. Comments by Tuck were featured in the *Defenders News and Views* 1 (Sept. 1955), copy in Tuck Papers.

and freedom. . . . I intend to resist with all the might I have this effort to distort the minds, to pollute the education, and to defile and make putrid the pure Anglo-Saxon blood that courses through the innocent veins of our helpless children. . . . In this matter there is no middle ground. There is no compromise. We are for integration or we are against it." [18]

In light of the passions which had thus been aroused, it was not surprising that the Gray plan came as a disappointment to many, since it did open the possibility of some integration. Under that plan, local school boards would be authorized to assign students to appropriate schools ostensibly according to criteria other than race—for example, aptitude, health, convenience of transportation, or "the welfare of the particular child, as well as the welfare and best interests of all other pupils attending a particular school." Such criteria (especially the latter) were sufficiently broad, the commission believed, to prevent integration in most cases; but, to take care of those instances in which integration did occur under the pupil assignment system, the plan called for state tuition grants to allow children in such schools to attend private segregated schools if they so desired. Further, it was recommended that the state's compulsory attendance law be amended so that no child would be forced to attend an integrated school. Implementation of the plan necessitated amendment of Section 141 of the state constitution which prohibited the appropriation of public funds for education in private schools. To expedite the change, a special session of the General Assembly, meeting in late November, set up a popular referendum for the following January in which the voters would decide whether a limited constitutional convention should be called for the purpose of amending the constitution so as to allow tuition grants.

Tuck was not at all happy with the Gray plan, writing Byrd, "I very much fear that the Governor and his Commission have not come out strong enough." Although the basic features of the plan were largely in accord with the recommendations which he himself had made to the commission earlier, Tuck, like many of his contemporaries, had grown more apprehensive in the interim; he now felt that even the minimal integration in some localities as envisioned by the Gray plan would be dangerous since it might weaken the resolve of segregationists in other

[18] Halifax *Gazette*, Oct. 27, 1955.

areas of the state. The pupil assignment plan and local option were thus perceived as constituting an entering wedge for full-scale integration.[19]

Despite his misgivings, Tuck, in response to the pleas of Governor Stanley, Peck Gray, and other organization leaders, worked diligently for passage of the tuition grant referendum. The vote was anticipated as an indicator of the strength of segregationist sentiment in the state—and the outcome was by no means viewed as certain. Gray, former Governor Darden, and Senator Byrd all expressed to Tuck their concern that the tuition grant plan might be defeated. As Byrd put it, "We have a long, hard and bitter fight ahead of us, and the local referendums will show what sections we can rely on when the cards are down."[20]

Such anxiety proved unwarranted. The plan was endorsed by an overwhelming vote of 304,154 to 146,164, with the widest margins coming, predictably, in the Southside, where over 80 percent of the vote was cast in the affirmative. The outcome left Tuck jubilant. "I have never been more proud of being a Virginian than I am now, and the Fifth District people have demonstrated that they are 'super Virginians,'" he exulted in the afterglow of victory. "I did everything that I could do, and at times I wondered if I wasn't even going a little too far. We tried to put the issue right on the line." Whatever Tuck did, it was effectual. His home county, where the population was 44 percent black (but with only 521 registered black voters as against 5,570 white), produced a well-nigh incredible 5,310 votes in favor, and only 677 in opposition.[21]

The segregationists' enormous margin of victory in the referendum elicited responses from sources far removed from Virginia. Columnist Arthur Krock, writing in the New York *Times*, commented that "by every democratic measurement of public opinion a great majority of

[19] Tuck to Byrd, Nov. 16, 1955, Tuck Papers. See also Tuck to North Carolina Governor Luther Hodges, Nov. 16, 1955, and Tuck to E. Blackburn Moore, June 6, 1956, ibid.

[20] Byrd to Tuck, Nov. 8, 1955, ibid. See also Stanley to Tuck, Dec. 6, 1955, Darden to Tuck, Dec. 19, 1955, and Byrd to Garland Gray, Dec. 16, 1955, copy, ibid.

[21] Wilkinson, *Harry Byrd*, p. 127; Tuck to Manly Aylor, Jan. 13, 1956, Tuck to Ben D. Lacy, Jan. 13, 1956, Tuck Papers; Gates, *Making of Massive Resistance*, p. 93.

one of the most law-abiding states of the Union, notable also for enlightened interracial conditions . . . , was registered against inflexible legal integration in the public schools." The *Wall Street Journal* similarly claimed that there was "nothing trivial about this protest. . . . Nor [was it] simply the voice of some rabblerousing demagogues hoisted to power upon one suspender. . . . Here is impressive testimony that the people who live closest to this ancient problem do not believe it can be resolved by a Supreme Court decree." [22]

The results of the referendum were of paramount significance in the decision of the Byrd organization to shift from the relatively mild approach of the Gray plan to a more defiant position—a position which Tuck and other Southside stalwarts had preferred all along. The organization's brain trust may well have figured that if the voters of the state were so in favor of limiting integration through the Gray plan (as was evidenced by the referendum results), they might be willing to accept, or even prefer, sterner measures which would prevent integration altogether. In any case, one thing was certain: the Southside, upon which the organization was heavily dependent for its success, had demonstrated conclusively in the referendum that it was firmly opposed to integration. From a purely political standpoint, the organization leadership realized the necessity of developing a policy which would retain the loyalty of that region. Thus did the more radical period of "massive resistance" begin to take shape.

It so happened that at the very time the decision was being made to go beyond the moderate approach contained in the Gray plan, a theory emerged which seemed to some segregationists to offer a means whereby the *Brown* decision could be completely circumvented: namely, the theory of interposition. Resurrected by a Chesterfield County lawyer (and college classmate of Tuck's) by the name of William Old, the theory was given wide circulation in late 1955 and early 1956 through a series of Richmond *News Leader* editorials which flowed from the brilliant pen of James Jackson Kilpatrick, the aggressive young editor of that paper. Interposition amounted to, in essence, a refurbishing of John C. Calhoun's antebellum doctrine of nullification—a hoary, and presumably discredited, theory which maintained that a state could nullify within its borders any federal act which it

[22] New York *Times*, Jan. 11, 1956; *Wall Street Journal* Jan. 11, 1956.

deemed invalid simply by asserting (or "interposing") its state sovereignty. Since the theory had not been used since the Civil War, and never used successfully, it seemed unlikely that it could be employed effectively to halt integration. Yet so vast were Kilpatrick's literary gifts, and so desperate were the segregationists, that the resisters gratefully embraced the chimerical theory of interposition as a veritable godsend. Tuck, for one, was encouraged by the possibilities. Having learned from Kilpatrick that an interposition campaign would be launched, Tuck wired the editor his "wholehearted approval," adding, "In my opinion it will electrify the South if not indeed the whole nation."[23]

When the 1956 regular session of the General Assembly met in January, following the referendum, much attention was focused on Kilpatrick's pet theory. Some, like Tuck, believed that interposition should become the keystone of segregationist opposition. "I hope you will get through the General Assembly a strong (not watered down) resolution on interposition," he wrote Garland Gray. "This is the only legal way that I know of that we can appeal from the decision of the Supreme Court. People all over the South are looking to Virginia for leadership and will follow us if we take a firm and persistent stand." The resolution which the Assembly did enact was, as it turned out, considerably "watered down"—a somewhat otiose expression of the members' resolve "to resist this illegal encroachment upon our sovereign powers, and to urge . . . prompt and deliberate efforts to check this and further encroachment by the Supreme Court, through judicial legislation, upon the reserved powers of the States."[24] In practical application, the effect of the resolution was nil. However, by seeming to provide a workable barricade, interposition served to embolden the segregationists and to nudge them toward a more extreme position.

Senator Byrd himself had become more adamant in his opposition during early 1956. On February 24, using the phrase which would come to identify Virginia's unyielding stance, Byrd announced, "If we can organize the Southern states for massive resistance . . . I think that

---

[23] Tuck to Kilpatrick, Nov. 18, 1955, Tuck Papers.
[24] Tuck to Gray, Jan. 18, 1956, ibid.; *Journal of the Senate,* 1956, p. 146.

in time the rest of the country will realize that racial integration is not going to be accepted in the South." Several weeks later, as part of the massive resistance plan, Byrd was instrumental in promulgating the "Southern Manifesto," a declaration of defiance which was signed by 101 members of Congress, Bill Tuck among them.[25]

The hard-line approach was precisely what Tuck wanted. Echoing Byrd's own phrase, he wrote the senator, "I am in favor of putting up an impregnable wall of massive resistance and keeping it there." How far was he willing to go? He flippantly told his friend Dan Daniel (who would later succeed him in Congress): "I am like the man who, when someone inquired whether he wanted his mother-in-law cremated, embalmed or buried, wired back, 'Make no mistake. Do all three'; and that is the way I am about this issue. I think we should hit it on every front." In a more somber mood he wrote another friend that he was "in favor of doing whatever is necessary to avoid integration, irrespective of what it may be, short of violence and insurrection."[26]

The means by which massive resistance would be effected in Virginia was devised during the summer of 1956. Tuck, one of the chief architects of the plan, hinted at what was to come when he wrote Farmville newspaper editor (and archresister) J. Barrye Wall, "We have just got to have a program [which will] draw the issue and separate the integrationists from the segregationists." That program began to take shape following a clandestine meeting of the inner circle of organization leaders at Byrd's Washington office on July 2. Several days later the senator directly requested Tuck to work with Congressmen Watkins Abbitt and Howard Smith to formulate a specific plan of action. Tuck was elated by the trend of events, gleefully informing Wall, "From all I can hear, it now looks as if we are getting ready to 'cook with gas.'"[27]

The strategy which emerged came to be known as the Stanley plan, though it actually owed less to the governor than to certain other organization wheelhorses from the Southside. The new approach was

[25] Richmond *Times-Dispatch*, Feb. 25, 1956; Muse, *Virginia's Massive Resistance*, p. 27.

[26] Tuck to Byrd, Mar. 29, 1956, Tuck to W. C. (Dan) Daniel, Feb. 10, 1959, Tuck to Isham T. Wilkinson, Mar. 21, 1956, Tuck Papers.

[27] Tuck to Wall, June 20, July 5, 1956, Byrd to Tuck, July 5, 1956, ibid.; Wilkinson, *Harry Byrd*, p. 130.

embodied in a package of bills enacted by the General Assembly at a special session summoned by Stanley in late August. The most significant provisions were those which required the governor to close any school under court order to integrate and to cut off state funds to any such school which might try to reopen in compliance with the court's edict. In the absence of state funds for public schools, a locality could attempt to operate its schools on an integrated basis using only local funds, or it could close its schools and secure tuition grants from state and local funds to provide for sending (white) students to private (segregated) schools.

The massive resistance legislation, because it envisioned the possible closing of schools, alienated many moderates, some of them organization loyalists, who had earlier stood by the Gray plan. Tuck took a dim view of such apostates. "If they won't stand with us, then I say make 'em," he snarled. "We cannot compromise. . . . If you ever let them integrate anywhere the whole state will be integrated in a short time." The very term "moderate" became an anathema to him. "We must not surrender," he told Byrd, "to the people who like to refer to themselves as 'moderates' or 'middle-of-the-roaders,' but who in fact are nothing other than full-fledged integrationists flying under false colors." He did not protest when the appellative "extremist" was applied to himself because, as he explained to a fellow resister, "even if those of us who oppose integration are extremists, we are serving the purpose of keeping the middle-of-the-roaders in the middle of the road, rather than having them come out openly for integration." [28]

As time passed, Tuck became known (along with Watt Abbitt perhaps) as the most massive of resisters among the state's major political figures. He assailed proponents of integration as "modern-day abolitionists and latter-day reconstructionists," declaring in one speech that the work of such people was calculated to cause a "merger of the races" which would ultimately result in a "hybridized human, if human it would be." Several groups in particular attracted his ire, among them the numerous ministers who advocated integration. He regarded them as hypocritical, commenting privately to Richmond attorney David J. Mays: "The churches never have and never will

[28] Richmond *Times-Dispatch*, July 28, 1956; Tuck to Byrd, Mar. 29, 1956, Tuck to J. Segar Gravatt, Nov. 19, 1954, Tuck Papers.

integrate. Unless and until they do, we should not give serious
consideration to integrating the public schools." Such ministerial
opposition did not deeply trouble him though because, he continued,
"The integrationists have many of the preachers, but we have the
congregations."[29] More vexatious to Tuck were the several newspapers
which opposed massive resistance, notably the Norfolk *Virginian-Pilot*
and the Washington *Post*—the latter once being described by Tuck as
"a veritable saturnalis of socialism and sin." Most reprehensible of all in
the congressman's view were those persons who professed allegiance to
the Byrd organization but who would not cooperate fully in the fight
against integration. Such individuals, he wrote Byrd, "appear to have
learned the science of termites, and that is to get on the inside to
disrupt and destroy."[30]

Tuck's contempt for those whose resoluteness fell short of his own
was counterbalanced by his esteem for those who stood firm. He
particularly admired the response of Prince Edward County, which had
been a party to the original desegregation suit before the Supreme
Court. Anticipating the possible closing of public schools, a group of
Prince Edward citizens in the summer of 1955 had formed a private
educational corporation to provide schooling for the county's white
children. Tuck lauded such action, assuring Barrye Wall, a leader of
the private school movement, "The determination of the Prince Edward people in this matter is certainly inspiring to patriotic Virginians
and Americans everywhere." Not content with mere words, he offered
financial support to the project. "I do not know the cost of sending one
child to school," he wrote Wall, "but I will contribute the full tuition
of one student . . . and you can put this down on the pledge book for
whatever amount that would be." Publicly he acclaimed the county's
efforts, perorating in one speech: "God bless old Prince Edward! May
she continue to lead Virginia in the trying days which lie ahead."[31]

While Tuck campaigned ceaselessly for massive resistance, the
school-closing laws which underlay that policy went untested for some
two years after their enactment. In the interim, J. Lindsay Almond,

[29] Speeches by Tuck, Jan. 5, 1956, Dec. 4, 1957, Tuck to Mays, June 23, 1955,
Tuck Papers. At the time Mays was serving as counsel to the Gray Commission.

[30] Speech by Tuck, May 3, 1958, Tuck to Byrd, July 18, 1955, ibid.

[31] Gates, *Making of Massive Resistance*, p. 47; Tuck to Wall, June 9, 1955, July 5,
1956, Tuck Papers; Halifax *Gazette*, Oct. 27, 1955.

having defeated the Republican Ted Dalton in a hard-fought contest, succeeded Tom Stanley as governor. Since the Tuck governorship Almond had served as the state's attorney general and in that capacity had consistently upheld the Byrd organization's position in the school controversy. Shortly after the *Brown* decision was delivered he stated his personal views to Tuck in a letter which, in retrospect, seemed remarkable. "I agree with you," he wrote,

that it is clearly manifest that integration in the public school system would virtually destroy secondary education in Virginia. It is also clearly evident that the people of Southside Virginia cannot and will not subscribe to any plan of integration. . . . It seems that some think the time has come in Virginia when a public official dare not voice his honest convictions. It is true that it is very difficult for me to conceal contempt. However, regardless of future consequences, I shall continue to let the people know exactly where I stand in this fight. . . . What the answer will finally be, the good Lord only knows. As far as I am concerned, the fight has just begun.[32]

Accordingly, it was as the guarantor of segregation that Almond ran for governor in 1957. Speaking in his behalf during the campaign, Congressman Tuck reduced the issue to what he regarded as its simplest terms: "Those favoring mixing of the races will naturally vote for Mr. Dalton. Those favoring separation will vote for Mr. Almond."[33] Thus aided, Almond was elected—a fact which Tuck and his fellow resisters were soon to lament.

Some nine months after Almond took office, the showdown came when schools in several localities were directed by court order to integrate at the opening of the fall 1958 term. Tuck was confident that the impending crisis would be successfully met. "The Governor has given every indication of fighting this to the very last ditch, and I certainly hope and believe he will do so," he informed Robert B. Crawford, state leader of the Defenders. Seeming almost eager for the confrontation, he continued, "We are in the position now where we will find out within the next few weeks who are the true Virginians and who are the renegades."[34]

[32] Almond to Tuck, Aug. 24, 1954, Tuck Papers.

[33] Charlottesville *Daily Progress*, Nov. 1, 1957. What Dalton actually favored was token compliance with the *Brown* decision through a locally administered pupil assignment plan.

[34] Tuck to Crawford, Sept. 13, 1958, Tuck Papers.

Under terms of the massive resistance laws, schools began to close in September—first in rural Warren County, then in the university town of Charlottesville, then in the state's largest city, Norfolk. As the schools ceased functioning, protests arose from concerned groups in the affected areas, from antiorganization politicians, and from 'the state press; in addition, significant influence was exerted by the business community, whose spokesmen feared that continued school closings would adversely affect the state's economy. For his part, Tuck, however, encouraged Almond to stand firm, urging him to "keep the schools on a segregated basis, if operated at all." With protest increasing, he assured the governor, "The people are one hundred per cent behind you in your determination to keep our schools from being integrated . . . and the harder and tougher the going is, the more the folks will unite behind you."[35]

By mid-January 1959 events were slipping beyond Almond's control. More school closings impended, and several court cases testing the resistance statutes were reaching their conclusions. Tuck still was unmoved, offering the beleaguered governor his continued support "in every honorable and just step you take . . . to resist this federal tyranny, and I am not in favor of taking any half-way measures."[36]

Tuck's bold words notwithstanding, the doom of massive resistance was sealed on January 19, when the state Supreme Court of Appeals and a three-judge federal court in Norfolk ruled, in separate decisions, that the school-closing laws violated both the Virginia and United States constitutions. In the face of those rulings, Governor Almond went on television the next day to deliver one of the most memorable addresses in modern Virginia history—an oration he later ruefully referred to as "that damn speech." Almond was perhaps the only politician in the state whose flights of rhetoric could rival Tuck's, and his performance of January 20 was extraordinary even for him. Addressing himself to, among others, "those who defend or close their eyes to the livid stench of sadism, sex immorality and juvenile pregnancy infesting . . . mixed schools," he roared, "let me make it clear for the record now and hereafter, as governor of this state, I will not

[35] Tuck to Almond, Sept. 8, 9, 1958, Almond Executive Papers, Virginia State Library.
[36] Tuck to Almond, Jan. 14, 1959, ibid.

yield to that which I know to be wrong. . . . We have just begun to fight!" Several days later he sounded the same theme privately, vowing, "I shall never surrender in this cause."[37]

Almond's speech won the plaudits of the hard-core resisters. Tuck wired the governor his congratulations on the message, which, he said, "should give our people great encouragement." Several days later, still cautiously optimistic, Tuck wrote to a personal friend: "I do hope and pray that Governor Almond will find the wisdom and courage with which to deal with the crisis which confronts us. It requires bold, determined and stern action. I feel confident that the situation can be effectively met if he will only do it."[38]

Alas for Tuck and the other massive resisters, the governor would not do it—or, more accurately, could not do it. The truth was that the strategy of all-out defiance had run its course, and Almond was as well aware of that fact as anyone. Only eight days after delivering what one writer called his "unfortunate rodomontade," the chastened governor appeared before the General Assembly and presented the astonished legislators with a program which amounted to the repudiation of massive resistance.[39] The basic feature of his plan called for a return to the local option approach, to be known thenceforth as "freedom of choice." At the same time he appointed a commission, headed by moderate state Senator Mosby D. Perrow, Jr., of Lynchburg, to make recommendations concerning further measures to be taken.

Almond's reversal immediately made him a pariah to those who, like Tuck, interpreted his actions as an abject capitulation. Byrd allegedly never spoke to him again; others sneeringly dubbed him "Benedict Almond" and castigated him for not "going the last mile"—that is, to jail. The Richmond *News Leader*, lately the advocate of interposition, commented patronizingly, "He did all that he could do (not all that Bill Tuck . . . might have done) but all that he, Lindsay Almond, was capable of doing."[40]

[37] Wilkinson, *Harry Byrd*, p. 146; Almond to W. C. Daniel, Jan. 23, 1959, copy in Tuck Papers.

[38] Tuck to Almond, Jan. 21, 1959, Almond Executive Papers; Tuck to Richard E. Byrd, Jan. 26, 1959, Tuck Papers.

[39] Dabney, *Virginia: The New Dominion*, p. 543.

[40] Ibid., p. 544; Richmond *News Leader*, Feb. 18, 1959. Indicative of the reaction in Southside Virginia was the editorial in Tuck's hometown newspaper: "When

Tuck, in fact, did continue to urge defiance, suggesting to Almond that he should utilize his inherent authority under the police powers of the state to block the enrollment of black students in previously all-white schools. It was clear, he said, that the state had the power, and the responsibility, to maintain order; at the same time he believed that violence might occur if black students attempted to enroll. Consequently, referring to the Roman dictum which he had cited as governor during the Vepco affair—"The public safety is the first law"—he contended that Almond should use his authority preemptively. "It is my opinion," he explained, "that it is preferable to use the police power to *remove* the irritant and thus *prevent* strife, rather than to use it for the purpose of *suppressing* public mischief and strife when it arises."[41]

When Almond failed to respond to his suggestion, Tuck's despair deepened. He contemptuously refused even to appear before the Perrow Commission, feeling (correctly, no doubt) that any such appearance would be futile. He explained his attitude to Circuit Court Judge Archibald M. Aiken of Danville: "The chairman, and I believe the majority of this commission, are not out to do us any good. It is obvious that they were appointed to integrate rather than segregate. Any plan submitted to them to bring about segregation will be ridiculed and spurned."[42]

In the meantime, on February 2, 1959, segregation ended in Virginia when twenty-one black children entered previously all-white schools in Arlington and Norfolk. The whole affair left Tuck, as he expressed it, "blue and depressed."[43] His disconsolation was understandable since, after almost five years of pleading, cajoling, and threatening in the attempt to stay the Supreme Court's edict, he saw his best efforts come to naught. From that point on, integration

Governor J. Lindsay Almond offered to turn the public schools over to the integrationists and the race mixers yesterday, he made Benedict Arnold look like a candidate for the Congressional Medal of Honor" (Halifax *Gazette*, Jan. 29, 1959).

[41] Tuck to William Old, Feb. 4, 1959, Tuck Papers.

[42] Tuck to Aiken, Mar. 5, 1959, ibid. State Senator William F. Stone of Martinsville agreed with Tuck's assessment, writing the congressman that "the new commission is stacked against people of our philosophy to the fullest extent. I can only count 11 sure votes out of the 40 for us" (Stone to Tuck, Feb. 3, 1959, ibid.).

[43] Tuck to Nathan B. Hutcherson, Jr., Feb. 3, 1959, ibid.

proceeded steadily and peacefully, albeit slowly, in the Old Dominion.[44]

In the midst of the struggle for massive resistance, one highly placed Byrd organization figure was alleged to have said (in what surely became the most frequently quoted comment in modern Virginia political history): "This will keep us in the saddle for twenty-five years. Why, we'll even have organized labor with us."[45] What he meant, of course, was that the integration issue was of such overriding concern that most voters would put aside all other considerations in a concerted effort to sustain the organization's defense of segregation. The spokesman was correct in assuming that almost all white Virginians were united in the goal of preventing integration; he erred in not recognizing that they differed sharply in the tactics which should be used to attain that goal. What, in fact, happened was that, far from unifying the various political elements under organization control, the policy of massive resistance tended to cause further fragmentation—not only widening the existing breach between Byrd and anti-Byrd Democrats but creating new fissures within the organization itself, as animosity developed between the moderates (like Almond, Battle, and Darden) and the all-out resisters (like Tuck, Abbitt, and Byrd himself).

Tuck minimized the disruptive impact of massive resistance. Writing at the time, he asserted that the newspapers had "overemphasized to a large extent and misstated the situation relative to a so-called split in the Byrd organization." Many years later he held the same opinion. Although admitting that the issue was "one of the most divisive . . . that has arisen in this century," he denied that it had any effect at all on the life of the organization.[46] However that might be, it could hardly be claimed that (as the anonymous spokesman had predicted) the issue in any way prolonged the Byrd hegemony.

---

[44] Prince Edward County was an aberration. Rather than accept integration, the county board of supervisors abolished all local funds for public education in 1959, thereby forcing the closing of public schools until 1964, when they were ordered reopened by the U.S. Supreme Court. For the full story of the Prince Edward situation, see Bob Smith, *They Closed Their Schools* (Chapel Hill: University of North Carolina Press, 1965).

[45] Quoted in Washington *Post*, June 19, 1957.

[46] Tuck to Mrs. R. W. Orrell, Feb. 16, 1959, Tuck Papers; Richmond *Times-Dispatch*, Nov. 9, 1975.

One contemporary observer, reportedly an organization sympathizer, was quoted as saying at the outset of the massive resistance campaign: "It might be good politics, but it will be bad history. And I think those responsible are going to be ashamed of it in the long run."[47] Bill Tuck was not ashamed: for him it was good politics—he was easily reelected time and again, usually without opposition, while the controversy swirled around him—and it was not bad history either, except insofar as it failed.

From the vantage point of over twenty years after the *Brown* decision, Tuck looked back on the era with some sadness. "It was the worst period . . . that I lived through," he recalled. "It was a heart-breaking experience." Yet he never recanted, never apologized; true to the beliefs ingrained in an earlier day, he maintained to the end that integration was hurtful both to education and to the two races generally. "But of course," he mused, "it's *fait accompli* now. It's like talking about the War Between the States and the Napoleonic War. It's all over. We have to accept it. . . . But I still don't like it."[48]

Tuck's actions during the era of massive resistance left him with a lasting reputation as a fire-eating archsegregationist. Some others who were criticized for a similarly adamant stand were either grudgingly commended for their devotion to principle, however reactionary, or else dismissed as hopelessly benighted; but Tuck, owing to the stridency of his rhetoric (the product of a lifelong penchant for the fulminant phrase), tended to be viewed as a demagogue.[49] He, of course, did not see it that way. During the controversy he wrote one friend, "I have learned long ago in life that you cannot compromise with evil." To another, while admitting that he "may have been too outspoken" at times, he professed that he had been guided throughout the crisis by a simple rhyme which he had once heard a minister recite:

> Dare to be a Daniel,
> Dare to stand alone,

---

[47] Quoted in Washington *Post*, June 19, 1957.

[48] Richmond *Times-Dispatch*, Nov. 9, 1975.

[49] See, for example, Washington *Post*, Mar. 11, 1956, for a contemporaneous view, and June 4, 1977, for a much later, but similar, assessment.

> Dare to have a purpose firm,
> Dare to make it known.[50]

Therein lay the explanation of his behavior as he understood it. Integration to Bill Tuck was patently evil, both morally and constitutionally, and to denounce it with all the vehemence he could muster was not in his opinion demagogic, it was his duty.

And, moreover, it was the only way he knew how.

[50] Tuck to J. Garland Hood, Feb. 19, 1959, Tuck to Myrtle Reynolds, Nov. 26, 1955, Tuck Papers.

Defender of the Conservative Faith
II. *The Forlorn Fight for "Sound Doctrine"*

> There are those in this country who would—like Delilah—exult
> in giving the South one of those celebrated haircuts for which she
> became so famous, depriving us of our strength and power. . . . I
> warn against this Samson-and-Delilah act, lest the pillars of the
> synagogue be pulled down and the temple destroyed—merry-
> makers, squanderers, wastrels and all.
>
> —*William M. Tuck (1956)*

> I knew I was just talking against the wind. There wasn't a chance
> of us winning, but I wanted my friends, and my children and
> grandchildren, to know that in this great, terrible and
> troublesome hour, I stood up for constitutional government.
>
> —*Tuck (1975)*

The defiance which Bill Tuck displayed toward school integration was
consistent with the unwavering conservatism which he manifested
from the very beginning of his tenure in Congress. That conservatism,
combined with his earthy, "good ol' boy" personality, made him
highly appealing to the traditionally Democratic (and almost lily-
white) electorate of the Fifth District. So great was his popularity that
he was not even challenged in five of the eight regular elections in
which he was a candidate.

In 1956, as the massive resistance controversy swirled about him,
Tuck was opposed for reelection for the first time. His Republican
adversary was Jackson L. Kiser of Galax, the nephew and law partner of
former state senator Floyd Landreth, who had run against Tuck for
governor in 1945. The contest presented a great contrast in age and
experience; the youthful (twenty-seven-year-old) Kiser had not even
been born when Tuck was first elected to the House of Delegates.[1]

Kiser's only chance of victory was to ride the coattails of President

---

[1] Richmond *Times-Dispatch*, Nov. 4, 1956.

Eisenhower, who had carried the Fifth District in 1952 and was running for reelection in 1956. Eisenhower's success in the district in the first campaign had been aided by Tuck's endorsement; however, by 1956, the congressman had become thoroughly disenchanted with Eisenhower's performance, mainly because of the *Brown* decision and the ensuing civil rights movement—developments which Eisenhower did not initiate or especially encourage, but for which he was nonetheless blamed by many southerners. "If Mr. Eisenhower is conservative," Tuck said in one speech, "let us all hope that Virginia may be spared from that brand of conservatism." [2] His disaffection with the president was sufficient to prompt his endorsement of Adlai Stevenson, whom he had scorned as the "Truman candidate" four years earlier.

Despite Tuck's efforts in behalf of Stevenson, Eisenhower again carried the Fifth District, including even Tuck's Halifax County—but all to no avail for Jackson Kiser; in the congressional contest, Tuck won easily by a vote of 39,771 (67.4 percent) to 19,263 (32.6 percent). Kiser did manage to win the Republican counties of Carroll, Grayson, and Wythe, as well as his hometown of Galax, but Tuck triumphed by amassing margins of almost five to one in the more populous counties of Halifax and Pittsylvania and the city of Danville. [3]

Having demonstrated his popularity by winning convincingly in a "Republican year," Tuck was not challenged in the three succeeding elections. By the time he faced opposition again in 1964 the Kennedy administration had come and gone, leaving Lyndon Johnson as president. Mainly because of his advocacy of civil rights, Johnson was intensely disliked in white Southside Virginia; his opponent in 1964, Barry Goldwater, in contrast claimed wide support in the area. Believing the conditions thus to be propitious for a Republican candidate, a South Boston grain mill owner named Robert L. Gilliam undertook to challenge the incumbent Tuck. Gilliam, not unlike Kiser in 1956, hoped to tar Tuck with the brush of Democratic liberalism by associating him with that party's presidential candidate. It was difficult, however, to tie the congressman to Johnson because he had consistently voted against both the Kennedy and Johnson administrations at

[2] Speech by Tuck, Sept. 18, 1965, Tuck Papers.

[3] All congressional vote totals in this chapter are taken from *Statistical Abstract of Virginia* (Charlottesville: University of Virginia, Thomas Jefferson Center for Political Economy, 1970), 2: 181. See also Richmond *Times-Dispatch*, Nov. 7, 1956.

almost every turn and during the campaign refused to endorse the president for reelection. As a result, even though the Fifth District went for Goldwater, Tuck won by a comfortable margin—39,867 (63.5 percent) to 22,946 (36.5 percent)—with Gilliam carrying only Carroll County. Two years later Gilliam again challenged the incumbent, waging an energetic campaign in which he assailed Tuck for his lack of leadership in Congress; but the result was essentially the same, even though Gilliam did manage to carry three counties plus the city of Martinsville, and did improve his overall share of the vote to a respectable 43.8 percent.[4]

During the time that he served in Congress, Tuck was occasionally mentioned as a possible candidate for other offices, most notably for the United States Senate in 1958. A furor arose that year when Senator Byrd, at the age of seventy-one, made the surprising announcement that he would not seek reelection that fall to the seat which he had held for a quarter-century. Democratic leaders throughout the state hastened to urge Byrd to reconsider, and the General Assembly, then in session, formally petitioned him to run again. Tuck publicly expressed his dismay at the senator's decision and met with him in Washington to prevail on him personally to reconsider. Emerging from the conference, he informed reporters, "I told him that he is at the very zenith of his usefulness, power and influence, and that there is an overwhelming demand from Virginians that he run again." In a letter to his close friend, Dan Daniel, Tuck said, "It is my earnest hope that Senator Byrd may yet reconsider."[5]

In the meanwhile, however, Tuck was surreptitiously lining up support to make a run for the vacated seat in the event Byrd did not reverse himself. "I had my announcement already written out," he recalled, "and in the hands of Ben Lacy [then clerk of the Virginia Senate] to be released to newsmen the minute Senator Byrd declined to reconsider." He felt certain that Byrd would not retract because, as he put it, "if Harry Byrd ever told you anything, you could go to bed on it year after next."[6] In this case, though, Byrd had reason to change his mind. The problem was that it soon became evident that former

[4] Richmond *Times-Dispatch*, Nov. 3, 1964, Nov. 9, 1966.
[5] Ibid., Feb. 19, 1958; Tuck to Daniel, Feb. 18, 1958, Tuck Papers.
[6] Richmond *Times-Dispatch*, Oct. 19, Nov. 7, 1975.

governor Battle was elso eyeing the Senate seat, and the prospect of a devastating intraorganization fight was appalling to Byrd. Such a bloodletting might allow an antiorganization candidate—perhaps Robert Whitehead—to slip through to the nomination and, beyond that, might leave the organization permanently enfeebled. Consequently, Byrd relented and agreed to seek another term.[7]

Byrd's reversal left political observers to speculate on the outcome of the abortive Tuck-Battle contest. One later commented that "Tuck had the support of the great majority of the political powers in the state, and he would have won hands down if there had been an election."[8] Tuck himself was not so sure. He felt, in retrospect, that Battle would have been supported by Governor Almond, who was then at the peak of his popularity, not yet having alienated the segregationists by his abandonment of massive resistance. He reasoned further that Battle would have been endorsed by a slight majority of the state legislators since more of them had served under Battle than under him. On the other hand, Tuck believed that he himself would have received the backing of the more flinty segregationists like Congressmen Howard Smith and Watkins Abbitt, as well as most of the Southside leaders. As for Byrd's own preference, "I reckon he would have supported me," Tuck surmised, "but I don't know."[9]

In later years Tuck could laugh about the whole affair. He recalled with amusement one incident which occurred during the time when he was about to announce his candidacy. He was driving from South Boston to Winchester, he related, when a blinding snowstorm forced him to take refuge at a service station. The attendant quickly recognized the congressman, and said: "You're Bill Tuck, aren't you? Well, I'm mighty pleased to make your acquaintance because I've always admired you." Tuck thanked him, and the man continued, "Ain't it a terrible bad thing about Senator Byrd retiring?" Tuck agreed, but was not ready for the man's follow-up: "Wouldn't it be a wonderful thing," he said, "if we could just persuade John Battle to run?"[10]

In truth, even though he could thus dismiss the affair with an anecdote in typical Tuck fashion, the congressman may well have been

[7] Interview with Tuck; Latimer, "Virginia Politics, 1950–1960," pp. 86–87.
[8] Halifax *Gazette-Virginian*, Sept. 18, 1975.
[9] Interview with Tuck; Richmond *Times-Dispatch*, Nov. 7, 1975.
[10] Richmond *Times-Dispatch*, May 7, 1967.

somewhat dispirited by the turn of events. He could scarcely conceal the fact that the prospect of moving to the more prestigious upper house was appealing to him, once wistfully commenting on Byrd's decision, "That's the only time in my life I ever knew him to change his mind." Yet he never admitted any disappointment outright. At the time of the incident he professed relief that Byrd had relented, and years later still maintained that he had considered running only because "I was afraid that things might take a turn that would not be so good for the organization."[11]

The year 1958 was not the only time during Tuck's congressional career that his name was bandied about as a possible candidate for statewide office. Some of the more ardent segregationists, particularly those who were members of the Defenders of State Sovereignty and Individual Liberties, encouraged Tuck to run for governor again in 1961. Although he much preferred the exercise of executive authority to his current legislative role, he refused to consider a second gubernatorial term. "For a least one hundred years," he wrote Defenders' leader Robert Crawford, "no person who has served as governor of Virginia has after the expiration of his term offered again for the office. I cannot get the consent of my mind to break that long-standing precedent."[12]

There was also repeated speculation that Tuck might eventually run for the Senate despite the rebuff in 1958. The *U.S. News and World Report* in early 1963 carried the "rumor," alleged to be going around Washington, that if Byrd did not offer for reelection the following year, he would support Tuck as his successor. Tuck claimed that he had no knowledge of such a development until he read about it in the magazine. In a letter to Fifth District Democratic Chairman Andrew A. Farley, he asserted that the story was "without any foundation whatsoever" and concluded, "I hope and have every reason to believe that Senator Byrd . . . will again offer for re-election in 1964."[13] As it turned out Byrd did run, and was methodically reelected.

A final attempt by some of his partisans to elect Tuck to the Senate came in 1966, following the surprising primary defeat of incumbent

[11] Ibid., Nov. 7, 1975; interview with Tuck.

[12] Tuck to Crawford, Jan. 10, 1961, Tuck Papers.

[13] *U.S. News and World Report* 54 (Jan. 14, 1963): 30; Tuck to Farley, Jan. 9, 1963, Tuck Papers.

Senator A. Willis Robertson by state Senator William B. Spong of Portsmouth. A group of conservative Democrats, unwilling to accept the moderate Spong, began a campaign to promote Tuck as a write-in candidate in the November general election. The movement was flattering to Tuck, he admitted, but also mildly annoying since he was at the time running for reelection to Congress against Gilliam. He speedily squelched the senatorial boomlet, announcing: "I am not a candidate for [the Senate]. I have not consented to the use of my name for such a purpose, and I cannot acquiesce in such a plan." [14] With that ended all serious talk of other elective office for Tuck, and he finished out his public life in the House of Representatives.

Bill Tuck's congressional career embraced the entire administrations of Eisenhower (except for about four months at the beginning), Kennedy, and Johnson. During most of that time the issues of paramount national importance were the spread of Communism, at home and abroad, and the movement for civil rights. Tuck was much concerned about both—as reflected in his two committee assignments, Un-American Activities (HUAC) and Judiciary—and he directed most of his energy toward those issues.

The fear of internal Communism had arisen in Virginia during Tuck's governorship, as indicated by a bill proposed in the 1948 General Assembly which was designed to outlaw the Communist party within the state. Debate on the floor of the legislature revealed utter detestation of the Communists on the part of many delegates. One of the patrons of the bill referred to them as "contemptible lice," and Robert Whitehead pleaded for passage of the measure in order to "tell these Communists: 'If you love Russia so much, go on back there.' Let's catch 'em and shake 'em like the rats they are." Tuck, as governor, took little active part in the anti-Communist drive, although he was clearly sympathetic to the objectives of the legislation (which was enacted in a somewhat softened form). "These Communists," he wrote privately, "are dangerous folks." [15]

That was in early 1948. By the time Tuck arrived in Congress five

---

[14] Richmond *Times-Dispatch*, July 26, 1966.

[15] Ibid., Feb. 27, 1948; Tuck to Hugh T. Williams, Jan. 26, 1948, Tuck Papers. The episode is discussed more fully in Crawley, "Governor William Munford Tuck," pp. 605–11.

years later the McCarthy era was at its peak, and the fear of the internal menace of Communism had become epidemic. Tuck, too, had grown more fearful. For one thing, he was convinced that the red hand of Communism lay behind the integration movement. The *Brown* decision, he claimed, was part of a plan "not only of the Supreme Court, the left-wingers, the one-worlders and other destructionists, but also of the Communists as well." The whole Communist idea, he maintained, was to foment such racial discord within America that the nation would easily fall prey to the Russians. He favored stern measures to combat the insidious threat, proclaiming in one speech, "Nothing we can do will satisfy them . . . and I, for one, am not interested in playing pacifier to pinks, punks or party-liners."[16]

While he believed that it was most imperative to "fight the Communists right here in America where they pose the worst threat," he also advocated a tough, active policy against Communism abroad, particularly in the Western Hemisphere. He was especially chagrined by the Cuban revolution in which the regime of Fulgencio Batista was overthrown by the Marxist Fidel Castro, thereby establishing a Communist haven at the very doorstep of the United States. "It is obvious to me as a matter of common sense," he wrote Andy Farley, "that we should have kept on a friendly basis with both Trujillo [of the Dominican Republic] and Batista. I do not condone their dictatorships, but both were friendly to the U.S., were anti-Communists, and kept order. Moreover, there was more personal liberty and safety under such governments than there is under Castro."[17] He regarded the developments in Cuba as an affront to the hallowed Monroe Doctrine—and one which should not be tolerated. "Castro must be deposed," he declared in one jingoistic speech.

Communism must be banished from our land and all the Americas. It should be done by diplomacy or by embargo or by . . . other methods of a similar nature, if possible, but if necessary it must be done by force. The Communists understand only the language of force. I am in favor, if necessary, of giving them a full dose of force and power, the only language they understand. . . . The Monroe Doctrine must be upheld, and America must be freed from the devastating influences of Communism.

[16] Speeches by Tuck, Dec. 4, 1957, Oct. 14, 1954, Tuck Papers.
[17] Speech by Tuck, Nov. 12, 1957, Tuck to Farley, June 15, 1961, ibid.

Tuck, usually no admirer of John Kennedy, was sympathetic to the president's stand on Cuba and was convinced that Communist subversive activities emanating from that island were responsible for Kennedy's assassination. "There is no doubt in my mind," he declared, "that some of the vicious attacks made on President Kennedy in relation to our Cuban policy were responsible in part at least for what [Lee Harvey] Oswald did."[18]

Tuck's militant anti-Communism, which could be seen in his fear of domestic infiltration and in his antipathy toward Castro, was most evident in his suspicion of and hostility toward the wellspring of Communism—the Soviet Union. The death of Joseph Stalin, which occurred in the month before Tuck entered Congress, was interpreted by some observers as heralding a new era of "peaceful coexistence" between the United States and Russia. Tuck did not buy such a theory of Soviet tractability, warning, "Let us never forget that . . . coexistence means nothing but gradual surrender." He accordingly counseled against any compromise with the still-treacherous foe. Some argued, he said in one speech, "that Communist terror and violence, particularly evident during the period of the late Soviet dictator's thirty-year rule, have been rejected as weapons by the Communists since Stalin's death. Such an inference is dangerously misleading, as the history of Hungary under Khrushchev demonstrates. . . . If de-Stalinization is one proper prerequisite for [better relations], then de-Khrushchevixion should without doubt be another one."[19]

Ever antagonistic toward the Russians, Tuck was infuriated by Khrushchev's visit to the United States in 1959. Fairly frothing with indignation, he portrayed the Soviet premier to one audience as "strutting our streets, applauding his own presence, with the innocent blood of tens of thousands of his victims literally dripping from his ruthless, merciless and murderous hands. You remember him," he continued, "his bullet head, his beady eyes . . . privy to every secret place; consorting with our President; posturing, posing, snapping as a bayed jackal at the impertinence of free men's questions. That was Khrushchev, made officially welcome to the land of the free. Welcome to the man who has said he would bury us. It was the saddest day in

[18] Speech by Tuck, Jan. 27, 1964, ibid.
[19] Richmond *Times-Dispatch*, June 16, 1963.

America, save one, and that was that fatal day in 1933 when the United States officially recognized these international blameworthys."[20]

In short, Tuck was a confirmed "Cold Warrior" who viewed foreign policy in terms of a continuous struggle for supremacy between Communism and the free world. He believed that the United States should not attempt to win that struggle through foreign aid, a program which he opposed as costly and ineffectual. Ridiculing such efforts in one speech, he remarked, "Even though Russia may get to the moon first, I dare say we will be ahead of them when it comes to foreign aid to the inhabitants of that faraway planet." In accordance with that view he voted against almost all expenditures for foreign aid, including appropriations for the Kennedy administration's much publicized Alliance for Progress and Peace Corps programs.[21]

The only way to assure American survival, in Tuck's opinion, was through maintenance of a strong defense, including a powerful military establishment with nuclear capability; above all, the United States must not cower in the face of Communist aggression. When he perceived American interests to be threatened by such an advance, as in Vietnam, he did not shrink from advocating a military response. Americans, he said, had historically "sought to avoid foreign entanglements and situations which might give rise to war. . . . But Americans should never be so desirous of peace, never so generous with our friendship, that we should permit ourselves to be pushed around at the expense of freedom."[22] Such a statement well characterized Tuck's basic philosophy of foreign policy—a philosophy which established him during his service in Congress as an unflinching anti-Communist and as a militant upholder of what he regarded as America's rightful preeminence in world affairs.

In domestic affairs Tuck was absorbed throughout his congressional

[20] Speech by Tuck, Feb. 11, 1960, Tuck Papers.

[21] Speech by Tuck, Jan. 27, 1964, ibid.; *Congress and the Nation* (Washington, D.C.: Congressional Quarterly Service, 1969), 2: 91a; Lerche, *The Uncertain South*, p. 300.

[22] Speech by Tuck, May 1, 1964, Tuck Papers. Tuck consistently supported appropriations for the prosecution of the war effort, including the controversial request for additional funds by President Johnson in 1966 (*Congress and the Nation*, 2: 21a).

years by the controversy over civil rights—the so-called "Second Reconstruction" which began almost simultaneously with his arrival in the nation's capital. In light of his earlier rejection of Truman on account of the president's civil rights proposals, and given his defiant attitude toward the *Brown* decision, it was only to be expected that he would oppose any attempts at passage of civil rights legislation. Indeed, his opposition was so vehement and so persistent that before his career ended, his reputation as a foe of civil rights tended to obscure all other facets of his service in Congress.

Tuck's attitude toward civil rights legislation was grounded in his racial preconceptions and was supported by his conviction that (since blacks were satisfied with the status quo anyway) changes such as those envisioned by civil rights advocates would be useless at best, and potentially disruptive of American society. Furthermore, on constitutional grounds he believed that federal legislation in behalf of blacks contravened the guarantee of states' rights embedded in the Tenth Amendment and was thus in violation of what he often referred to as "sound doctrine."

Tuck seldom ventured into the well of the House to deliver a formal speech. It was therefore significant that his first such address, like most of those which followed, was a declamation against a pending civil rights bill—the Eisenhower administration–sponsored Civil Rights Bill of 1957. The proposed legislation called for the establishment of a permanent Civil Rights Commission with broad powers of subpoena; for the creation of a new office of assistant attorney general, to be charged specifically with protecting voting rights; and for authorizing federal courts to issue injunctions to force compliance with voting rights guidelines.[23] The whole package was repugnant to Tuck. Its enactment, he cried, "would release upon the country a horde of political bloodsuckers and harpies clothed with the badge of power who could, and no doubt would, in instances reduce us to a 'police state.'" His anger was increased because the bill was supported by Eisenhower, who as a candidate three years before had pledged himself—and Tuck quoted him—to uphold states' rights. "I am sorry," said Tuck, "that he [now] has seen fit to place the influence and power of the office of President behind proposals that will utterly destroy the

---

[23] *Congress and the Nation*, 1: 1622.

principles which he claims to espouse."[24] Despite the opposition of Tuck and other members of the (largely southern) conservative coalition, the measure eventually passed, thereby becoming the first civil rights legislation enacted by Congress in eighty-two years.

The Civil Rights Act of 1957 came to seem mild in comparison to subsequent legislation on the subject. Tuck suspected that sterner measures were in prospect when Kennedy received the Democratic presidential nomination in 1960. "I do not recall that I have ever been in such a quandry [sic]," he wrote his friend Ben D. Lacy. "I know that I will never be able to get up any enthusiasm [for] people who are for enforced integration, for the FEPC, for the unions and against the public, and for squandering the nation's financial resources."[25] Kennedy's election soon brought Tuck's fears to fruition, as the new administration threw its weight behind the most extensive civil rights program since Reconstruction.

Tuck attacked the proposed legislation in every forum available to him. On the lecture circuit he decried it in a succession of speeches as "that heinous, obnoxious, flagitious . . . Civil Rights Bill," which was being foisted upon the public by "the President and his Attorney General brother" at the behest of the NAACP—"the National Association for the Agitation of Colored People."[26] When the bill reached the Judiciary Committee, of which Tuck was a member, he endeavored to speak against it but was prevented from doing so, he claimed, by the liberal chairman of the committee. "I recall distinctly," he told one audience, "that after repeatedly unsuccessful efforts to gain recognition, I stood at my desk and pounded as hard as I could with a heavy ashtray, but . . . the chairman [Emanuel Celler, a Democratic representative from New York] refused to recognize me for any purpose, although I have served on the Committee for nearly ten years." The bill which survived the committee was conceded to be a more moderate version than had been originally proposed, with changes having been made ostensibly in deference to the southern opponents. Tuck, nevertheless, was far from satisfied. The measure was being promoted as "watered down," he complained, but "the only water on it was the

[24] Congressional Record, 85th Congress, 1st Session, 1957, 103: 8655, 8656.

[25] Tuck to Lacy, Aug. 2, 1960, Tuck Papers.

[26] Speeches by Tuck, Oct. 4, Aug. 6, 1963, ibid.; Congressional Record, 86th Congress, 2d Session, 1960, 106: 5306.

polluted water of political intrigue brought about . . . under the influence of such organizations as the Congress of Racial Equality, NAACP and like sinister groups." [27]

When the bill came up for debate before the full House, Tuck carried his opposition directly onto the floor. In a contumacious speech laced with vintage Tuck verbiage, he lambasted the entire bill, title by title, singling out certain provisions for especially vicious criticism. [28] The section dealing with public accommodations, he declared, was written in such a manner as to "lead one to believe that the sanctimonious sentences contained in it were formulated by none other than a modern day Apostle Paul." "But irrespective of this pretense of piety," he continued, "one of the accomplishments of this section would be to deprive the owner of a place of public accommodation his right to operate his own business, to decide with whom he will deal, who will eat at his table, or will sleep in his beds. This section would confer upon the political hirelings and myrmidons of the ever growing bureaucracy of Washington the power . . . to compel submission of innkeepers and landlords to the dictatorial edicts of the overlords in Washington." Such a proposal, he claimed, was a prostitution of the Fourteenth Amendment, whose guarantee of "equal protection of the laws" was intended to proscribe only certain state, not individual, actions.

The section designed to desegregate public facilities was scored by Tuck mainly on account of the unwarranted power for enforcement which it conferred upon the attorney general—"autocratic power such as may befit a commissar of justice in a totalitarian country, but which is incompatible with our system of jurisprudence, and constitutes a stench in the nostrils of all right-thinking people." The section calling for the creation of a vigorous Civil Rights Commission was condemned as "repugnant to every concept of liberty" because of the vast investigatory authority which it would possess. Predicted Tuck, "It will flare back to haunt those who empower it to intimidate, bullyrag and torment an already aggravated citizenry." The effects of the section designed to prohibit discrimination in federally assisted programs were

[27] Speech by Tuck, Feb. 17, 1964, Tuck Papers.

[28] The entire speech is found in the *Congressional Record*, 88th Congress, 2d Session, 1964, 110: 1586–92; all of the following quotations are taken therefrom. For exact provisions of the bill, see *Congress and the Nation*, 1: 1638.

so potentially far-reaching as to be "nauseating" to the congressman. "This," he snarled, "puts into the hands of these Washington factotums a hundred-billion-dollar blackjack to browbeat the people of America into submission."

Having deprecated the bill in all of its particulars, Tuck drew on his biblical resources to lecture those of his colleagues who favored the legislation. "There are those who advocate these stringent measures with the view and desire of punishing . . . [the] Southern states. But," he sermonized, ". . . let me remind those of you who so complacently support this bill that in a few years you may find yourselves in the plight of Haman of old, who constructed a scaffold upon which to hang Mordecai. But it was Haman himself, not Mordecai, who was hung on that scaffold. And Mordecai was there to witness the hanging while he luxuriated in the luscious arms of Haman's paramour."

By the time the bill came up for final consideration on the House floor, President Kennedy had been assassinated and advocates of the bill were calling for its passage as a tribute to the fallen leader. Tuck concluded his oration with a rebuttal to such pleas. "It has been suggested that these proposals should be regarded as a symbol of love in memory of the late President," he said. "Surely history would regard it as a poor memorial. . . .for the Congress to violate the Constitution in his name." Ultimately, of course, all of Tuck's impassioned eloquence and the parliamentary maneuvering of his conservative cohorts proved insufficient to prevent passage of the bill, and the Civil Rights Act of 1964—the most significant legislation in that area in almost a century—became the law of the land.

The Civil Rights Act was only the first, and perhaps most egregious, of numerous developments which Tuck found abominable during the Johnson administration; indeed, he opposed virtually every major piece of Great Society legislation which came before Congress. One of the most objectionable to Tuck, because it struck directly at Virginia, was the Voting Rights Act of 1965, which, among other provisions, abolished literacy requirements such as existed in Virginia and gave federal officials increased authority to supervise voter registration in the South.[29] Failing to acknowledge that in some areas blacks were uniformly discouraged from voting through various subterfuges, Tuck

---

[29] For a summary of the contents of the bill, see *Congress and the Nation*, 2: 362–64.

maintained that the setting of voter qualifications was the responsibility of the individual states and categorically denied the right of the federal government to intervene. The Voting Rights Act, he said scornfully, would force the registration of everyone, "irrespective of a person's ability to write his name or read one word of English."[30]

For failure to meet the test of the "sound doctrine" which he preached—that is, because they were in his view either prodigal of tax money or violative of states' rights—Tuck endeavored to obstruct the passage of a plethora of Johnson administration measures, prominently including Medicare ("nothing more than socialized medicine"), the Federal Housing Act ("a particularly dangerous rathole"), the Elementary and Secondary Education Act, and all attempts to extend urban renewal, rent subsidy, and antipoverty programs.[31] He even voted against some proposals which, on their face, seemed advantageous to his home district; he opposed them, he explained, because "Congress enacts a law in broad general terms and then turns it over to a department for implementation [which] takes the form of 'guidelines,' the magic word which spells control."[32] There were a few occasions when he supported administration measures, as in the case of the Truth-in-Lending Act and an omnibus crime bill; and there were even rarer occasions when he opposed the administration successfully, as in the fight against repeal of Section 14-B of the Taft-Hartley Act (which, had it been repealed, would have abrogated the Virginia Right-to-Work Law passed during Tuck's governorship). By and large, however, Tuck's pleas went unheeded as the heavily Democratic Congress, under the lash of a dynamic president, proceeded to enact the most extensive program of social and economic legislation since the New Deal. The old conservative warhorse looked on with dismay and anxiety. "The extinction of our liberty," he predicted, "will be the price we shall have to pay for the so-called Great Society."[33]

[30] *Congressional Record*, 89th Congress, 1st Session, 1965, 3: 15720.

[31] Speeches by Tuck, Oct. 8, 1965, Sept. 30, 1965, Tuck Papers. During 1965, the year when much of the Great Society legislation came before Congress, Tuck voted against the administration 60 percent of the time and with the "conservative coalition" 98 percent of the time (Wilkinson, *Harry Byrd*, pp. 361–62).

[32] Speech by Tuck, Nov. 17, 1966, Tuck Papers.

[33] Speech by Tuck, Oct. 8, 1965, ibid. For a summary of Tuck's votes on key legislation during the Johnson administration, see *Congress and the Nation*, 2: 9a–39a.

By the late 1960s many had begun to believe with Tuck that the reform attempts of the Johnson years were ineffectual, if not counterproductive. With crime infesting many cities, riots shattering black ghettos, and protests disrupting college campuses across the land, Tuck's dire predictions seemed to be coming true. The congressman could not forbear a reminder to his colleagues in a speech delivered shortly after the assassination of the Reverend Martin Luther King, Jr. He deplored the murder of the black leader, he said, and expressed his hope that the "senseless murderer be brought to justice speedily . . . and given the extreme penalty of the law." Yet he was by no means an admirer of King, he continued, for "although . . . he openly advocated nonviolence, he fomented discord and strife between the races. . . . [He] trampled upon the laws of our country with impunity, and the Stokely Carmichaels and the Rap Browns were spawned in the waters of hate agitated by his public utterances. . . . Violence followed in his wake wherever he went, until he himself fell a victim to violence." Turning to a more general discussion of the existing situation, he resurrected his well-worn analogy of Haman, and said:

I made the prediction in 1957 that the adoption of this initial so-called Civil Rights Bill would be marked by countless future years of irritation and acrimony. . . . The proponents of the measure contended that the legislation was needed because it would bring peace and tranquility. Where is that peace? . . . I cannot see that the legislation of this nature has done us one iota of good. On the contrary . . . the situation has become infinitely worse and has reached desperate stages.[34]

Though he believed that civil rights agitation was at the root of the chaos which seemed to be enveloping the nation, he recognized that resentment against the war in Vietnam was also a contributing factor. The erstwhile Marine did not, however, propose to abandon his support of the war but instead urged that the protests against American involvement—"Communist-planned and Communist-directed"— be suppressed. In particular he railed against the antiwar activities which were then commonplace on college campuses. "The professors and students taking part in these demonstrations must be dealt with sternly," he declared to a Danville audience. "The professors should be dismissed from the faculty and the students expelled from the cam-

[34] *Congressional Record*, 90th Congress, 2d Session, 1968, 114: 9535.

pus. . . . [I am] thankful that we still have men and women in this country who would much prefer to be dead than to be either yellow or red."[35]

As continued civil disturbances seemed to portend the disintegration of American society, Tuck became an outspoken champion of "law and order," the breakdown of which he attributed in no small part to the recent decisions of the Warren Supreme Court (*Escobedo* v. *Illinois*, *Miranda* v. *Arizona*, etc.) which extended the protective rights of accused criminals. Utilizing one of his favorite metaphors, Tuck assailed the chief justice, proclaiming, "He is not a synthetic Samson. He is genuine, for like Samson of old he is not only blind, heedless, desperate and destructive, but he has also pulled down the temple."[36] The congressman's own prescription for treating the problem of lawlessness was uncomplicated. "I think much of the trouble we have had recently would have been spared us," he told a HUAC hearing, "if the police had used a bit more of those nightsticks and a few bullets once in a while. That's the kind of law I was taught."[37]

On May 3, 1967, Tuck unexpectedly announced that he would not seek reelection. There was much speculation as to what had prompted the surprising decision. Some observers, citing the fact that his margin of victory had dipped in the previous election, suggested that political considerations were paramount—in short, that he feared that he might be defeated if he ran for what would have been his ninth term.[38] Tuck denied that theory, and subsequent events did render it implausible, since the man who replaced him, Dan Daniel, was easily elected and reelected while holding views essentially the same as Tuck's.

The congressman himself had a simple explanation for his decision to retire. "It's like making a speech," he said. "If they're applauding and enjoying it, stop. I think this is a good time to stop."[39] But there was more to it than that. Several personal considerations played a part: first, even though Tuck's overall health seemed good (despite a chronic

[35] Speech by Tuck, Jan. 12, 1966, Tuck Papers.

[36] Quoted in John D. Weaver, *Warren: The Man, The Court, The Era* (London: Victor Gollancz, 1968), p. 4. During his governorship Tuck had dubbed John L. Lewis a "synthetic Samson."

[37] Richmond *Times-Dispatch*, April 25, 1968.

[38] Ibid., May 7, 1967.

[39] Ibid.

weight problem), his eyesight was deteriorating as the result of cataracts; second, his wife was terminally ill with Parkinson's disease, which by 1968 had necessitated her confinement at home; and third, Tuck was deeply grieved by the tragic death of his eldest grandson, William Munford Tuck Dillard, who had succumbed to an injury received in a high school football game the previous fall.[40]

Added to such considerations was the fact that Tuck had become increasingly disenchanted with his ability to make any real impact on the House. His tenure in Congress was, in the main, bereft of meaningful accomplishment—and he knew it. "All you could do," he said disgustedly, "was try to block them." Yet, even in his self-proclaimed role of obstructionist, he had little success. Though he had kept up the fight, he did not delude himself about his effectiveness, commenting frankly on one occasion, "I don't amount to anything in Congress."[41]

When the time came for him to leave, he was bade farewell with an hour-long session of flowery testimonials in the House chamber. Many of the plaudits went well beyond perfunctory expressions of politeness, and many were delivered by members who had been diametrically opposed to Tuck on almost every issue. The personal (as distinct from political) affinity which those colleagues felt was revealed in columnist Charles McDowell's recollection that one "[Johnson] administration leader, who probably could count as little on Bill Tuck's vote as any in the House, found no embarrassment in gazing at him and saying, 'I can only say I love him.'"[42]

The accolades of his colleagues notwithstanding, Tuck was not reluctant to leave the Capitol. "I'll miss this, of course," he told one reporter, his voice lacking conviction. "But I'll be happier at home, . . . back down there on my poor, rocky farm."[43]

[40] Ibid.; interview with Tuck.

[41] Interview with Tuck.

[42] *Congressional Record*, 90th Congress, 1st Session, 1968, 114: 28404–18; Richmond *Times-Dispatch*, Sept. 29, 1968.

[43] Richmond *Times-Dispatch*, Dec. 13, 1968.

Conclusion

Home Again to Halifax
12. The End of a Career—and an Era

Tuck was like a little boy walking down a road and spotting a
hornet's nest. Instead of whistling peacefully and avoiding it,
Tuck felt obliged to pound it with a stick, stir up the hornets, and
deal with them one by one, and in droves.

—Charles McDowell

A country boy by birth, and always one at heart, Bill Tuck happily
returned to his rural Southside in 1969 at the age of seventy-two. As
had happened at the end of his governorship, there were those who
urged that he remain active in politics. The Richmond *News Leader* for
example, suggested obliquely that he return to the General Assembly.
"It would be a fine thing for Virginia, even at this late date," commented that paper, "if an opportunity could be found for the Governor
[as he was uniformly referred to by his admirers] to serve the Commonwealth. These are times that cry out for men . . . who stand up
unafraid. Mr. Tuck is such a man. There is no one quite like him." [1]

This time, however, the retirement from public life was to be
permanent, though he remained quite active for a number of years.
Much of his daily routine involved the leisurely practice of law in his
old South Boston office. The firm by then had become a large one by the
standards of that part of the state, but Tuck professed to be only a
"country lawyer." As such, he once said, his clientele consisted of
"strumpets, bootleggers, corporations—whoever comes along," adding with a sly smile, "You have to try to be on the right side of every
case, of course." [2]

With his wife increasingly enfeebled up to the time of her death in

[1] Richmond *News Leader*, May 4, 1967.
[2] Richmond *Times-Dispatch*, Feb. 22, 1970.

late 1975, Tuck seldom ventured far from home. His social life consisted mainly of relaxing with Halifax cronies and chatting with old-time associates who came periodically to visit. His political activity was infrequent. From time to time he attended Democratic affairs such as the annual Jefferson-Jackson Day fete, and occasionally he bestirred himself to endorse a candidate whom he deemed sufficiently conservative (a vanishing breed, by his lights), but by and large he abjured participation in the hurly-burly of politics. Even so, his name continued to appear intermittently in the news. Any discussion of labor relations in Virginia was likely to include reference to the events of his governorship.[3] His stand on massive resistance was not soon forgotten either, especially by those who disagreed with him. As late as 1977, liberal gubernatorial candidate Henry Howell assailed his opponent in the Democratic primary, Andrew P. Miller, for having consorted with Tuck, declaiming to one predominantly Jewish audience, "You all remember Bill Tuck. He thought massive resistance was 'Jim Dandy' . . . the greatest thing since matzoh ball soup."[4]

Despite the low profile which he generally exhibited in retirement, Tuck maintained a strong interest in public affairs, as evidenced in a memorable series of conversations between him and former governor Colgate Darden which was produced in 1975 for public television.[5] Showing that time and events had neither altered his views nor mellowed his rhetoric, he denounced such earlier vexations as the 1965 Voting Rights Act. "Under this law, the only test you can require to register and vote is whether you can breathe," he said, and proceeded to dramatize his point in the inimitable Tuck fashion: "You roll a man up to the registrar in a wheelbarrow. Can this man talk? No. Can this man see? No. Can he hear? No. Can he read? No. Can he write? No. Well, what qualifications does he have to register? Well, he's breathing.

---

[3] See, for example, the Fredericksburg *Free Lance-Star*, Mar. 17, 1977.

[4] Washington *Post*, June 3, 1977. Howell was referring to the fact that when Miller visited South Boston earlier in the campaign he had been photographed with Tuck.

[5] The series, entitled "The Living History Makers," was produced jointly by Central Virginia Educational Television and the Richmond *Times-Dispatch*. Based on the program interviews, Latimer wrote a series of newspaper articles which were later compiled in a booklet, *Virginia Politics: The Way It Was* (Richmond: Richmond Newspapers, Inc., 1975).

In retirement at Buckshoal Farm in Halifax County, 1975. (Courtesy of the South Boston *Gazette-Virginia*)

That's the only requirement left under this so-called voting rights act: Can he breathe? It seems to me some test of intelligence should be allowed." [6]

With regard to another area of longtime concern to Tuck, he admitted, reluctantly, that he had accepted racial integration of the schools, but inveighed against busing as a means of achieving that end. "According to that theory, if it's carried to its logical conclusion," he said, "we could be carrying them from here to Nebraska to school." Somewhat less hyperbolically (at least in terms of geography) he pursued his argument:

There are probably only three or four colored families in Carroll County. They have practically no integration. If integration is beneficial, if it's impossible to educate colored or white unless they are educated together, then there's no way for them to have good schools unless they send down here [Halifax County] and get some of our colored people, and we send up there and get some of their white people. It just doesn't make sense to me. [7]

One of his last major public appearances came in September 1975, when a Halifax civic group staged "Bill Tuck Day" in his honor. As a country music band serenaded the outdoor crowd of several thousand with such Tuck favorites as "You Are My Sunshine," the political elite of Virginia assembled to praise his career—Governor Mills E. Godwin, Jr., Lieutenant Governor John Dalton, Attorney General Andrew P. Miller, Senator Harry F. Byrd, Jr., Congressman Dan Daniel, former governors Colgate Darden, Albertis Harrison, and (Tuck's one-time nemesis) J. Lindsay Almond, as well as a panoply of state and area officials. It was, according to the Washington *Post*, "an unprecedented and unashamedly emotional tribute" to one of the eldest of Virginia's "elder statesmen." [8] The audience, significantly, was almost entirely white, save the local high school band, which was fully integrated.

The celebration was essentially Tuck's last hurrah. A little more than a year later he was felled by a stroke which left him unable to walk

---

[6] Latimer, *Virginia Politics: The Way It Was*, p. 7.

[7] Ibid., p. 20.

[8] Washington *Post*, Sept. 21, 1975. See also Danville *Register*, Sept. 21, 1975, and Richmond *News Leader*, Sept. 22, 1975.

except with considerable difficulty; by that time, too, his vision had dimmed and his hearing had deteriorated. His mind, however, remained clear, his wit sharp, his memory unerring. Determined to recover from the disabling effects of his illness, he usually appeared optimistic, but sometimes became depressed at the thought of so many of his personal friends and political associates who had died. "But I can't worry about it," he mused. ". . . I've had a full life." [9]

The political life of William Munford Tuck was indeed a full one by any standard. Born while Grover Cleveland was president of the United States, Tuck entered public life while Warren Harding was in the White House; by the time he departed, Richard M. Nixon was president-elect. In the course of nearly a half-century of service, Tuck went before the electorate a score of times and was never defeated, or even seriously threatened. During that time he served for seven years in the Virginia House of Delegates, nine years in the state Senate, four years as governor, and, after a three-year hiatus, nearly sixteen years in the United States House of Representatives. His career was coeval with that of the Byrd organization, to whose principles he was dedicated: established just as Tuck was entering politics, the organization flourished during Tuck's salad days, reached its peak during his governorship, and declined as his public career drew to a close.

Tuck's political longevity was basically attributable to the simple fact that his states' rights theory of government and his adherence to the status quo accorded well with the essential conservatism of the Virginia voting public at the time. But it was not merely his political philosophy which accounted for his continued popularity; there was always the matter of his unique (for Virginia) personality which endeared him to the voters. Indeed, throughout his career Tuck was something of an anomaly, in that while he espoused the views of the aristocracy, he exhibited the personality of a populist. In so doing he emerged, remarked J. Harvie Wilkinson, as "such a lovable and colorful individual that he ranked as a Virginia political institution of the first order." [10]

There was no doubt that Tuck's greatest prominence was achieved

[9] Interview with Tuck some six months after his illness occurred.
[10] Wilkinson, *Harry Byrd*, p. 25.

while he was governor. Whether he was big-sticking the labor unions, sparring with President Truman, or coaxing a tax increase out of a reluctant legislature, Tuck engaged the attention of Virginians, giving them an administration which was both competent and, in the view of most voters, enjoyable. "It was like watching Shakespeare," commented journalist Guy Friddell, "Caesar bestriding the world, or better still, an entire troupe performing Henry IV, Part I. He dominated the scene, and Virginia became a spectator state."[11]

If, as Friddell suggested, the Tuck administration was evocative of *Henry IV*, then the protagonist of that administration was more than a little reminiscent of Falstaff. Massive, jovial, and spirited, Tuck possessed "a sizzling temper that boiled down to a funny story as often as not." A gifted raconteur with a knack for mimicry, he freely embellished his tales with borrowings, alternately and even simultaneously, from the Bible and from his "monumental repertoire of profanity." Possessing a full complement of human foibles, he admitted to claustrophobia, to fear of ghosts, and to what he termed an "alone complex," by which he meant a dread of being without companionship.[12] He was, above all, a man who plainly liked to have a good time, which to him included listening and dancing to hillbilly music; dining on such delicacies as chitlins, turnip greens, and black-eyed peas; and swilling bourbon tinctured but slightly with water. To Virginians accustomed to staid, straitlaced (and basically drab) FFV sorts as their political leaders, Tuck was a rousing iconoclast—and a novelty: a man with whom they could identify.

The years from 1946 to 1950 constituted for Tuck, as for the Byrd organization, a "golden age" of power; in succeeding years, it was a different story for both. The organization managed to maintain a tenuous hold on state politics for a decade and a half thereafter, but its grasp was progressively weakened by internal dissension and, more importantly, by demographic, constitutional, and ideological changes which, try as it might, it could not control.[13] As for Tuck, even though he remained successfully in active politics for a score of years

[11] Friddell, *What Is It about Virginia?*, pp. 62–63.
[12] McDowell, "Bill Tuck," p. 8; Richmond *News Leader*, Oct. 3, 1967.
[13] These developments are analyzed in Wilkinson, *Harry Byrd*.

yet, he did not again achieve the acclaim which he had known as governor.

The congressional years were never truly satisfying for Tuck; it was as governor that he had found his métier. Having become accustomed to wielding executive authority as governor, he found the role of congressman tedious and woefully lacking in real power. (Even elevator operators, he said with disdain, had more prestige than a mere congressman.)[14] To be sure, he remained to the end a popular figure, both with his constituents and his colleagues. In the House he was affectionately referred to as the "jolly warrior of the South" or the "member most likely to secede" by appreciative colleagues who regarded him, said one observer, "as their private Will Rogers."[15]

Withal, the personal adulation could not make up for the fact that his record in Congress was one of virtually unrelieved negativism, of constant warring against ideas and programs whose time had come. Engulfed by the tide of liberalism which rose during the 1960s, Tuck found it nearly impossible to bring his conservative views to bear significantly at the national level. "He became immensely popular in the House," concluded the Richmond *News Leader*, "but his 'sound doctrine' made small impression. Much of the time he seemed an old-fashioned figure, an aging ship of the line amidst a flotilla of snappy speedboats."[16]

Nevertheless, for years, even though his efforts in behalf of conservatism were increasingly futile, Tuck had at least been comforted by fighting beside his longtime brethren in the Byrd organization. Gradually, however, they had fallen away: Congressman Howard Smith defeated in the 1966 primary by the liberal George Rawlings; Senator A. Willis Robertson defeated at the same time by the moderate William B. Spong; and, most devastatingly of all to Tuck, Senator Harry Byrd himself cut down in 1965 by a malignant brain tumor which led to his death the following year. By 1967 Tuck alone of the old guard was left to man the battlements of states' rights and "sound

[14] Richmond *News Leader*, Jan. 2, 1969.
[15] Houston, *Virginians in Congress*, pp. 13–14; Richmond *Times-Dispatch*, Nov. 20, 1960.
[16] Richmond *News Leader*, Jan. 2, 1969.

doctrine." Physically and philosophically he was virtually alone, isolated, in Washington. It was thus with unfeigned relief that he departed from what had been all along a largely hostile environment to return to the rural setting in which he had been nurtured.

The world of the 1970s was a vastly different place from the world into which Tuck had been born; even from the time that he was governor until the end of his congressional career, changes occurred which were profound and pervasive. Through it all, Tuck held fast to the ideals of an earlier time—ideals concerning the proper role of government (limited), the proper relationship between the races (separated), the proper place of America in the world (preeminent). For much of his career those ideals served him well, but near the end they were increasingly out of harmony with the prevailing consensus, and his stature as a public leader was diminished accordingly. Yet there was no chance that he would abandon those ideals, because to him they were not ephemeral, they were not mutable; they were verities.

For his uncompromising stand Tuck was acclaimed by his conservative friends as the courageous defender of a glorious heritage, and simultaneously castigated by his liberal critics as the reactionary relic of a bygone era. From whichever end of the political spectrum it might be viewed, the close of his career marked the passing of one whose like had seldom been seen before and would never be seen again in Virginia politics; beyond that, it symbolized the passing of the old Virginia which Tuck had represented, and had loved.

Bibliographical Note
Index

Bibliographical Note

The national setting within which the events of this book took place may be viewed in such popular works as William Manchester's glib narrative history, *The Glory and the Dream* (Boston: Little, Brown, 1973), and Eric Goldman's informal but solid *The Crucial Decade—and After: America, 1945–60* (New York: Knopf, 1960), Vintage edition. The best one-volume survey of Virginia history is Virginius Dabney, *Virginia: The New Dominion* (Garden City, N.Y.: Doubleday, 1971). The background of modern Virginia politics is discussed in Allen W. Moger, *Virginia: Bourbonism to Byrd, 1870–1925* (Charlottesville: University Press of Virginia, 1968).

The most helpful, indeed essential, study of state politics during the period of Bill Tuck's career is J. Harvie Wilkinson III's readable and insightful *Harry Byrd and the Changing Face of Virginia Politics, 1945–1966* (Charlottesville: University Press of Virginia, 1968); from the time of its publication it has remained the starting point for any investigation of the Byrd organization. Monographic studies of the Byrd era are rare, except for the period of "massive resistance" which has inspired a number of works including James W. Ely, Jr., *The Crisis of Conservative Virginia: The Byrd Organization and the Politics of Massive Resistance* (Knoxville: University of Tennessee Press, 1976), a thoroughly researched and nicely balanced study; Robbins L. Gates, *The Making of Massive Resistance: Virginia's Politics of Public School Desegregation, 1954–1956* (Chapel Hill: University of North Carolina Press, 1962), an analysis written from the perspective of a political scientist; and Benjamin Muse, *Virginia's Massive Resistance* (Bloomington: Indiana University Press, 1961), a work short on research and long on animosity toward the Byrd organization. A view of the organization from the standpoint of one of its most articulate critics is Francis Pickens Miller, *Man from the Valley: Memoirs of a 20th Century Virginian* (Chapel Hill: University of North Carolina Press, 1971).

For the day-to-day developments in Virginia politics during the Tuck years the basic sources are the major state newspapers, particularly the Richmond *Times-Dispatch* and *News Leader* and the Norfolk

Virginian-Pilot, each of which enjoyed notably capable editorial direction during that time (respectively, Virginius Dabney; Douglas Southall Freeman and James J. Kilpatrick; and Lenoir Chambers). Useful newspapers for providing various regional views throughout the state include the Charlottesville *Daily Progress*, Danville *Register*, Fredericksburg *Free Lance–Star*, Lynchburg *News*, and Roanoke *World-News*. The Washington *Post*, the major daily in northern Virginia, takes a consistent antiorganization position. The views of the black press are to be found in the Richmond *Afro-American* and the Norfolk *Journal and Guide*.

For an understanding of the inner workings of politics, the indispensable source is the personal correspondence of the participants. The period under consideration in the present work lies at just such an historical remove that a number of important manuscript collections became available while the study was in progress—a fact which lent continuing excitement to the research effort, even as it necessitated revisions. The most significant collections now accessible include the papers of organization leaders Harry F. Byrd and Howard W. Smith, at the University of Virginia, and William M. Tuck and A. Willis Robertson at the College of William and Mary; and those of antiorganization activists Martin A. Hutchinson, Robert Whitehead, and Francis Pickens Miller, all at the University of Virginia. The executive papers of Tuck and the succeeding governors are deposited at the Virginia State Library; the Tuck and Almond collections are most enlightening. The papers of Virginius Dabney and James J. Kilpatrick, both deposited at the University of Virginia, reveal the insights of two of the state's most astute observers.

For years to come students of twentieth-century Virginia history will be indebted to Professor Edward Younger of the University of Virginia. Under his direction a wealth of doctoral dissertations has been produced covering almost the entire political history of the Commonwealth from Reconstruction to the present. The most helpful for the years of Tuck's career are Alvin L. Hall, "James H. Price and Virginia Politics, 1878 to 1943" (1970); Robert Thomas Hawkes, "The Career of Harry Flood Byrd, Sr., to 1933" (1975); Ronald L. Heinemann, "Depression and New Deal in Virginia" (1968); Peter Ros Henriques, "John S. Battle and Virginia Politics, 1948–1953" (1971); and Jonathan J. Wolfe, "Virginia in World War II" (1971).

Other informative unpublished studies include Herman L. Horn, "The Growth and Development of the Democratic Party in Virginia since 1890" (Ph.D. dissertation, Duke University, 1949), and James R. Sweeney, "Byrd and Anti-Byrd: The Struggle for Political Supremacy in Virginia, 1945–1954" (Ph.D. dissertation, University of Notre Dame, 1973).

For more detailed information on the sources consulted or cited for this work, see the author's "The Governorship of William Munford Tuck, 1946–1950: Virginia Politics in the 'Golden Age' of the Byrd Organization" (Ph.D. dissertation, University of Virginia, 1974), pp. 720–44.

Index

Abbitt, Watkins, 232, 233, 239, 245
Acuff, Roy, 52
Aiken, Archibald M., 238
Almond, J. Lindsay, 144, 213, 264; and school desegregation, 226, 235–39; as attorney general, 129–30, 164, 174; as gubernatorial candidate, 234–35; as speaker, 174, 236–37; relationship with Tuck, 130, 235–39
American Federation of Labor, 70, 81–82, 98, 111–13, 124
American Legion War Voters Act, 46
Americans for Democratic Action, 213
Anderson, Henry W., 8
Anderson, James A., 131
Anderson, Sherwood, 81
Antiorganization Democrats, 11, 61, 116, 119, 226, 239, 245; and Democratic state convention of 1948, 162–64; and poll tax reform, 193–97; and presidential election of 1948, 163–65, 172–79; and presidential election of 1952, 212–13; in gubernatorial primary of 1945, 65–72; led by James H. Price, 38–41; opposition to "anti-Truman bill," 148–49, 151–52; opposition to Tuck labor legislation, 99, 105, 118, 119, 121–22, 123; weakness of, 65, 133–34
"Anti-Truman bill," 143–79, 198–99
Arnold, Remmie, 118
Atkinson, Alfred V., 125–26

Bagwell, Donald P., 207
Barbour, John S., 4, 8
Barkley, Alben, 171, 177
Battle, John S., 56, 60–62, 174, 197; as possible Senate candidate, 244–46; at Democratic national convention of 1952, 209–12
Bennett, J. Gordon, 93
"Bill Tuck Day," 264–65
Birth of a Nation, 221
Blacks, 12, 70, 111, 135–36, 139, 148–49, 158, 171, 175, 183–85; *see also* Tuck, and civil rights; Tuck, racial views
Bland, James A., 221
Booker, Marshall B., 28
Boothe, Armistead, 147
Bradford, John H., 100
Brown, Sinclair, 67
Brown decision, 184, 219–20, 222–23, 230, 243, 248
Bruce, David K. E., 42, 207
Burch, Thomas G., 36, 38, 43, 59, 193
Burton, Frank P., 174
Byrd, Harry F.: admiration for Tuck, 99, 105, 106, 108, 144, 198, 214, 218; and Democratic national convention of 1952, 209–13; and John L. Lewis, 110; as organization leader, 4–16, 69, 74; attitude toward New Deal, 35–38, 56; attitude toward Truman, 135, 137, 142–46, 165–67, 171, 174–76; death, 267; early career, 5–10; economic views, 6–7, 185, 188; for president, 121–22, 136, 153; opposition to school desegregation, 220, 229, 231–32; origin of relationship with Tuck, 30–31, 34–35; relationship with Tuck as governor, 80, 99, 105, 106, 108, 144, 150–52, 158, 178, 188, 192, 194, 196; rumored retire-